SAVING
THE
BILL OF
RIGHTS

SAVING
THE
BILL OF
RIGHTS

**EXPOSING THE LEFT'S CAMPAIGN TO
DESTROY AMERICAN EXCEPTIONALISM**

FRANK MINITER

Since 1947
**REGNERY
PUBLISHING, INC.**
An Eagle Publishing Company • Washington, DC

Cataloging-in-Publication data on file with the Library of Congress
ISBN 978-1-59698-150-8

Published in the United States by
Regnery Publishing, Inc.
One Massachusetts Avenue, NW
Washington, DC 20001
www.regnery.com

Manufactured in the United States of America
10 9 8 7 6 5 4 3 2 1

Books are available in quantity for promotional or premium use. Write to Director of Special Sales, Regnery Publishing, Inc., One Massachusetts Avenue NW, Washington, DC 20001, for information on discounts and terms or call (202) 216-0600.

Distributed to the trade by:
Perseus Distribution
387 Park Avenue South
New York, NY 10016

To all the people who secured our individual rights…

To Plato, Socrates, and Aristotle for lighting the way

To the Magna Carta, the Bible, and the U.S. Constitution

To John Milton for *Areopagitica*

To John Locke for *Two Treatises of Government*

To Thomas Hobbes for *Leviathan*

To Montesquieu for *Spirit of the Laws*

To Adam Smith for *Wealth of Nations*

To Thomas Paine for *Common Sense*

To Thomas Jefferson for the Declaration of Independence

To James Madison, Alexander Hamilton,
and John Jay for the *Federalist Papers*

To Benjamin Franklin, George Washington, George Mason,
and the rest of the Founding Fathers who knew government
needs to be restricted to its constitution

To John Stuart Mill for *On Liberty*

And to Alexis de Tocqueville, Ludwig von Mises, Lord Acton,
Harriet Beecher Stowe, and to countless other defenders of
human freedom who added their wisdom and sometimes their blood
to the fight for individual liberty that has given the world
everything it now takes for granted.

CONTENTS

THE PREAMBLE

Liberty Isn't Liberalism

*"The only good bureaucrat is one with a pistol at his head. Put it
in his hand and it's good-by to the Bill of Rights."[1]*
—H. L. Mencken

Though my wife made me promise to behave, I just couldn't fabricate a fake chuckle when a professor at a New York cocktail party quipped to a group of academics, "As Jon Stewart said, 'If the events of September 11 proved anything, it's that the terrorists can attack us, but they can't take away what makes us American—our freedom, our liberty, our civil rights. No, only conservatives can do that.'"

Half a dozen acolytes laughed like school children, but the professor, who teaches English at a New York State university, noticed my poker face. A moment later he deftly moved within whispering distance before asking under his breath, "You're a conservative, aren't you?"

I replied, "I cling to my guns and religion."

His eyes flared mirth and he raised his wine glass to me as he said, "Sorry to be divisive, but you know, I really don't understand you conservatives. But I do try. I even went to a Tea Party just to write down all the stuff on their signs. Then I went to my office and studied the slogans thinking I could use them in class, you know, as examples of free speech turned hate speech or something, but I still couldn't make sense of what those people were so miffed about. So I'll ask you, just what liberties do you conservatives think you're losing to us progressives?"

The professor had an open-minded expression and a Ph.D. from U.C. Berkley. He sported carefully trimmed sideburns, a silver-stud earring, and clothes that fell out of style with Archie Bunker. He thought of himself as tolerant, worldly, and *en vogue*. He referred to himself as a "citizen of the world." He'd protested against the Patriot Act when President George W. Bush was still in office. He believed gays should be able to marry and that marijuana should be legalized. I was the starchy conservative, so he didn't see how I could possibly be a defender of individual liberty.

So I fired both barrels in the hope he'd do the same: "Let's see, I'm disturbed when the Supreme Court redefines the Fifth Amendment to say it's okay for state and local governments to seize land from one private person so they can give it to someone they prefer. I'm opposed to any government that, despite what the Second Amendment protects, says law-abiding citizens can't defend their lives and families with firearms. I'm rattled that the U.S. Congress was able to take away corporations' First Amendment rights during elections, even as Congress passes taxes targeting particular industries. I find it remarkable that our federal government has been able to discount our Tenth Amendment, the right that stipulates that all powers not expressively given to the federal government in the Constitution are reserved for the states or the people. I am dismayed when I see a progressive movement afoot attempting to shackle our First Amendment freedom of the press with censorship spun into a Fairness Doctrine or net neutrality. I'm troubled that the Fourth Amendment's 'right of the people to be secure in their persons, houses, papers, and effects, against unreasonable searches and seizures' has not always included my computer and cell phone. I'm horrified when my government requires me to buy, not just health insurance, but their version of health insurance, even as they exempt themselves. I'm aghast that our government is spending so recklessly, it is putting American independence in the hands of Chinese communists. Basically, I'm tired of a government that treats my life as a puppeteer all the while assuring me it's for the collective good."

Aware that I was rudely filibustering, I relinquished the floor.

His eyes tightened, then crossed. He really didn't know what to say. He finally raised his wine glass again, smiled, and began his counterattack: "I can counter all those points you know, but I'll start by saying you conservatives too often let religion get in the way of the peoples' rights, but thankfully we have a wall, from our First Amendment, separating your churches from the state, a wall you'd like torn down."

"There is no 'wall,'" I replied.

As his eyebrows hit the ceiling, I continued, "Actually, in 1947 Justice Hugo Black pulled the phrase 'wall of separation between Church and State' out of a letter President Thomas Jefferson sent to the Baptist Association of Danbury. Justice Black used the quote out of context. When read in its entirety, the letter clearly states that Jefferson saw the First Amendment as a restriction on the federal government's ability to sanction a state religion—hence the First Amendment's establishment clause."

"*Hmm*, I'll have to look into that," he pondered aloud as his eyes searched his shoes before rising back to mine, "but you know, what the Christian Right really can't reconcile is the science Darwin unearthed, and so, like people, the government must evolve."

"No, you're not being accurate," I replied. "The truth is actually more interesting then your ahistorical view. Here's what I mean: it's ironic that liberals today embrace Charles Darwin's theory of evolution—the belief that the strong prevail in nature while the weak go extinct—while at the same time they place Adam Smith's *Wealth of Nations* under their collective heels, a book that can be boiled down to an argument that government should simply provide a just arena so that businesses can attempt to outcompete their competition. True capitalism assures us that only the fittest survive, just like in nature. It's actually all the more ironic when you realize that Darwin was clearly guided by Smith's invisible hand. Darwin most certainly studied Smith."

"But religious conservatives attacked Darwin from the start," pointed out the professor as his voice wavered uncertainly.

I was shaking my head as I answered, "Sorry professor, that's revisionist history. People have forgotten that Darwin's *Origin of Species* wasn't that controversial when it was first published in 1859. Even the church didn't have a big problem with it then. It was Darwin's publication of *The Descent of Man* in 1871 that was controversial. That book, unlike *Origin of Species*, was not substantiated with scientific evidence but was built on suppositions."

"Maybe," he said, "but come on, you conservatives don't like evolution now."

"No, I know very few conservatives who completely tank the theory of evolution. What conservatives find objectionable is the false premise that evolution must mean, if true, that atheists are right."

"But how can you draw any other conclusion?" he asked.

"Here's what you're missing," I answered. "In the second edition of *On the Origin of Species*, published in 1860, Darwin added the phrase 'by the Creator' to the closing sentence.[2] In fact, Darwin's stated view at the time was that God created life through the laws of nature. This is something even the Catholic Church is okay with; in fact, in 1950 the Vatican stated its official position with a papal encyclical stating evolution is not inconsistent with Catholic teaching."[3]

"Is that really true?" he asked doubtfully.

"Yes, it is," I answered, "in fact, I'd like to know why atheists believe evolution can give people an id, an ego, and a super ego, as well as minds that can comprehend the atom and the universe, but can't grasp the notion that evolution could give us a soul? Why is being soulless a precondition to agreeing with Darwin?"

He smiled a smile that must swoon female undergraduates and said, "Perhaps what happens after death is something we can't know. Perhaps it is metaphysical. But, you know, as a progressive I believe individual rights are not infringed when a decision is made for the greater good. For our own benefit, the Constitution needs to be considered according to our evolving values."

Again laughing in surprise at his candor, I countered, "You do realize there is a constitutional process for amending the Constitution? That process gave us the income tax and, after a war, did away with slavery, so the will of the people and their 'evolving values' can and has been taken into account; so then you must realize that what you're *really* saying is that courts and legislators should be able to create your liberal utopia without that pesky old Constitution getting in their way."

"I'm not sure I like the way you put that," he said. "I'd say we need experts to evolve the Constitution into what's best for us collectively, for what we really want and need but maybe the masses can't quite articulate."

"So," I said, "you think the state must do these things whether the people want them done or not? You believe in some version of a meritocracy, as opposed to a constitutional republic, yet you think you're for fair and impartial individual rights?"

He shrugged, "Oh, let's be honest, it's the definition of what constitutes life, liberty, and property that we disagree on, isn't it? We don't really disagree on the text of the Constitution or the Bill of Rights, but what it all means, and words and concepts evolve. So, for example, I contend that if you're squatting on a piece of property that a community needs to develop to add jobs and revenue, then I'd say you're harming other individuals so the government must step in for the greater good. I mean, at the nation's founding they had a frontier that seemed limitless, right? And now we are fighting over overdeveloped space. So times have changed as has our Constitution."

"Ah, now we're getting somewhere," I replied. "According to the Fifth Amendment, property can be taken for public use with just compensation. But remember, it says *public* use, such as for a highway or a reservoir, not for private hotels and housing. The definitions of the words 'private' and 'public' have not changed. 'Public use' does not mean, as liberal justices have asserted, 'public purpose.'"

"The Supreme Court disagrees with you on the Fifth Amendment's right to property."

"Yes," I answered, "and property rights is one of the liberties that have been weakened by you progressives."

"Maybe we disagree in application," he thought aloud.

I parried his obfuscation by insisting, "No, we disagree in the fundamentals. You can't subjugate the individual to the state's collective will, or maybe its loving benevolence, while saying you're for individual rights to life, liberty, and property. It's the individual's right to succeed or to fail without the state's telling them how to invest or what property he or she must sell or how many widgets to make that gave us this wine glass, this palatable bargain-price Italian Chianti, and the trucks and ships to send it around the world to little cocktail chats like this."

He looked at me through his wine glass and spun his red wine around as he smiled again, his smile looking like a Cheshire cat's through the glass, before he attacked from another angle, "Those slave-owning Founding Fathers you love didn't let women and blacks in on the Bill of Rights. It was the liberals who did that."

I was waiting for that one: "Many of the Founding Fathers were abolitionists, were anti-slavery. And besides, it was the Republicans who, behind President Abraham Lincoln, defeated the slave states; in fact, it was the due process clause in the Fourteenth Amendment, an amendment that incidentally was passed in 1868 right after the American Civil War by Republicans, that was used in *Brown* v. *The Board of Education* to give equal schooling to all citizens."

"Well," he countered, "I concede that I might have been a Republican in those bygone times, but times have changed. It was Democrats who fought and won the civil-rights movement."

"No, it wasn't that simple," I answered. "Look back and you'll find the division wasn't so much along party lines as it was along regional ones–southern Democrats fought to keep black Americans in the backs of buses."

Actually, the U.S. House of Representatives passed the Civil Rights Act of 1964 by 289 to 126, a vote in which 79 percent of Republicans and 63 percent of Democrats voted yes. When the bill came before the full Senate for debate on March 30, 1964, a "Southern Bloc" of eighteen southern Democratic senators and one Republican senator led by Democrat Senator Richard Russel from Georgia launched a filibuster to prevent its passage. The Senate vote was 73 to 27, with 21 Democrats and 6 Republicans voting no.

The professor shrugged and said, "I think you're wrong somewhere, but I'll have to look into it."

"Please do," I said, "but you may not like what you find. The Southern Democrats even actively disarmed African Americans after the Civil War and passed laws to keep them disarmed so they could keep them from voting—this was an infringement of their Second Amendment rights."

"Oh, you conservatives go to extremes," he said, finally showing some exasperation. "I'm sure that happened a few times, but anyway I don't understand why you people are so scared of the state. The government needs to equalize things and to make sure minorities get what they've been long denied, and the government needs to protect the environment from greedy capitalists, and sometimes lands need to be given to someone who will do something that will benefit the community and tax base, and to administer social justice, and so on."

I was shaking my head again as I said, "Now we've exposed the gaping fissure between our viewpoints. You think the state should guide the populace to some politically correct good at the expense of individual rights while I say individual rights must check state power. Your government-enforced fairness, your social justice in place of equal justice, is assaulting every tenet of the Bill of Rights. Now do you understand the conservative point of view with regards to our lost liberties?"

He smiled again as he said, "Yes, you're individualists. That's a very selfish way of living."

"No, quite the opposite," I countered, "individualism safeguards the republic by keeping the government's penchant to grow toward authoritarianism at bay."

Then, as he shrugged, I really picked a fight: "Actually, we just illustrated why the conservative in contemporary American society is the more open-minded; after all, conservatives don't care if someone is an environmentalist, a fundamentalist, an atheist, or even a pantheist, just as long as that person doesn't try to force them to be one or all of those things; meanwhile, liberals argue that, for our own good, we must accept their worldview hook, line, and sinker. And if we don't, they label us as racists or extremists or militia members as they try to change the laws and our

Constitution to force us to adopt their way of thinking. The liberal, or progressive, wants to tell us whether we can smoke or pass the salt or tell off-color jokes or buy eight-cylinder autos or own and carry guns, while the conservative leaves these decisions up to the individual."

He turned up his nose at me and said, "Oh yeah, what about gay rights?"

I asked, "Why aren't gay-rights activists satisfied with civil unions? I don't know why they require everyone to collectively apply the word *marriage* to their same-sex union? And why do they need judges to give them marriage licenses? Shouldn't state legislatures, via popular will, decide the issue? Or, even better, shouldn't the state just get out of the business of *holy matrimony*?"

He shrugged and said, "How about abortion, we liberals are for a woman's right to choose?"

I said, "An unborn child is an individual with rights."

He said, "What about marijuana? I think individuals have just as much of a right to have a beer as they do to smoke a reefer."

I said, "Many libertarians agree with you. I say there are types of alcohol and even cheese that are illegal and I wonder why liberals don't have a problem with those regulations. But you know, I'm a conservative, not an anarchist. I'm not opposed to all government restrictions, especially when they're equally and justly administered for moral reasons and are decided by a voting public, not by activist judges. You don't have anarchist contradictions mixed with your socialism do you?"

Then he really laughed. He was really a very jolly progressive. And then thankfully our wives stepped between us and pointed out that we'd been very rude standing all by ourselves and talking so seriously for such a length of time. And, of course, they were right.

I recap this slightly combative cocktail party debate in detail because its openness showcased the philosophical attacks many liberals now use to curb individual freedom, even as they're so certain they are the protectors of liberty. Conservatives see the contradictions in liberal-progressive ideology, yet don't always do a good job of putting it all together. Putting it all together so we can save the Bill of Rights is what this book is about.

Americans need to understand what is happening to their Bill of Rights; after all, many of the precedents established by progressive judges are designed to be complex theorems so people who don't have law degrees won't clearly see that another liberty has been taken or weakened. To retake our lost rights, and to save the rights we still have from this ever-growing government, we have to fully understand our Bill of Rights. As Thomas Jefferson warned, "If a nation expects to be ignorant and free in a state of civilization, it expects what never was and never will be."[4]

For example, when we hear progressive politicians claim the Constitution is "a living document," we must expose that what they mean by "living" is their desire to create a document they can either ignore or that they can use to create additional rights—such as a woman's right to choose—that aren't in the Constitution.

To this end we must fully understand that President Barack Obama attacked the Constitution when he said the Constitution is just a "charter of negative liberties." We must comprehend exactly what he intends to do when he says the Constitution "says what the states can't do to you, says what the federal government can't do to you, but it doesn't say what the federal government or the state government must do on your behalf."[5] We must know he means that, like President Franklin D. Roosevelt (FDR), he wishes to pass a new statist list of "positive rights" that the government must provide to the people, new rights that would give the federal government a mandate to take away individual rights in order to provide new collective directives.

In his State of the Union address on January 11, 1944, FDR outlined what is often referred to as his "second bill of rights":[6]

> This Republic had its beginning, and grew to its present strength, under the protection of certain inalienable political rights—among them the right of free speech, free press, free

worship, trial by jury, freedom from unreasonable searches and seizures. They were our rights to life and liberty.

As our nation has grown in size and stature, however—as our industrial economy expanded—these political rights proved inadequate to assure us equality in the pursuit of happiness.

We have come to a clear realization of the fact that true individual freedom cannot exist without economic security and independence. "Necessitous men are not free men." People who are hungry and out of a job are the stuff of which dictatorships are made.

In our day these economic truths have become accepted as self-evident. We have accepted, so to speak, a second Bill of Rights under which a new basis of security and prosperity can be established for all—regardless of station, race, or creed.

Among these are:

1. The right to a useful and remunerative job in the industries or shops or farms or mines of the nation;

2. The right to earn enough to provide adequate food and clothing and recreation;

3. The right of every farmer to raise and sell his products at a return which will give him and his family a decent living;

4. The right of every businessman, large and small, to trade in an atmosphere of freedom from unfair competition and domination by monopolies at home or abroad;

5. The right of every family to a decent home;

6. The right to adequate medical care and the opportunity to achieve and enjoy good health;

7. The right to adequate protection from the economic fears of old age, sickness, accident, and unemployment;

8. The right to a good education.

FDR was relying on the populace's panic near the end of the greatest financial crisis in United States history to wrestle individual rights from the people so he could place them squarely in the loving death embrace of the state. FDR wanted a nanny state erected on the pillars of collective mandates that would trump individual rights. President Barack Obama said he would like to finish FDR's work when, just before winning the 2008 presidential election, he said, "We're just five days away from fundamentally transforming the United States of America." Obama knows such mandates placed upon a government would create a constitutionally backed welfare state, an entitlement-enslaved populace that would permanently function as a Democratic base in defense of his statist ideal. FDR's second bill of rights would not be additions to an individual bill of rights, they would be a collectivist's bill of rights, decrees which would give the federal government the power to decide who is hired and fired, how much people make, who gets the operation for cancer, and so much more.

FDR didn't get his second bill of rights in the 1940s, because Americans still believed in the American dream, because we the people wanted to succeed by the toil of our own hands and minds. The American people knew centralized control, whether from a king, a dictator, or a bureaucracy, is what people from all over the world have always come to America to escape. Most Americans agreed with a quip attributed to Mark Twain: "Don't go around saying the world owes you a living. The world owes you nothing. It was here first."

Still, FDR's second bill of rights is worth remembering, because history may be repeating itself. FDR's first sweeping moves to disregard the Constitution and American capitalism were first halted with a series of 5–4 decisions from a conservative Supreme Court, much as President Obama's politics were thwarted with a 5–4 Supreme Court decision that struck down parts of The Bipartisan Campaign Reform Act of 2002 (more popularly known as "McCain-Feingold"). Obama's worldview, if not his legislation, was also curbed by two 5–4 Second Amendment decisions from the high court.

FDR pushed back against the Court with the Judiciary Reorganization Bill of 1937, a bill better known as the "court-packing plan." After winning the 1936 presidential election, FDR swung for the fences. Although the bill aimed to overhaul the federal court system, its most controversial provision would have granted the president power to appoint an additional justice to the Supreme Court for every sitting member over the age of 70.5, up to a maximum of six. Since the Constitution does not limit the size of the Supreme Court, FDR sought to counter the constitutional checks-and-balances from the high court's opposition to his political agenda by expanding the number of justices to create a pro-New Deal majority on the bench.

The legislation was unveiled on February 5, 1937, and was the subject of one of FDR's Fireside Chats; however, shortly after his radio address, the Supreme Court upheld a Washington state minimum-wage law in *West Coast Hotel Co.* v. *Parrish* by a 5–4 ruling. Conservative Justice Owen Roberts had suddenly joined the progressive side. Because Roberts had previously ruled against most New Deal legislation, his about-face was widely interpreted as an effort to maintain the Court's judicial independence. Roberts' move came to be popularly known as "the switch in time that saved nine."

About six weeks after this flip-flop, Justice Willis Van Devanter, one of the consistent opponents of the New Deal, announced his retirement from the bench.

FDR then nominated Justice Hugo Black to the high court, a former Democratic senator. The U.S. Senate confirmed Black, and FDR's progressive policies began to pass the Court's constitutional tests.

As of the winter of 2011, President Obama had a similar court structure to that which FDR had before 1937, with Justice Anthony Kennedy being the swing vote. Kennedy ruled that the Second Amendment is an individual right, but he also ruled that the Fifth Amendment allowed New London, Connecticut, to seize land from one private person to give to another private entity.

If history repeats itself, President Obama—who has already gotten two Supreme Court picks—could turn the Court far to the Left if a conservative justice retires or passes on. This would give Obama the opportunity to fundamentally change America as FDR did, with a majority of the Court justices being liberal and/or progressive.

For a view of what an Obama Court would do to the Constitution, consider his own thoughts. He wrote in his senior seminar paper while attending Columbia University: "The Constitution allows for many things, but what it does not allow is the most revealing. The so-called Founders did not allow for economic freedom. While political freedom is supposedly a cornerstone of the document, the distribution of wealth is not even mentioned. While many believed that the new Constitution gave them liberty, it instead fitted them with the shackles of hypocrisy."[7]

To save our Bill of Rights, we need to look back to the beginning, to what gave us everything. As John Stuart Mill wrote, "A people, it appears, may be progressive for a certain length of time, and then stop. When does it stop? When it ceases to possess individuality."[8] For progress to occur in a society, its people need to have individual rights, the ability to take risks, and the chance to profit from their boldness. So to keep statism from slaying our individual rights, we must take back what has been lost. In America this reckoning begins with the Bill of Rights.

AMENDMENT I

Congress shall make no law respecting an establishment of religion, or prohibiting the free exercise thereof; or abridging the freedom of speech, or of the press; or the right of the people peaceably to assemble, and to petition the Government for a redress of grievances.

*"You do not define the First Amendment. It defines you. And it is
bigger than you. That's how freedom works."[1]*
—Charlton Heston

ll around the Capitol Hilton's Presidential Ballroom in Washington, D.C., thousands of Life Members of the National Rifle Association were seated at hundreds of tables and having a hell of a time. So when this middle-aged woman with a grimace that would depress a clown sat next to me in what was apparently the last empty seat in the boisterous ballroom, I thought she seemed out of place. When everyone at the table tried to welcome her to the party, she responded by standing, spinning her chair around, and sitting down with her back to the table and her scowl facing the stage; we all knew something wasn't right. Yet no one knew this woman was poised to rowdily showcase a crass misunderstanding of the First Amendment.

Senator Mitch McConnell (R-KY) had just finished speaking. He left to a standing ovation. The Constitution-thumping gun owners packing the enormous ballroom had flown in from all over America. It was a Friday afternoon, and they thought coming to hear politicians pander during the lead-up to the 2008 presidential election was a splendid excuse to spend a weekend in the nation's capital. So the spirited people around the table ignored the woman's rudeness and then hushed as Senator John McCain (R-AZ) walked out on stage.

It was September 21, 2007, and McCain wanted to run for president, again. This audience didn't like McCain's First Amendment restrictions in the Bipartisan Campaign Reform Act of 2002, popularly known as "McCain-Feingold," a bill that silenced corporations, unions, and associations (such as the NRA) near elections. They also didn't like McCain's support for lawsuits started by President Bill Clinton's administration that attempted to hold firearm manufacturers liable when criminals used American-made guns to commit crimes. Despite these attacks on the Bill of Rights, though, they were willing to hear McCain out.

McCain began by thanking the thousands in attendance for giving him the opportunity to address them, but before he could really get going, the woman with the earned frown leapt out of her seat and pulled a cloth sign from beneath her sweater. Her sign read "End the War Now." She began screaming at the top of her shrill voice, "I'm with CodePink and I'm here to use my freedom of speech—"

But before the CodePink activist could finish her first sentence a fast-thinking man at our table reached over and snatched the sign from her fingers.

The activist whirled around, seething, "Give that to me. It's mine. I have the First Amendment right to say what I want!"

He passed the sign under the table to me.

She pounced at me liked a riled housecat, claws out, but before her nails shredded my face I passed the cloth sign under the table to a woman on my right. Around the sign went with the activist in pursuit like a hamster on a wheel.

By the time she was on her third lap, security had her by the arm.

As that CodePink activist was being dragged away still screaming about her constitutional right to be heard, someone to my right grumbled, "Well, I suppose this is a small price to pay for freedom."

Everyone nodded agreement. He would have been correct on the street, but not at this private event. The activist actually embodied a commonly held misunderstanding of the First Amendment, a misinterpretation now laying the philosophical basis for restrictions on the freedom of speech in America.

Every fourth grader knows the First Amendment's protection of the freedom of speech and of the press are fundamental liberties that were earned on the battlefield and later safeguarded within the Bill of Rights; however, few Americans today, including that protester, understand that the First Amendment is not a positive right the government is required to enforce, but rather a restriction designed to keep the government from infringing upon our basic human liberties. The First Amendment doesn't prevent a restaurant owner, for example, from telling a patron to put away their cell phone or leave. The right to the freedom of speech doesn't bar censorship by individuals on their private property, it only restricts the government from unreasonably censoring speech. This original intent rests on the belief that government does not grant inalienable rights, such as the right to speak one's mind, but rather that the freedom of speech is a natural human liberty the government can't unreasonably restrain.

Flip-flopping the First Amendment into a right the government has created and therefore is required to enforce—instead of a natural liberty the government can't unreasonably take away from the people—grants the government the power to define what free speech is and how we may utilize our right to speak or even get news over the Internet and radio. This topsy-turvy, statist view that many people today accept—and that many public schools teach—can be construed to allow the government to decide what free speech is permissible during elections. It can be used to permit the government to regulate what can be said or allowed on the Internet with net neutrality, a concept that gives the government the power to equalize speech on the Web and therefore the ability to censor the "fairness" of speech on the Internet. This misreading of the First Amendment can empower government bureaucrats to equalize opinions on the radio with a Fairness Doctrine; it can give the government the authority to censor speech all over America with hate speech laws and other regulations; and it can, in different ways, give the government the ability to legislate and enforce otherwise unconstitutional regulations that are supposed to enhance national security. As a result, this statist attempt to put the government in charge of defining our rights is not only counterintuitive, it also semantically subjugates the individual to the will of the state. The Bill of Rights was supposed to constrain the federal government to the will of the people, not the people to the whims of government.

The American Revolution freed the American colonies from an English king and Parliament. The revolutionaries who fought and suffered for freedom from foreign control didn't want, after their unlikely victory, a central government in the United States to grow as tyrannical as King George III. So they restricted the new federal government to the powers listed in the Constitution. Subsequently, the first U.S. Congress passed the Bill of Rights, which the states then ratified, to prevent the new federal government from infringing upon the rights of the people and, in the Tenth Amendment, from usurping the rights and authority left to the states. In this way the Bill of Rights didn't grant new rights to the people, but rather restricted the federal government from taking away the freedom the people had just won in revolution.

To understand and thereby save the First Amendment, it's necessary first to understand this basic premise. Next, it's important to realize that though the First Amendment was originally only designed to be a constraint on the federal government, in *Gitlow* v. *New York* (1925) the Supreme Court held that the "due process" clause of the Fourteenth Amendment incorporated the First Amendment. From then on the First Amendment also restrained state and local governments from inhibiting the freedom of speech and the press. However, by deciding *Gitlow*, the Supreme Court didn't twist the First Amendment into a positive right that gives the federal government a free hand to force its definition of "fairness" or "equality" of free speech upon the states and the people, though that is the way some liberal-progressive Supreme Court justices began to view the First Amendment.

Perhaps this backwards reading of the First Amendment is why that leftist CodePink activist thought the amendment is a positive right the government gave her, a right she could use to interrupt a private proceeding. Her perverted version of a right to the freedom of speech would, of course, result in anarchy, as it would allow any town hall meeting, concert, or court proceeding to be interrupted by anyone at any time for any reason. She also didn't seem to comprehend that by yelling during McCain's speech, she was actually curtailing McCain's constitutional right to speak to an audience who had come to hear him, and others, speak.

But then again, perhaps she did, as she's not really a proponent of the First Amendment. CodePink has defended Venezuelan president Hugo Chavez's efforts to turn Venezuela from a democracy into an autocracy. To achieve this, Chavez has systematically dismantled the freedom of speech and of the press in Venezuela and has even censored political dissent on the Internet. CodePink, however, doesn't seem to care about Chavez's means; they only care about his ends. After a visit to Caracas, CodePink's cofounder Medea Benjamin—who "monitored" a polling station—penned an article for CodePink's website that portrayed Chavez as a champion of the lower class, even though Chavez has been busy damning the lower classes to serfdom as he takes away their individual rights.[2] CodePink has shown similar support for Fidel Castro's Communist Cuba, a place where an outspoken critic of the government is jailed or worse. CodePink seems to think the freedom of speech and of the press are good things only when they support their liberal, socialist causes. They are dishonest to the marrow.

CodePink's activists are actually an extreme example of a movement—mostly found on the left fringe of the Democratic Party—now attempting to redefine the First Amendment, not as an individual protection from government censorship, but as a tool the federal government can use to silence its critics with net neutrality, the Fairness Doctrine, and with other statist assaults on the First Amendment.

The First Amendment is necessarily open to these attacks because, though the First Amendment plainly says, "Congress shall make no law … abridging the freedom of speech, or of the press," the government has always been able to reasonably restrict the freedom of speech and of the press with defamation laws, copyright laws, noise ordinances, and with other laws designed to prevent people from infringing upon the rights of others. The First Amendment also doesn't afford individuals the right to sing in a courtroom, to shout obscenities in a private restaurant, or to scream "fire" in a crowded theatre—unless, of course, there's really a fire.

Nor can we legally heckle someone off a stage because we don't like their politics. As a result, there will always be constitutional quibbling about what these legitimate restrictions on the freedom of speech actually entail, and there should be, but this debate doesn't alter the basic premise that the First Amendment constrains the government, not the private citizenry as liberal-progressives say it does. To safeguard this fundamental right, the Supreme Court is supposed to treat regulations that affect the First Amendment according to its most stringent standard of judicial review, called "strict scrutiny."

Here's another premise necessary to understanding the First Amendment that many on both sides of the political aisle have lost sight of: the "press" hasn't historically been granted rights that are not held by every American. No court has established a definition of "press" that defines it as a specially protected class. Any differentiation between the press and the people that was once even vaguely definable has since been further blurred by blogs, Twitter, Facebook, and other social media sites. As far back as *Lovell* v. *City of Griffin* (1938), Chief Justice Charles E. Hughes defined the press as "every sort of publication which affords a vehicle of information and opinion." This includes everything from newspapers to blogs to WikiLeaks. As journalist A. J. Liebling (1904–1963) famously quipped, "Freedom of the press is guaranteed only to those who own one."[3] Today, we all own one.

This is because the only way to decide who qualifies as "press" would be for the government to license the media just like it gives press badges for access to the White House. If such an unconstitutional thing were to occur, then the media could go around and haughtily flash their official media badges like a bunch of Junior G-men while the rest of us would be second-class citizens. Though amusing, this is a frightening concept, as government media licenses would allow politicians to decide who gets to interview them, who gets to write about them, and who is permitted to opine about them and their policies. Such government control of the press could never be compatible with the First Amendment. This is why the people are the press.

The First Amendment has historically given the press—except for a few dark periods in American history—the freedom to hunt down and print the truth. In fact, in *The New York Times* v. *United States* (1971) the Supreme Court ruled that the *Times* could publish the "Pentagon Papers," a series of top-secret U.S. Department of Defense papers that outlined the history of the U.S. political and military involvement in Vietnam from 1945 to 1967. Because WikiLeaks is considered to be press just as much as the *New York Times* or Joe the Plumber, WikiLeaks is protected by the First Amendment and can't be prosecuted for printing the top-secret information it released in late 2010 any more than *USA Today* can. However, they could be prosecuted if they obtained the information by hacking or by otherwise stealing it, by paying a government employee for the espionage, or by breaking other laws to obtain the classified information. Simply printing the information is constitutional, unless of course the Supreme Court wishes to set a new precedent by redefining the freedom of the press right out of the First Amendment.

WikiLeaks could be prosecuted, as could anyone, if they published false or misleading information. In *The New York Times* v. *Sullivan* (1964), the Court decided that for written words to be libel they must be, first of all, false. In fact, these protections from government restrictions are so strong they include a right to ignore mandates from the government: a website, newspaper, or television network cannot be required to publish advertisements for a political opponent, even if they normally accept commercials from politicians.

All of these precedents came under attack in late 2010 when some Republicans and Democrats began calling for the U.S. Justice Department to use the Espionage Act of 1917—an act that was used as a political weapon by President Woodrow Wilson and his administration—to prosecute Julian Assange, the Australian director of WikiLeaks. This overreaction could be detrimental to our First Amendment protections of free speech and of the press. If the Supreme Court were to get behind allowing the U.S. government to jail Assange for merely publishing material, then the government would be handed a frightening new power that could be used to curb the individual expression of every American citizen, as it would prevent journalists from developing government sources and could even be used to put whistleblowers in jail. Or if legislation such as "The Shield Act," which was promoted by Senators John Ensign (R-NV), Joe Lieberman (I-CN), and Scott Brown (R-MA) in December of 2010 as a way to prosecute those who publish classified material, becomes law, and perhaps is even deemed to be constitutional by the courts, then the government could begin to expand its reach and prosecute anyone who even unknowingly prints true criticism of the government and its policies that is deemed to somehow adversely effect national security.

In the case of Julian Assange, instead of setting such precedents, the U.S. Justice Department should simply investigate whether the material released by WikiLeaks was obtained illegally. If it was, they could prosecute Assange. Meanwhile, they should prosecute whoever gave WikiLeaks the material. Pushing the case further by attacking the press could reduce the peoples' right to check the government by finding and publishing true information.

The U.S. government certainly has a longstanding constitutional right to negotiate with foreign governments in private by classifying information. Conversely, the American people have the right to check government power with Freedom of Information Act requests and by utilizing their First Amendment-protected freedoms to investigate their local, state, and federal governments. Allowing the government to prosecute those who print the truth would mean Bob Woodward should be locked away for life for his reporting on Watergate. Is that the America the Founders created or that United States citizens today want to live in? In this age of massive over-classification of documents, it is imperative that the American people keep the First Amendment intact so they can continue to hold their government accountable.

Over-classification of documents is so rampant that in October 2010, the U.S. Congress passed, and President Barack Obama signed into law, the "Reducing Over-Classification Act." The Act created a "Classified Information Advisory Officer" to reduce the scope of classified documents because, according to the bill: "Over-classification of information causes considerable confusion regarding what information may be shared with whom, and negatively affects the dissemination of information within the Federal Government and with State, local, and tribal entities, and with the private sector." This act addressed the issue in a superficial way—by hiring a government bureaucrat to propose changes—but at least it acknowledged that every memo and report shouldn't automatically be withheld from the public.

Keeping the government responsible to the people by maintaining a strong First Amendment is all the more important in an age when politicians were so recently able to protect their positions and policies by silencing capitalists and associations near elections. In a nation with First Amendment protections of the freedom of speech and of the press, this next statist attack was only possible because much of the American populace has lost sight of what the First Amendment really means, and much of the so-called "mainstream media," which had an exemption from these regulations, was willing to go along with the government censorship.

How Progressives Silenced Capitalists

While climbing the wide marble steps of the U.S. Supreme Court building on a late summer morning in 2009, David Bossie looked up to the words carved over the face of the building: "Equal Justice Under Law." He paused a moment. He wanted to remember this scene. A rising sun was lighting the dome of the United States Capitol building. All around him, people in dark business suits were striding up the long, white steps into the Court with all the seriousness of Sunday morning parishioners. He thought the somberness of the scene fitting. He was coming to see if the Supreme Court would wrestle his First Amendment rights back from Congress, or if the nine overseers of the Constitution would rule that "equal justice" no longer includes business owners, leaders of associations, and corporations. He was coming to see if America was still the land of the free.

With the scene imprinted in his mind, he tread up the remaining steps to the court's 252-foot-wide oval plaza, where he passed between a pair of marble statues holding swords and scales—symbols of justice—as well as The Three Fates, weaving the thread of life. He walked across the plaza to the main steps of the court where a statue to his left, a female figure, is known as the Contemplation of Justice, and on his right, a male figure is deemed the Guardian of Law. Capping the entrance above him was the sculpture representing Liberty Enthroned, guarded by Order and Authority. On the opposite side of the building he knew were the sculptures of Moses, Confucius, and the Athenian statesman Solon along with the phrase "Justice the Guardian of Liberty."

He walked between the bronze doors on the west front, each of which weighs six and one-half tons, and stepped into the main corridor, following a current of well-dressed people into what is known as the "Great Hall." At each side were the double rows of monolithic marble columns rising to a coffered ceiling. Busts of all former chief justices are there, set alternately in niches and on pedestals.

From the Great Hall he passed into the Court Chamber, a room that measures eighty-two by ninety-one feet. Its twenty-four columns are Old Convent Quarry Siena marble from Liguria, Italy; its walls and friezes are of Ivory Vein marble from Alicante, Spain; and its floor borders are Italian and African marble.

David Bossie had come to these marbled halls to find out if all this decadence and historical idealism had been reduced to an aesthetic frame around a warped, progressive view of justice. He was there to see if he would get equal justice under law or if the Court would decide "equal justice" could be defined as something progressives call "social justice," a phrase that can mean anything at all.

Bossie is president of Citizens United, a conservative nonprofit group that primarily makes political documentaries. He was at the Court to witness the second oral hearing for *Citizens United* v. *Federal Election Commission* (2010), a legal fight Bossie picked after Congress had taken his freedom of speech away. Bossie had served as chief investigator for the U.S. House of Representatives Committee on Government Reform and Oversight. During President Bill Clinton's two terms, he'd led investigations ranging from the Whitewater land deal to foreign fundraising in the 1996 Clinton re-election campaign. Bossie is the author of political books, such as *The Many Faces of John Kerry*, and has been the head of Citizens United since 2000, where he has overseen the production of more than a dozen conservative documentaries.

Born in 1965, Bossie is a volunteer fireman with short-cropped hair and a direct way of speaking. He is the kind of pundit/activist who makes left-wing ideologues hyperventilate. In fact, no freedom-loving journalist at the *New York Times* or the *Washington Post* or at ABC, CBS, or NBC, or at President Barack Obama's favorite news site, the *Huffington Post*, seemed to care that the government made it a felony for Bossie to sell a political movie on Hillary Clinton near the 2008 election. It seems the media elite thought Evelyn Beatrice Hall's famous declaration—"I disapprove of what you say, but I will defend to the death your right to say it"[4]—is only suitable for idealistic journalism school students. The press got an exemption from the Bipartisan Campaign Reform Act of 2002, also known as "McCain-Feingold"; as a result, many journalists didn't seem to care that people like Bossie, or as the owner of the corner grocery and the CEO's of Fortune 500s, had gotten muzzled.

As of November 6, 2002, McCain-Feingold prevented leaders of industry, associations, and small businesses from using their First Amendment rights within thirty days of a primary and sixty days of a general election to run political ads that name a federal candidate. As primaries stretch across any political year, this meant national political ads paid for by corporations and associations were illegal during the entire election cycle.

When McCain-Feingold was passed, all the aforementioned media outlets largely took the government's side. During the Senate debate on McCain-Feingold, Senator McConnell challenged Senator John McCain (R-AZ) on the U.S. Senate floor.

McCain had repeatedly alleged that the bill's restrictions on political speech must be put in place to reduce "corruption." So McConnell said,

> I am interested in engaging in some discussion here about what specifically–which specific senators he believes have been engaged in corruption. I know [McCain] said from time to time the process is corrupt. But I think it is important to note, for there to be corruption, someone must be corrupt. Someone must be corrupt for there to be corruption. So I ask my friend from Arizona what he has in mind here in suggesting corruption is permeating our body and listing these [spending] projects for the benefit of several states as examples.

McCain gave a long, rambling response with no specifics.

So McConnell continued: "I ask the senator from Arizona, how can it be corruption if no one is corrupt? That is like saying the gang is corrupt but none of the gangsters are. If there is corruption someone must be corrupt....I repeat my question to the senator from Arizona: Who is corrupt?"

McCain, whose temper was then etching his voice, replied, "First of all, I have already responded to the senator that I will not get into peoples' names."[5]

Individuals can defend themselves, but groups have less protection, especially when allegations fit a believable narrative. Though sold as "fairness," this case amounted to something as basic as a power struggle between government and industry. Progressives like McCain and President Barack Obama hadn't always claimed that the words "corporation" and "corruption" were synonyms; after all, in 1991 Justice Thurgood Marshall, a hero to the Left, argued in a dissenting opinion to *Renne* v. *Geary* that the gratitude a candidate feels toward his supporters "is not a corruption of the democratic political process; it is the democratic political process." Stopping groups of people, whether in associations or corporations, from publicly supporting or attacking a candidate is an attack on democracy itself, as the people's right to petition the government, whether individually or in groups, is explicitly what the First Amendment protects. As Alexander Hamilton wrote in *Federalist 35* published in 1788:

> Is it not natural that a man, who is a candidate for the favor of the People and who is dependent on the suffrages of his fellow-citizens for the continuance of his public honors, should … be willing to allow them their proper degree of influence upon his conduct? This dependence, and the necessity of being bound himself, and his posterity, by the laws to which he gives his assent, are the true, and they are the strong chords of sympathy, between the representative and the constituent.

To this end, Senator McConnell thought the government should be restricted to investigating actual cases of alleged bribery of public officials. Silencing groups and corporations because their money might influence a candidate is clearly unconstitutional; after all, the First Amendment protects the right to "petition the Government for a redress of grievances."

It is actually quite extraordinary to expect corporations, by law, to have to filter their messages through the media, as newspapers and other media outlets often officially endorse candidates who may very well be anti-business. However, despite this glaring hypocrisy, partly because of the complexity of the issue, and partly because corporations are reluctant to stick their necks out for fear of impacting their bottom lines, Senator McCain prevailed and the law passed. President George W. Bush then signed McCain-Feingold, despite what Bush called "reservations about the constitutionality of the broad ban on issue advertising."[6]

Instead of vetoing the infringement on the First Amendment, Bush appeared to expect the Supreme Court to nullify McCain-Feingold for him. Bush seems to have forgotten that the Supreme Court is not the only protector of the Constitution; each branch of government has this responsibility. In the end, Bush's political calculation backfired; in December 2003, the Court upheld most of the legislation in *McConnell* v. *FEC* by a 5–4 majority.

After *McConnell* v. *FEC* was decided mostly in favor of silencing corporate political speech, Justice Antonin Scalia scathingly pointed out the liberal justices' hypocrisy: "Who could have imagined that the same court which, within the past four years, has sternly disapproved of restrictions upon such inconsequential forms of expression as virtual child pornography, tobacco advertising, dissemination of illegally intercepted communications, and sexually explicit cable programming, would smile with favor upon a law that cuts to the heart of what the First Amendment is meant to protect: the right to criticize the government."[7]

After all this brouhaha, Bossie was hoping the Constitution would get a better hearing in 2009, as Chief Justice John Roberts had since replaced Justice Sandra Day O'Connor on the Court. (O'Connor had voted with the liberals to uphold McCain-Feingold's muzzle on corporate speech in *McConnell* v. *FEC.*) Roberts was Bush's pick, so to be fair, maybe Bush's political calculation would pay off in the end, as Roberts seemed to understand that the Federal Election Commission (FEC) shouldn't be instructed to treat political ads near elections as potential felonies.

Bossie found a seat on a crowded pew beneath the Court Chamber's 44-foot ceiling. Over a mahogany rail in front he could see former Bush solicitor general Ted Olson, the attorney representing Citizens United, and attorney Floyd Abrams representing Senator McConnell. These two would argue that the First Amendment clearly protects the political speech of every American, whether they own a business or not.

On the other side Bossie saw the government attorneys, President Barack Obama's U.S. Solicitor General, Elena Kagan (who, in August 2010, became a U.S. Supreme Court justice), and Seth Waxman, an attorney representing Senator John McCain.

The nine justices shuffled austerely out in black robes and took seats around a wing-shaped bench. As someone slammed a gavel, Bossie, as the president of Citizens United, knew he wasn't a lone victim hoping he'd regain the right to advertise and sell political documentaries. He represented every factory owner, CEO, union leader, small-business owner, nonprofit group, and even every artist who was incorporated. He stood for every corporate leader and owner of a mom-and-pop business who wanted to back politicians who promised to fight for business freedom, for the right to make a profit and thereby drive the American economy. He stood for every corporate leader who wanted to publicly oppose politicians whose policies they thought would harm their businesses and their employees. This is why groups from the National Rifle Association (NRA) to The American Civil Liberties Union (ACLU) to the U.S. Chamber of Commerce had presented amicus briefs to the Supreme Court arguing that these First Amendment restrictions must be found unconstitutional. (Though the left-leaning ACLU later had a board fight over its opposition to McCain-Feingold and sent the issue to its special committee on campaign finance for further consideration.)

This law was muzzling Americans, not just inanimate corporations. David Bossie couldn't stomach the idea that American business owners could be popularly reviled as corrupt bourgeoisie. In times past, the American business owner was an iconic figure, someone living the American Dream, someone others wanted to emulate. Names such as William Randolph Hurst, John D. Rockefeller, and Andrew Carnegie were synonymous with success. They were called "captains of industry." One such captain of industry, J. P. Morgan, actually bailed out the U.S. government in 1895. After the Sherman Silver Purchase Act was largely responsible for spiraling the U.S. government into debt, Morgan and his group (J. P. Morgan & Company) came to the rescue by replenishing the U.S. gold reserve with $62,000,000 in gold. In these bloated times, the federal government has grown too big for a Morgan to bail out, and in government's desire to grow it now even sees business leaders as threats that must be silenced, not as assets shaping America's future in a competitive world.

Today, to get its way, the government must silence people such as Steve Sanetti, the CEO of the National Shooting Sports Foundation (NSSF), a trade group representing 5,500 firearms manufacturers, retailers, and more. Members of the NSSF include companies such as Remington Arms Co., the oldest continuously operating firearms manufacturer in North America. But some legislators in the U.S. Congress are embarrassed that companies such as Remington are in business in America, even though Remington supplies police forces with Model 870 shotguns, the special forces with Model 24 sniper rifles, and millions of American hunters with firearms. Some politicians would like to see America's firearms manufacturers go bankrupt. They're after their livelihood. And then they silenced them with McCain-Fiengold. Why?

In 2002, as McCain-Fiengold—backed by Senators John McCain and Russell Feingold (D-WI)—took away people's free speech, progressive politicians were conspiring to put American firearm manufacturers out of business. President Bill Clinton's administration had thought it fair play in the late 1990s to sue firearms manufacturers on behalf of thugs who use guns to rob, rape, and kill. If a rifle blows up due to poor design, then the manufacturer should be held liable, just as Chevy should be liable if its Suburban explodes due to a faulty gas line. But if someone drives their Toyota Prius down a crowded sidewalk, then Toyota shouldn't be held responsible. Similarly, when someone uses a legally obtained Winchester to commit murder, Winchester shouldn't be held accountable; the murderer should. But the government thought they could use lies and emotional public appeals to hold Remington, Winchester, and so on liable for the actions of criminals. Such was the gist of a series of lawsuits from Democratic mayors and Clinton's Justice Department, designed to bankrupt firearms manufacturers.

So America had an age-old manufacturing sector being bankrupted by government lawsuits that wasn't allowed to publicly fight back against the peoples' elected representatives within sixty days of a federal election. Despite these undemocratic impediments, after years of lobbying by American manufacturers, Congress finally passed the Protection of Lawful Commerce in Arms Act, an act signed into federal law in 2005 that still allows firearms manufacturers to be sued for product liability, but not for criminal misuse of their products. Without the NSSF and the NRA's millions of members and its dedicated lobbyists, the Protection of Lawful Commerce in Arms Act would never have passed. Such examples illustrate that lobbying by corporations is a self-defense mechanism against government. Corporations have to defend themselves from intrusive regulations, taxes, and sometimes from frontal attacks by government entities. Lobbying and paying for issue ads aren't inherently good or bad any more than free speech is inherently good or bad; it's the First Amendment right to "petition the government" and to speak one's mind that is good and the loss of it that is bad.

This is why every industry now has to hire lobbyists to make sure unfair taxes and regulations don't target them—taxes such as the 10 percent sales tax "found" in President Obama's Health Care and Education Reconciliation Act of 2010 that specifically targets tanning salons. In fact, this is how major corporations have learned that the Washington elite can make or break them. During the financial meltdown of 2008, Washington, behind President George W. Bush's administration, bailed out Bear Stearns, but then let Lehman Brothers sink in the ensuing panic, before later riding to the rescue of Goldman Sachs by bailing out AIG. Then, in 2009, President Barack Obama used similarly open-ended discretionary power (and money appropriated for another purpose) to give major stakes in the auto industry to labor unions that support him. Industry, more than ever before, has to actively engage Washington politicians.

The ethanol industry is a stark example of how government can affect private industry. The ethanol industry exists almost entirely today because of subsidies from taxpayers. And ethanol is just a small part of the government's "green economy." Indeed, the prospect of the Obama administration passing cap-and-trade legislation that would put a price on carbon emissions and then allot credits to certain companies started a gold rush among some large corporations because the carbon allotments could be worth billions of dollars. This is why the *American Spectator* reported that companies hired some 2,500 lobbyists in 2009 to lobby for cap-and-trade.[8] Washington has made itself the Godfather of industry, and all the companies have to come to it for favors and to avoid being penalized. Those favors require lobbying and donations. McCain-Feingold's silencing of corporate free speech near elections only made lobbying more important, which then made corruption, by McCain's definition, more likely.

Bossie found himself in this mad conundrum where government has the power not only to pick corporate winners and losers, but also to silence corporations. Bossie was running a non-profit corporation, Citizens United, that specializes in making political documentaries which it couldn't advertise to the American public because the films might imperil a politician's political aspirations. Bossie naturally wanted his freedom back. He also didn't want to commit a felony in the process; ironically, the government would punish Bossie individually for breaking the law, even though they claimed corporations didn't have individual rights.

So before the 2004 presidential election, Citizens United sent a letter to the FEC asking if they could market a documentary on Senator John Kerry (D-MA) and a book Bossie had written about Senator Kerry. FEC Chairman Bradley A. Smith responded on September 9, 2004:

> [O]ur Advisory Opinion finds that Citizens United may not benefit from the press exemption for broadcasting its documentary because of a lack of record producing documentaries, and because it was to pay for the broadcasting of the documentary, rather than be paid by broadcasters for the right to use it. Also, Citizens United may not pay for advertisements for Mr. Bossie's book because those expenditures would not "appear in a news story, commentary or editorial" and would not be part of a normal media function.[9]

They even censored ads for Bossie's book! The public, however, still didn't grasp that McCain-Feingold was government censorship of capitalists, associations, and other groups. This lack of public awareness largely occurred because the press either didn't much care or had chosen sides—McCain-Feingold, after all, gave the press an exemption. This is hypocritical, as many newspapers—including the *New York Times,* the *Los Angles Times,* and the *Washington Post*—endorse candidates during every national election cycle. And many of the major media companies are owned by huge corporations. The *Los Angles Times* is owned by Tribune Company, ABC is owned by Disney, and NBC is owned by General Electric. Yet Congress decided it could deem who could and who couldn't publicly support a candidate? And the press largely stayed mute?

Thus in 2008, Bossie, through Citizens United, produced *Hillary the Movie*, a partisan film that investigated Hillary Clinton's career and politics. Bossie says he planned to use the government's censorship of this film to again challenge the First Amendment infringement McCain-Feingold created. Citizens United sued and subsequently lost lower court decisions, but everyone knew those rulings didn't matter; this was a constitutional question for the Supreme Court to readdress. Finally, on appeal, the Supreme Court said it would take the case.

On March 24, 2009, the Court held its first oral hearing for *Citizens United* v. *FEC.* Kagan's deputy, Malcolm L. Stewart, represented the government and argued it was constitutional for McCain-Feingold to prohibit corporations and unions from spending funds to elect or to defeat political candidates; however, when asked how much censorship power the Obama administration thought was constitutionally permissible, Stewart stumbled. When Chief Justice John Roberts asked Stewart what would happen if a corporation published a 500-page political book that ended with a single sentence endorsing a particular candidate, Stewart answered that such an endorsement would constitute "express advocacy" and therefore a corporation could only fund the publication of the book through a political-action committee. "And if they didn't, you could ban it?" asked the chief justice. "If they didn't, we could prohibit publication of the book," Stewart replied.

That alarming testimony is thought to be what prompted justices to call for an unusual second oral hearing for the case. This is what Bossie had come for on September 9, 2009. Citizens United's attorney, Ted Olson, spoke first. He didn't say anything surprising, though Justice Ruth Bader Ginsburg voiced the progressive opinion that corporations shouldn't have the same rights as individuals, as if someone who starts a successful business loses his or her First Amendment rights because other people pay for their products or services. What people were waiting for was how the government would parse its book-banning power.

When the government's turn came, U.S. Solicitor General Elena Kagan, instead of her deputy, stood at the podium before the Court. Justice Ginsburg asked Kagan whether it was still the government's position that it was constitutional for McCain-Feingold to ban TV, radio, and newspaper ads, and even political books.

"The government's answer has changed," Kagan replied, causing the people in the benches to break the rule mandating they be silent, by laughing.

Of course it had, but how?

Kagan conceded that although the statute in question did cover "full-length books," it would be subject to "quite good" challenges if it were ever used to ban a book. Moreover, she pointed out that the FEC had never enforced the law with respect to books.

Chief Justice Roberts didn't like her contrived answer. He said, "We don't put our First Amendment rights in the hands of FEC bureaucrats." Then he asked, "If you say that you are not going to apply it to a book, what about a pamphlet?"

Kagan answered, "I think a pamphlet would be different. A pamphlet is pretty classic electioneering, so there is no attempt to say that 441 b only applies to video and not to print."

On hearing this exchange, Bossie sighed with relief. He felt that even the liberals on the bench couldn't condone censorship of a pamphlet; after all, Thomas Paine's *Common Sense*, which in 1776 articulated why Americans had to try to end English rule, has long been considered a pamphlet.

During a subsequent series of questions, Kagan attempted to reassure the justices that a book containing hundreds of pages would not be banned even if it endorsed a candidate; she seemed to think they should just forget what her deputy had said a few months earlier. However, Kagan did imply that if the book engaged in "express advocacy," then it could be banned; as a result, if her contrived view of the law were put into effect, the FEC would have been required to define the differences between books and pamphlets. Is it a book if it has more than 100 pages? How about 150? Is a paperback a book, or is it really a pamphlet? FEC bureaucrats would also have had to decide what constitutes "express advocacy." Does a political candidate have to be named? Would a politician's catch phrases, such as "spread the wealth around," count? Such decisions would require FEC staffers either to become book reviewers or a de facto censorship committee.

When the hearing ended, Bossie walked out with his attorney past the statues dedicated to justice, intoxicated with the optimistic view that his freedom of speech would be returned.

Months later, in January 2010, the U.S. Supreme Court ruled 5–4 to un-gag union leaders, CEOs, and small-business owners alike. 5–4? The four liberals on the Court are okay with the FEC banning political pamphlets? Bossie says he still can't believe the vote was a 5–4 close call.

The majority ruled: "If the First Amendment has any force, it prohibits Congress from fining or jailing citizens, or associations of citizens, for simply engaging in political speech."

Chief Justice Roberts wrote:

> The Government urges us in this case to uphold a direct prohibition on political speech. It asks us to embrace a theory of the First Amendment that would allow censorship not only of television and radio broadcasts, but of pamphlets, posters, the Internet, and virtually any other medium that corporations and unions might find useful in expressing their views on matters of public concern. Its theory, if accepted, would empower the Government to prohibit newspapers from running editorials or opinion pieces supporting or opposing candidates for office, so long as the newspapers were owned by corporations—as the major ones are. First Amendment rights could be confined to individuals, subverting the vibrant public discourse that is at the foundation of our democracy. The Court properly rejects that theory....The First Amendment protects more than just the individual on a soapbox and the lonely pamphleteer.

Justice Scalia's words were even stronger:

> The notion which follows from the dissent's view, that modern newspapers, since they are incorporated, have free-speech rights only at the sufferance of Congress, boggles the mind.... If speech can be prohibited because, in the view of the Government, it leads to "moral decay" or does not serve "public ends," then there is no limit to the Government's censorship power.

Days after the ruling, during his 2010 State of the Union speech on January 27, President Barack Obama literally looked down on six of the justices in the United States Capitol Building as he condemned their ruling on national television:

> With all due deference to separation of powers, last week the Supreme Court reversed a century of law that I believe will open the floodgates for special interests—including foreign corporations—to spend without limit in our elections. I don't think American elections should be bankrolled by America's most powerful interests, or worse, by foreign entities. They should be decided by the American people. And I'd urge Democrats and Republicans to pass a bill that helps to correct some of these problems.[10]

It's strange that President Obama doesn't think U.S. business owners qualify as "American people." And how do you define: "America's most powerful interests"? A famous person could be a powerful interest, as could a politician. This mixed-up logic prompts an ironic question: Because the Bill of Rights is a list of restrictions on the government, how can we leave who gets and who doesn't get the freedoms safeguarded from the government to the government?

Justice Samuel Alito didn't buy President Obama's spin. During President Obama's rebuke, television cameras caught Alito mouthing the words "not true." Alito's act of defiance was then played for weeks on news broadcasts.

President Obama, however, still thought he had a safe populist position, so he went on to call the Court's decision "a major victory for big oil, Wall Street banks, health insurance companies, and the other powerful interests that marshal their power every day in Washington to drown out the voices of everyday Americans."[11] Other progressive politicians and liberals also recoiled at the notion that American businessmen and women could again legally strike back during elections at politicians who vote for anti-business policies.

Representative Alan Grayson (D-FL) hyperbolically called the ruling "the worst Supreme Court decision since the Dred Scott case."[12] (In *Dred Scott* v. *Sandford*, the Supreme Court held that slaves were property without rights.) Representative Donna Edwards (D-MD) said she'd like to reverse the decision with a constitutional amendment.[13] Representative Leonard Boswell (D-IA) formally introduced legislation to amend the constitution.[14] Senator John Kerry (D-MA) also called for a constitutional amendment to silence America's business community.[15]

Senator McCain said he was "disappointed by the decision of the Supreme Court and the lifting of the limits on corporate and union contributions," but he wasn't particularly surprised by the decision, as he said, "It was clear that Justice Roberts, Alito and Scalia, by their very skeptical and even sarcastic comments, were very much opposed to BCRA."[16]

The *New York Times* opined in an editorial: "The Supreme Court has handed lobbyists a new weapon. A lobbyist can now tell any elected official: if you vote wrong, my company, labor union, or interest group will spend unlimited sums explicitly advertising against your re-election."[17]

This causes an educated, freedom-loving electorate to holler, "Good, that's called the democratic process."

The *Los Angeles Times* explained why so many Democrats were angry that the business community might get a chance to defend themselves in the court of public opinion: "Many analysts predict the ruling will benefit Republicans in next fall's [2010] midterm elections."[18]

Maybe so, thought Democrats. So to again curb the free speech of those paying the highest percentage of taxes, in April 2010 Senator Charles E. Schumer (D-NY), former Chairman of the Democratic Senatorial Campaign Committee, and Representative Chris Van Hollen (D-MD), Chairman of the Democratic Congressional Campaign Committee, introduced legislation in the Senate and House, respectively, designed to muzzle the business community. Subsequently, on June 24, 2010, H.R.5175 (The Disclose Act) passed by 219–206 in the U.S. House of Representatives–217 of the "yes" votes were from Democrats.

When the Disclose Act passed the House, Senator Schumer boasted that the legislation "will make [corporations] think twice" before attempting to influence election outcomes, and that this "deterrent effect should not be underestimated."[19]

R. Bruce Josten, executive vice president for government affairs at the U.S. Chamber of Commerce, didn't underestimate the Disclose Act's deterrent effect. He noted that the Disclose Act would exempt money transfers between affiliated entities–including individuals rather than organizations–up to $50,000. This tweak in the law would exempt unions, which are dues based, not corporations. Josten, who long referred to the Bipartisan Campaign Reform Act of 2002 as the "Democratic Incumbent Protection Act," knew he had a fight on his hands if the American business community was going to retain the freedom to speak freely during elections.

Josten put out a statement saying, "Just when you think the special interest backroom deals can't get any worse, House leadership inserts a carve-out designed to even further butter the breads of labor unions and squelch free speech. Unions would be able to shift unlimited amounts of money around through various affiliated entities, completely absolved of any disclosure requirements. This is a brazen case of rewarding political allies at the expense of everyone else, and is corrupt politics at its worst...."

Strong words, but the U.S. Chamber of Commerce isn't the powerhouse it might be on this issue. The Chamber is located across Lafayette Park from the White House. It represents more than 3 million businesses, as well as state and local chambers and industry associations. Some 96 percent of its members are small businesses with 100 employees or fewer. The Chamber had submitted an amicus brief for *Citizens United* v. *FEC* calling for an end to the restrictions on its members' free speech. The Chamber's gaudy lobby and large office building on the Hill insinuate power, yet Josten says the Chamber wasn't willing to legally challenge McCain-Feingold. Nor were its members. It took a small, independent nonprofit, Citizens United, to pose the constitutional question to the courts.

Why was the business community so unwilling to slug it out for its free speech?

The complexity of the laws was the first reason. In an attempt to educate the Chamber's members on what McCain-Feingold outlawed, Josten invited representatives from Chamber member businesses to a conference. He booked the Chamber's largest room, thinking he'd have droves of business leaders in who wanted to learn how to navigate the nearly unintelligible campaign-finance law. But only eighteen people showed up. Josten led them to a smaller room. He then found that even the people who did show up were clearly confused by the law's exemptions and clauses. Josten realized the whole topic was too convoluted and complex for people busy watching their bottom lines and stock prices to deal with. Actually, calling it a complex issue is a gross understatement; after all, even the U.S. Supreme Court's first dalliance with McCain-Feingold in *McConnell* v. *FEC* resulted in a 273-page, horribly intricate decision.

To deal with the law and the *McConnell* decision, Josten says, "Either businesses had to hire attorneys to interpret and comply with these dense new regulations, or they just had to stay out of politics. Most pulled out of the process for fear of making a mistake and thereby committing a felony, even though they knew doing so was at their own peril."[20]

Another reason the business community was reluctant to challenge the loss of their free speech was that politicians had successfully defined them as "special interests." This is why even after the Court struck down McCain-Feingold, American businesses still hadn't won in the court of public opinion. Many Americans buy the narrative that lobbyists–the people corporations and groups hire to represent them on complex issues–are by definition corrupt special interests. The truth, however, is more interesting than the demagoguery: the number of lobbyists is actually proportional to the size of the federal government. The bigger and more intrusive the government gets, the more unions, associations, and corporations have to hire lobbyists to defend their interests. Lobbying is a necessary self-defense measure against a government that passes favors to its friends and tosses targeted taxes onto the backs of the not-so-well-connected.

Nevertheless, the American public doesn't see lobbyists as a necessary defense against burdensome government; in fact, lobbyists are held in such low esteem that, prior to the 1980s, lawmakers rarely walked out of elected positions and into lobbying firms. The profession was once upon a less onerous time considered to be degrading for former congressmen; however, as corporations desperately sought lobbyists with enough influence to defend them from the ever-growing federal government, congressmen started being offered enough money to make sweet-talking former colleagues worth the loss of face. In fact, Public Citizen, a group that lobbies on behalf of "the people," published a report entitled "The Journey from Congress to K Street" which analyzed hundreds of lobbyist registration documents filed in compliance with the Lobbying Disclose Act and the Foreign Agents Registration Act, and found that between 1998 and 2005, 43 percent of the 198 members of Congress who'd left government registered to lobby their former peers.

The public's perception of lobbyists is why Democrats didn't see any political price to pay for pushing the Disclose Act. Senator Schumer said the Disclose Act would:[21]

1. Enhance Disclaimers: Make CEOs and other leaders take responsibility for their ads.
2. Enhance Disclosures: It is time to follow the money.

3. Prevent Foreign Influence: Foreign countries and entities should not be determining the outcome of our elections.
4. Shareholder/Member Disclosure: We should allow shareholders and members to know where money goes.
5. Prevent Government Contractors from Spending: Taxpayer money should not be spent on political ads.
6. Provide the Lowest Unit Rate for Candidates and Parties: Special interests should not drown out the voices of the people.
7. Tighten Coordination Rules: Corporations should not be able to "sponsor" a candidate.

Take a look again at number six: the Disclose Act would not only criminalize corporate free speech while giving unions exemptions, it would also "provide the lowest unit rate for candidates and parties." Democrats didn't just want to shut up the business owners who, incidentally, pay the largest share of taxes; they wanted to make sure they got the cheapest rate for their free speech from media corporations. As for number seven's ban on corporate endorsements, would this include the newspapers that are corporations? Many of the other requirements, such as getting shareholders to approve all political expenditures, would slow corporations down so much they couldn't react to a changing political climate. These requirements would also result in battles within corporations—if, that is, any publicly owned corporation would be insane enough to attempt to run this gauntlet.

As a result of these limitations on free speech, Republicans in the Senate stayed unanimously opposed to the Disclose Act. The Senate then voted 57–41. Though they had a majority, this vote didn't give the Democrats the three-fifths majority they needed to end debate on the Disclose Act. The bill, which would have been enacted thirty days after its passage, would have been in time to silence critics during the 2010 Midterm Elections.

Anyone wondering how disclosure muzzles corporate speech needs to look no further than what happened in August 2010 when MN Forward, a Republican-leaning political group, reported accepting $150,000 from the retail outlet Target. Democrats and gay advocacy groups pounced on Target by threatening to boycott its stores. MoveOn.org even launched a TV ad urging shoppers to boycott the chain. MN Forward was supporting Tom Emmer, the Republican candidate for Minnesota governor, who was an outspoken opponent of same-sex marriage, just like 80 percent of Americans and, officially, President Barack Obama. The attack on Target was especially fraudulent because Target has sponsored gay pride events and offers benefits to domestic partners; in fact, Target received a 100% score on Human Rights Campaign's 2010 Corporate Equality Index, a scoring system that rates companies on their policies regarding gay rights.

MoveOn.org, along with the gay rights advocacy group Human Rights Campaign, didn't care. They were after political points. So they told Target it must contribute $150,000 to pro-gay-rights candidates before they'd leave the company alone. When Target didn't comply—stating they were supporting the Republican's pro-business positions, not necessarily his disdain for same-sex marriage—MoveOn.org pushed its boycott campaign. In an editorial, even the liberal *Los Angeles Times* condemned this move: "For MoveOn.org, the fight is at least as much about corporate money as it is about gay rights.... [B]y pointing out Target's involvement in Emmer's campaign and obtaining an apology, MoveOn and Human Rights Campaign had already won; their calls for a boycott and attempt to strong-arm money from the company are deeply counterproductive."[22]

To avoid such shakedowns, Josten maintains that corporations should be able to contribute money to the DNC or the RNC or to the U.S. Chamber of Commerce's general political-action fund and so on without having to endorse a specific policy position, as they now can; after all, simply giving money to a candidate or a political party shouldn't have to be construed as express advocacy for a specific policy position. But that is what the Disclose Act was about—silencing corporate speech by forcing companies to assume ideological positions that would likely harm their bottom lines by chasing away consumers who disagreed.

This rancorous, complex, and hyperbolic battle over corporate free speech is unfortunately in keeping with American history. Just after the start of this nation, Federalists quelled criticism of their government with the Alien and Sedition Acts of 1798. President John Adams signed the acts into law. The Anti-Federalist press was the chief target of the Alien and Sedition Acts. Federalists viewed the Anti-Federalists as opponents of "genuine liberty"[23] for their criticism of the Adams administration. Thus, for example, Matthew Lyon, a Vermont congressman and the editor of the newspaper *The Scourge of Aristocracy*, was fined $1,000 and sentenced to four months in prison for criticizing the government. And famously, when President John Adams stopped in Newark, New Jersey, en route from Philadelphia to Quincy, Massachusetts, he was greeted by a crowd and by a committee that saluted him by firing a cannon. After the cannon went off, a bystander hollered, "There goes the President and they are firing at his ass." Then another bystander, Luther Baldwin, loudly replied that he did not care "if they fired through his ass." Baldwin was indicted and convicted in federal court for speaking "sedicious words tending to defame the President and Government of the United States."[24]

The Alien and Sedition Acts subsequently became a major political issue in the elections of 1798 and 1800. Although the Federalists hoped the Alien and Sedition Acts would muffle the opposition during the election, many people still spoke and published criticisms of the Federalists and made the Alien and Sedition Acts into a principal election issue. President Adams then lost his reelection bid to Thomas Jefferson, and the Alien and Sedition Acts were allowed to expire.

Nearly 120 years later, progressive president Woodrow Wilson signed The Espionage Act of 1917 into law. A year later, The Sedition Act of 1918 was added as amendments to The Sedition Act, making it a crime to utter, print, write, or publish any disloyal, profane, scurrilous, or abusive language about the United States. In James Mock's 1941 book, *Censorship 1917,* he noted that most U.S. newspapers "showed no antipathy toward the act" and, as with McCain-Feingold's restrictions on free speech, Mock found that "far from opposing the measure, the leading papers seemed actually to lead the movement in behalf of its speedy enactment." Hundreds of people were jailed during World War I for speaking out against the war, controversial publications were stopped in the mail, and mail to people suspected of sedition by the postmaster general was sent back, stamped "Mail to this address undeliverable under Espionage Act."

In *Abrams* v. *United States* (1919) the Supreme Court voted 7–2 to uphold the convictions of three people who had been imprisoned under the Espionage Act. Justices Oliver Wendell Holmes and Louis Brandeis dissented and said that the more protective "clear and present danger" standard ought to be used to overturn the conviction. Decades later the precedent was overturned in *Brandenburg* v. *Ohio* (1968), where the Court adopted the "incitement to imminent lawless action" standard, a test even more speech protective than the "clear and present danger" standard. Holmes thought a 20-year sentence against the defendants for printing a few leaflets was an unconstitutional punishment for advocating their beliefs. He wrote: "When men have realized that time has upset many fighting faiths, they may come to believe even more than they believe the very foundation of their own conduct that the ultimate good desired is better reached by free trade in ideas."

Ultimately, both attempts to muzzle political dissent backfired. For the same to happen today, this issue needs to be clearly understood for what it is by the American public. Arguments for freedom and justice, such as this summation from Justice Scalia from *Citizens Untied* v. *FEC*, must be heard:

> Dissent says that when the Framers "constitutionalized the right to free speech in the First Amendment, it was the free speech of individual Americans that they had in mind." That is no doubt true. All the provisions of the Bill of Rights set forth the rights of individual men and women—not, for example, of trees or polar bears. But the individual person's right to speak includes the right to speak in association with other individual

persons. Surely the dissent does not believe that speech by the Republican Party or the Democratic Party can be censored because it is not the speech of "an individual American."

Here Come the Thought Police

Attacks on the First Amendment by progressives don't stop with capitalists; they also include people the attackers just plain think should shut up. For example, Florida urologist Dr. Jack Cassell put up a sign on his office door declaring, "If you voted for Obama, seek urological care elsewhere. Changes to your health begin right now, not in four years." Dr. Cassell's congressman, the ever-quotable Representative Alan Grayson, (D-FL), accused Dr. Cassell of racism. "Well, in fact," said Grayson, "where [Cassell] lives, in Mount Dora, which is in my district, many, many of the Democrats who live in Mount Dora happen to be African-Americans. So, by saying that he will not treat somebody who supported Obama, he's saying that he's not going to treat a large number of African-Americans in this country."[25] Somehow Grayson made this into a racial issue. Perhaps that is just part of the reason why Grayson lost his reelection bid in 2010.

Though Dr. Cassell told everyone who would listen that the purpose of the sign was to point out that Obamacare would harm patients and that he wasn't literally turning down patients, Representative Grayson publicly toyed with the idea of passing legislation to silence Dr. Cassell. Since that move wasn't politically feasible, Grayson called Dr. Cassell a racist, in an attempt to silence Dr. Cassell with false accusations and thereby stop public dissent of a controversial Democratic bill.

For the same reason, many on the Left, including the Speaker of the U.S. House of Representatives Nancy Pelosi and the U.S. Senate Majority Leader Harry Reid, insinuated that anyone who criticizes President Barack Obama must be a white-hooded racist, especially those who go to Tea Party rallies.

They believe you're allowed free speech, just not speech they don't approve of. For example, in October 2009 President Obama signed a defense authorization bill that included a "hate crimes" provision. Democrats slipped the hate crimes language into a defense-spending bill after a stand-alone bill written to make homosexuals a specially protected class had failed to pass Congress year after year. "After more than a decade of opposition and delay, we've passed inclusive hate crimes legislation to help protect our citizens from violence based on what they look like, who they love, how they pray, or who they are," Obama boasted.[26]

The hate crimes provision allows the U.S. Justice Department to seek harsher penalties against someone who allegedly attacked another because the person is gay, a woman, or has a disability. People whom the government views as targets of hatred were added to the already-covered race and religion categories. The problem with levying more severe penalties based on motive is that it constitutes punishing "thought crimes." Judges, attorneys, and juries will now have to try to get into peoples' minds to decide if they acted out of hate.

Prosecuting people for what they think violates the American principle of equal justice under the law; after all, every violent crime is a hate crime, and every victim has equal rights—some people aren't more special than others. But a party that backs affirmative action (which constitutes giving some people advantages based on their race or gender, while disadvantaging others based on the same criteria) has already turned up its nose at equal justice under the law.

Incredibly, this hate-crimes law actually lays the legal foundation for investigating, prosecuting, and thus jailing anyone who says or even is thought to have racial or sexual beliefs someone else might find offensive. This is Orwellian. In the novel *1984* by George Orwell, a "thoughtcrime" is an illegal type of thought. The novel's main character, Winston Smith, writes in his diary: "Thoughtcrime does not entail death: thoughtcrime is death." Orwell's Thought Police use psychological surveillance to find and eliminate members of society who are capable of the mere idea that could challenge the ruling authority. Orwell's Thought Police were inspired by the methods used by the Third Reich and by Joseph Stalin's Communist empire. So now they're being created in America?

Many constitutions in democratic countries explicitly protect the freedom of thought. For instance, the First Amendment says laws may not be made that interfere with religion "or [prohibit] the free exercise thereof." Indeed, even the liberal Supreme Court Justice Benjamin Cardozo reasoned in *Palko* v. *Connecticut* (1937): "Freedom of thought ... is the matrix, the indispensable condition, of nearly every other form of freedom. With rare aberrations a pervasive recognition of this truth can be traced in our history, political and legal."

Freedom of thought is also a vital part of international human rights law. In the United Nations' Universal Declaration of Human Rights, freedom of thought is listed under Article 18: "Everyone has the right to freedom of thought, conscience and religion; this right includes freedom to change his religion or belief, and freedom, either alone or in community with others and in public or private, to manifest his religion or belief in teaching, practice, worship and observance."

As it is impossible to know with certainty what another person is thinking, giving this power to the state grants the government an open-ended, impossible-to-define check on First Amendment rights. Such a power could turn a bureaucrat into a member of the Gestapo. To caution against this form of censorship the Bible, in Ecclesiastes 8:8, says, "There is no man that has power over the spirit, to retain it; neither has he power in the day of death." And Queen Elizabeth I (1533–1603) actually revoked a thought censorship law because, according to Sir Francis Bacon, she did "not [like] to make windows into men's souls and secret thoughts."[27]

Liberals are not willing to dispense these hate-speech laws fairly. For example, after Marine Lance Corporal Matthew A. Snyder was killed while serving in Iraq, his family arranged for a private funeral at St. John's Catholic Church in Westminster, Maryland. When the family arrived at the church they found Fred Phelps there with his Kansas-based cult, consisting mostly of members of a single family, holding placards saying things such as: "God Loves Dead Soldiers," "Semper Fi Fags," and "Thank God for IEDs."

Albert Snyder, the father of the fallen soldier, only wanted to bury his son in peace. Meanwhile, Phelps, who has called America a "sodomite nation of flag-worshipping idolaters," was there to say he was glad Snyder's son was dead.

Phelps is a disbarred lawyer who has run for public office in Kansas five times, as a Democrat. Phelps and his cult members travel around the country and hold signs outside military funerals because they believe the reason American soldiers die in wars is that God abhors America's tolerance of homosexuality—one of the Left's especially "protected" classes of people.

Snyder was so incensed he sued Phelps' cult group for emotional distress and won a $5 million judgment from a jury. But on appeal, the Fourth Circuit Court of Appeals reversed the ruling, finding in favor of protecting the protesters' First Amendment rights to free speech. Snyder next appealed his case to the Supreme Court, which heard the case (*Snyder* v. *Phelps*) on November 2, 2010. The court had to decide whether the tort of "intentional infliction of emotional distress" (IIED) can justly exist in a country with a First Amendment. The tort of IIED bars speech or conduct that is specifically intended to inflict emotional distress, such as "hate speech." The Second Restatement of Torts (1965) defines IIED as conduct "so outrageous in character, and so extreme in degree, as to go beyond all possible bounds of decency, and to be regarded as atrocious, and utterly intolerable in a civilized community."

If you're going to have a First Amendment infringement, such as hate-speech laws, then you have to at least apply the laws equally. Most liberals refused to get behind this father's right to bury his son in peace. Many conservatives, meanwhile, find the very idea that the government can decide who is "atrocious and utterly intolerable" to run counter to the First Amendment's restriction on government censorship. Of course, most IIED claims—typically based on name-calling and other petty affronts—are tossed out of court. But if a cult holding signs saying "God Loves Dead Soldiers" at a bereaved family's funeral, a place where the family has no choice but to be, isn't practicing hate speech, then the laws should be ruled unconstitutional, as they can't be applied equally.

On March 2, 2011, the Supreme Court voted 8–1 that Phelps' cult group has the First Amendment right to heckle bereaved families as they bury their fallen heroes. The majority opinion, written by Chief Justice John Roberts, ruled that:

> Speech is powerful. It can stir people to action, move them to tears of both joy and sorrow, and—as it did here—inflict great pain. On the facts before us, we cannot react to that pain by punishing the speaker. As a Nation we have chosen a different course—to protect even hurtful speech on public issues to ensure that we do not stifle public debate.

This was a narrow decision in which Justice Roberts wrote: "[O]ur opinion here is limited by the particular facts before us." Justice Roberts made a point of leaving states with the authority to restrict when and where activists can protest in order to preserve the rights of people who want to do law-abiding things like go to funerals without being verbally assaulted.

Justice Samuel Alito was the lone dissenter in this case. He wrote, "Our profound national commitment to free and open debate is not a license for the vicious verbal assault that occurred in this case." He thought that Snyder just wanted "to bury his son in peace. But respondents, members of the Westboro Baptist Church, deprived him of that elementary right." Justice Alito noted that Phelps' activists issued a press release in an effort to turn the funeral into "a tumultuous media event" and then "launched a malevolent verbal attack on Matthew and his family at a time of acute emotional vulnerability."

As a First Amendment protection from government censorship, *Snyder* v. *Phelps* is a narrow ruling that allows states to legislate protections for private and bereaved individuals. It didn't give the nanny state a new power to decide who gets to speak. If the Supreme Court now begins to treat all protesters with this same hands-off standard, then perhaps hate-speech laws designed to favor some groups over others will also be struck down as other cases come before the Court. Indeed, if a case against anti-abortion protesters makes it once again to the Supreme Court, it will be interesting to see if the liberal justices on the bench will consistently side with First Amendment protections from government censorship, as they did in this case, or if they'll rule that certain "protected groups" (as the Left likes to call them) should get special rights to privacy—rights Albert Snyder and his family didn't get.

Politically Correct Speech Only

Today's Thought Police may be just getting their regulations in order, but recently the Left twisted an existing law in an attempt to make felons out of people who broadcast speech they don't like. In 2004 Robert Stevens, a resident of Virginia, found himself in an area of speech progressives would like to squelch.

Stevens thought he was living in a free country. He thought he had the right to free speech. He knew that in practice, the right to freedom of speech is not absolute, that it is subject to limitations, such as not inciting a riot. But he didn't think producing videos on pit bulls in which he broke no laws could itself constitute a felony. But then Stevens found himself in court embroiled in a case ultimately headed to the Supreme Court, a First Amendment case that could make it a felony to air a documentary on dog training or hunting or anything a government bureaucrat might deem objectionable.

Baffled? So was Stevens. He'd published a book titled *Dogs of Velvet and Steel: Pit Bulls*, as well as DVDs on pit bulls. He thought he was a law-abiding example of the American dream. But then Stevens was charged under Section 48 of Title 18, United States Code, which stated, "Whoever knowingly creates, sells or possesses a depiction of animal cruelty with the intention of placing that depiction in interstate or foreign commerce for commercial gain, shall be fined under this title or imprisoned not more than 5 years, or both."

This federal statute defined "depiction of animal cruelty" as "any photograph, motion-picture film, video recording, electronic image or sound recording of conduct in which a living animal is intentionally maimed, mutilated, tortured, wounded, or killed, if such conduct is illegal under Federal law or the law of the State in which the creation, sale, or possession takes place, regardless of whether the maiming, mutilation, torture, wounding, or killing took place in the State." Yeah, that's right, *Field & Stream* magazine could break this law by simply mailing an issue containing a bear-hunting article to someone in Florida, a state with no bear season.

The statute passed through Congress and was signed into law by President Bill Clinton with virtually no opposition, because Congress never intended to curb First Amendment rights by condemning an entire, law-abiding industry (hunting media), or dog trainers who use shock collars, or someone making a documentary with animal footage shot in another country.

Stevens thought this ideological overreach wouldn't stand. He was certain he'd beat the silly charge and go home. Meanwhile, the national media ignored the story. Stevens wasn't a very sympathetic person, not to them. He was writing books and selling videos on pit bulls, a breed with a very poor reputation. Many in the national media thought bureaucrats should go after politically incorrect people like Stevens.

Stevens hired an attorney and appeared in a federal court in Pittsburgh in 2004. He was the first person to be prosecuted under the decade-old statute. Stevens' documentary on pit bulls covers the breed's history, their misuse as fighting dogs, and details their practical uses for home-protection and for legal hunting methods. He included pit bull fight footage (recorded in Japan) as an example of how this breed has been misused.

Then, in January 2005, a jury that had been instructed it had no choice but to apply the law as the government saw it convicted Stevens of a felony and sentenced him to thirty-seven months in prison for making and selling the films. They did this even though there was never any allegation that Stevens engaged in dog fighting or any act of animal cruelty. They took away his right to vote and to own a gun and sentenced him to prison.

Stevens' attorney, Patricia Millett, commented, "The notion that Congress can suddenly strip a broad swath of never-before-regulated speech of First Amendment protection and send its creators to federal prison, based on nothing more than an ad hoc balancing of the 'expressive value' of the speech against its 'societal costs' is entirely alien to constitutional jurisprudence and a dangerous threat to liberty."[28]

Naturally, Stevens appealed. The Third Circuit Court of Appeals overturned the conviction as unconstitutional based on the First Amendment; however, before Stevens could sing "God Bless America," the government appealed to the Supreme Court, which scheduled the case for September 2009. Stevens and his attorney didn't know what the high court would do.

In the oral hearing for *U.S.* v. *Stevens* (2009), the government argued it had a "compelling interest" to prevent people from profiting from animal cruelty. The federal prosecutors said they were just after people who sell things like "crush" videos, in which women, with their faces unseen, are shown stomping rabbits or puppies to death with spiked-heel shoes. By using such horrific examples, the government attorneys tried to make the case about animal cruelty, even though Stevens was never charged with a single act of animal cruelty. Stevens didn't crush puppies; he showed dogfight footage someone else had recorded in Japan, where it is legal.

To understand why the government was reaching, you need look no further than the statute's exemption: "Subsection (a) does not apply to any depiction that has serious religious, political, scientific, educational, journalistic, historical or artistic value." So, if the conviction were reinstated, the federal government would have had the legally vague authority to determine "value." They could later have used this moral mandate to jail people they don't approve of, such as hunters and trappers and some moron who makes a home video of a dog on a trampoline. This is why

U.S. v. *Stevens* was about the First Amendment, not animal cruelty; after all, animal cruelty is already illegal in all fifty states.

After the oral hearings at the Supreme Court and the months of waiting for a decision, the Court struck down the federal animal-cruelty statute with an 8–1 ruling, thereby clearing Stevens' record.

Chief Justice John Roberts wrote for the majority:

> The Government … proposes that a claim of categorical exclusion should be considered under a simple balancing test: "Whether a given category of speech enjoys First Amendment protection depends upon a categorical balancing of the value of the speech against its societal costs…." As a free-floating test for First Amendment coverage, that sentence is startling and dangerous. The First Amendment's guarantee of free speech does not extend only to categories of speech that survive an ad hoc balancing of relative social costs and benefits. The First Amendment itself reflects a judgment by the American people that the benefits of its restrictions on the Government outweigh the costs. Our Constitution forecloses any attempt to revise that judgment simply on the basis that some speech is not worth it.

Instead of allowing an attorney in the U.S. Department of Justice to determine if you can be prosecuted for selling a hunting video, in which you broke no laws, the high court found that the First Amendment protects the right to share activities—and, thankfully, even most of the liberals on the Court couldn't go along with this attack on the First Amendment.

The Supreme Court even ruled that if the statute were allowed to stand:

> The only thing standing between defendants who sell such depictions and five years in federal prison—other than the mercy of a prosecutor—is the statute's exceptions clause.

> Subsection (b) exempts from prohibition "any depiction that
> has serious religious, political, scientific, educational, journal-
> istic, historical, or artistic value." The Government argues that
> this clause substantially narrows the statute's reach: News
> reports about animal cruelty have "journalistic" value; pictures
> of bullfights in Spain have "historical" value; and instructional
> hunting videos have "educational value."

Allowing the government to determine the "value" of your free speech
would allow censorship of anything the government didn't deem to be
politically correct.

Justice Samuel Alito was the only justice who didn't concur. But his
dissenting opinion only disagreed with the scope of the decision. He didn't
want to throw out the entire statute. He instead argued for judicial restraint
by simply narrowing the scope of the statute to what the U.S. Congress
had originally determined it to read, not to what some progressive U.S.
attorneys decided it could mean.

Allowing the government to censor speech based on "value" would
have opened the door to restrictions of all kinds. It would have muzzled
public dialogue on important topics. John Stuart Mill, in his book *On
Liberty* (1859), outlined this potential dilemma by saying:

> First, if any opinion is compelled to silence, that opinion may,
> for all we can certainly know, be true. To deny this is to assume
> our own infallibility.
>
> Secondly, though the silenced opinion is an error, it may,
> and very well commonly does, contain a portion of the truth;
> and since the general or prevailing opinion on any object is
> rarely or never the whole truth, it is only by the collision of
> adverse opinions that the remainder of the truth has any
> chance of being supplied.
>
> Thirdly, even if the received opinion is not only true, but
> the whole truth; unless it is suffered to be, and actually is,

vigorously and earnestly contested, it will, by most of those who receive it, be held in the manner of prejudice, with little comprehension or feeling of its rational grounds.

Some statists don't think everyone should be able to speak freely. They would like to silence corporate speech and to jail Stevens for selling a video in which he broke no laws simply because they don't like his "values." As Mill explained, this government-led, politically correct censorship would result in a dumbing-down of the human mind.

Next, Liberal Regulators
Move to Censor the Internet

On April 6, 2010, the U.S. Court of Appeals for the District of Columbia ruled that the Federal Communications Commission (FCC) doesn't have the power to regulate any Internet provider's network. Comcast had filed suit after the FCC tried to stop it from controlling traffic over its network to a popular file-sharing site. The court ruled that the FCC didn't have "express statutory authority" from the U.S. Congress to regulate the Internet. At the time, most thought this would stop the FCC cold. However, this court ruling didn't squelch the FCC's attempt to regulate, and thereby censor, the Internet with "net neutrality" regulations.

How the FCC ignored this federal court ruling and Congress isn't simply another example of bureaucratic overreach; it is, rather, an audacious and illegal power grab in a larger ongoing war to decide if the American people, or government bureaucrats, are in charge of Internet content and pricing.

On December 20, 2010, the FCC's five-member board approved net neutrality rules. The vote was 3–2, with the two Republican members voting "no." Julius Genachowski, the Obama administration's chairman of the FCC's five-member board, staged this partisan vote a few days before Christmas after a stealthy campaign that would have impressed Sun Tzu. They did it even though the public wasn't behind their takeover.

For example, just weeks after the vote, Rasmussen found that only 21 percent of likely voters want the FCC to regulate the Internet as it does radio and television.[29]

Nevertheless, as liberal dominance of the media has waned under the shadow of FOX News, conservative talk radio, and websites such as the Drudge Report, some in the Democratic Party have been looking for creative ways to maintain, or regain, the "mainstream media's" liberal clout. Net neutrality is one way to attain their goal of dominating the media. Genachowski is a former law school pal of President Barack Obama. This gave him all the access he needed to the president. The White House's official visitor logs show Genachowski had at least eleven meetings with the president or his staff leading up to this 3–2 vote. President Obama had also publicly backed the FCC's move to regulate the Internet. So, with the president's support, Genachowski had the air support to take new ground.

Genachowski explained that all he wants to do is use net neutrality to make sure Internet service providers (ISPs) can't prevent consumers from accessing Internet content, applications, and services. He also says he doesn't want broadband providers to "discriminate" against particular Internet content or applications by giving more bandwidth (speed) to companies that pay for the privilege. Chairman Genachowski wants to take capitalism out of the marketplace by, for example, preventing Comcast from charging Netflix for all the bandwidth its customers are using on Comcast's networks. Genachowski sees this as a chance to make the government the central player. Instead of standing aside and letting the companies battle for customers, Genachowski wants them to pay for Beltway influence.

Genachowski's goals at first don't sound like First Amendment infringements, so why have conservative writers and commentators purported that net neutrality would lead to censorship? Why did Rush Limbaugh say, "[N]et neutrality is the Fairness Doctrine of the Internet"?[30]

Common sense. Content-based regulation of television and radio have been upheld by the Supreme Court because there is a limited number of frequencies for non-cable television and radio stations, therefore the government is permitted to regulate radio and TV with licenses. In this way, the Supreme Court determined the FCC could restrain radio and TV broadcasters, though only on a content-neutral basis. The problem of scarcity, however, does not allow the FCC to infringe on the First Amendment, but some savvy, statist lawyers at the FCC have long seen this as a chance to define what "content-neutral" entails. The Fairness Doctrine, which President Ronald Reagan's FCC terminated, was an offshoot of this line of thinking. It allowed the government to decide what was content neutral. This allowed the FCC to fine radio and TV stations, or even to revoke their licenses, if it didn't think broadcasts were fair and balanced, or if the station aired profanity, hate speech, or other offenses; as a result, many radio stations simply stayed out of politics.

Net neutrality would give the FCC oversight of every Internet service provider in the country. Government could expand because each Internet service provider would need clarification when applying new net neutrality regulations. Innovation would decrease in such a new regulatory regime, as some of the Internet service providers' funds will have to go towards hiring people to deal with the FCC, as well as complying with regulations and lobbying for better regulations. Since the late 1990s, private companies have spent hundreds of billions of dollars developing America's Internet. This money could dry up if the companies can't make profits from their investments.

A dampening of entrepreneurship might not be what President Obama and FCC Chairman Genachowski are after—it is more likely just a side-effect of their ambition. Establishing that the FCC has the authority to regulate the Internet is what they're after, as it gives the FCC a Trojan horse—a gift they've framed as a safeguard to Internet freedom, but one that is full of bureaucrats ready to slip out and take over the Internet. In other words, these simple regulations which will supposedly keep the Internet open and fair can next be grown into a governing authority over Internet content, as once happened in radio.

To ensure "fairness," the FCC would have to create and enforce guidelines that would affect search results and Internet access. This would inevitably affect speech; after all, if a search engine has to load liberal views as quickly as it does conservative ones, and vice versa, then the views from the most popular or most topical, or the websites of advertisers would have to be moved down the list to ensure "fairness." This censors a search engine's owners' right to free speech, as it controls what they say and how they present the information. (The White House is certainly aware how important search results are; for example, in December 2010, *Politico* reported that the Obama administration had paid Google, with tax dollars, to load www.healthcare.gov when someone searches for the term "Obamacare.")[31]

Now, if the First Amendment protects anything, it prevents the government from silencing speech, as the Bill of Rights was written and ratified as restrictions on the government, not the people. The FCC's regulations by definition would begin to strangle the marketplace for Internet speech; as a result, it's disingenuous for the FCC to suggest that by regulating speech it's going to promote the widest dissemination of all forms of speech. Just ask yourself this: has any government agency ever been a neutral enforcer?

Also, the FCC's use of net neutrality would subject Internet access to Title II of the Telecommunications Act of 1996. Title II outlines how the FCC can grant licenses for the broadcast spectrum; the terms of broadcast licenses; the process of renewing broadcast licenses; restrictions on over-the-air reception devices; and much more. Giving the FCC the power to control Internet service providers with licenses (and the renewal of these licenses pursuant to how much bureaucrats like or dislike them) would put all ISPs under the thumb of the FCC. This would also apply a vague rule preventing "discrimination," which was designed to manage radio's limited number of stations on the dial, to Internet access and searches. Put another way, under net neutrality regulations, the FCC could establish rules on "reasonable" network management practices, and the FCC would get to define what is "reasonable."

Letting the government micro-manage how ISPs run their networks would allow government regulators to fine Yahoo!, for example, if a search for "net neutrality" turned up more negative than positive opinions. But how would Yahoo! label which opinion is pro and which is con? To do so, they'd have to decide that CNN is Democratic-leaning and FOX News is Republican-leaning and so on for every website, as rating every article would be impossible. Or maybe the government, after lawsuits had been filed, would be happy to do it for them. Okay, then we would have an official government list of friends and foes–depending on which party is in power. This would inevitably lead to censorship. Without much speculation, it's easy to see how net neutrality results in a Fairness Doctrine for the Internet. Limbaugh is exactly right.

But after the April federal circuit court ruling saying the FCC didn't have the authority, without Congress, to regulate the Internet, how did they pull this off?

Chairman Genachowski is President Obama's law school buddy, but for the guidelines for establishing net neutrality they relied on the ideas of Robert W. McChesney, a socialist University of Illinois communications professor and author who founded the liberal lobby Free Press in 2002. In 2008 McChesney wrote in the Marxist journal *Monthly Review*: "Any serious effort to reform the media system would have to necessarily be part of a revolutionary program to overthrow the capitalist system itself."[32] The central goal of McChesney's group, Free Press, which says it has 500,000 members, has long been to give the FCC the power to regulate the Internet via net neutrality. Why? According to McChesney: "Instead of waiting for the revolution to happen, we learned that unless you make significant changes in the media, it will be vastly more difficult to have a revolution. While the media is not the single most important issue in the world, it is one of the core issues that any successful Left project needs to integrate into its strategic program."[33]

There is even a personnel link between the FCC and McChesney's group, Free Press. FCC Chairman Genachowski's press secretary, Jen Howard, used to handle media relations for Free Press. Also, the FCC's chief diversity officer, Mark Lloyd, co-authored a Free Press report calling for regulation of political talk radio.[34]

Free Press has obtained much of its funding from liberal foundations such as Pew Charitable Trusts, the Joyce Foundation, George Soros' Open Society Institute, the Ford Foundation, and the John D. and Catherine T. MacArthur Foundation. The investment paid off. Free Press's main goal has been to validate the alleged problem of Internet traffic disruptions, manipulations perpetuated by evil capitalists who want to profit from their investments. They knew this would enable the FCC to tie on its cape and fly in to solve the fake problem with net neutrality. McChesney and Genachowski had to create the problem because, when asked, people pretty much like how the Internet works.

To substantiate this false premise so the FCC could take control of the Internet, in 2009, Free Press commissioned a poll on net neutrality. The Harmony Institute did the poll and reported that "more than 50% of the public argued that, as a private resource, the Internet should not be regulated by the federal government." The poll went on to postulate that because "the public likes the way the Internet works ... messaging should target supporters by asking them to act vigilantly" to prevent a "centrally controlled Internet." That's a savvy way to spin the public's distaste for FCC Internet regulations. They decided to tell the public that the FCC, and only the FCC, can stop corporations from creating a "centrally controlled Internet."

To make this spin a reality, FCC Chairman Genachowski, in 2009, hired Harvard University's Berkman Center for Internet and Society to conduct an "independent review of existing information ... [to] lay the foundation for enlightened, data-driven decision making." The Berkman Center is hardly nonpartisan on this topic. They are a left-leaning advocacy group. Commissioning them was like hiring the Democratic National Committee (DNC) to do a study for the Federal Election Commission (FEC) that would lead to real policy detailing who should be allowed to monitor polling places.

The Berkman Center's FCC-paid-for report, entitled "Next Generation Connectivity," was also funded by the Ford and MacArthur Foundations— groups that had funded Free Press and that had spent years advocating for net neutrality. So liberal groups that wanted net neutrality paid for research that would be the FCC's official rationale for whether or not to pass net neutrality. That's pretty bold.

FCC Chairman Genachowski, with support from President Obama, then passed net neutrality by a party-line, 3–2 vote. They did all this despite an unfavorable court ruling and without approval from Congress. What they're counting on is a public that either buys their rationale that the FCC is a neutral regulator or a populace that finds this entire issue too complex to fathom.

Of course, if the FCC's net neutrality regulations are really just about controlling access to Netflix-type content, why are there so many leftist public policy groups involved? And why have they spent so much money to pass net neutrality? The answer is simple: the statists want control. This is a Trojan horse that, if left standing, will give the FCC control of Internet content.

As this book was being written, the battle over Internet freedom, thankfully, wasn't over. FCC Commissioner Meredith Attwell Baker, a Republican, said she didn't support the FCC's Internet power grab; the agency decided to regulate the Internet "because it wants to, not because it needs to."[35] This is true. The public has not seen a problem with the way the Internet works. And the private industry that built the infrastructure for the Internet did so at a breathtaking speed that the U.S. government couldn't accomplish. The private sector has also continued to invest billions of dollars annually in upgrading and improving networks they expect to earn profits from. This is largely due to a lack of government meddling.

The other Republican on the FCC's board, Robert M. McDowell, said this move by the Democrats on the board to regulate the Internet is "jaw-dropping interventionist chutzpah," and he added, "[T]he FCC [has] bypass[ed] branches of our government in the dogged pursuit of needless and harmful regulation."[36]

Meanwhile, Democratic FCC Commissioner Michael Copps said, "In my book, today's action could, and should, have gone further."

So the battle lines have not only formed, but the FCC has broken through. The counterattack will need to come from Congress. As of late

2010, over 300 House and Senate members had signed a letter opposing the FCC Internet takeover. This opposition grew in 2011. Senator Mitch McConnell (R-KY) called the FCC vote to regulate the Internet "flawed" and said Republicans would move to prevent the FCC from exceeding its authority.

Over the last decade, some in the U.S. Congress have tried and failed at least five times to pass net neutrality, so the fight over Internet regulation and censorship is hardly over. Democrats want to regulate, tax, and secure their definition of "fairness" on the Internet. Republicans want the Internet to continue to be a free, open market for free speech and innovation. In a climate where we already have the Department of Homeland Security confiscating web-domains behind very weak due process, government control over the Internet would only be the beginning of centralized control. The only way to stop it, and to keep our freedom on what is surely the printing press of the twenty-first century, is for the public to understand what net neutrality can do to their First Amendment freedoms.

How about Talk Radio's Free Speech?

Meanwhile, many on the Left have tried to revive the aforementioned Fairness Doctrine in order to resuscitate left-wing media dominance. The Fairness Doctrine was a policy enforced by the Federal Communications Commission. Introduced in 1949, it required the holders of broadcast licenses to present controversial issues in a way that was, in the FCC's view, honest, equitable, and balanced. In *Red Lion Broadcasting Co.* v. *FCC* (1969), the Supreme Court upheld the FCC's general right to enforce the Fairness Doctrine where channels were limited, though the Court didn't rule that the FCC had to regulate this speech. In *Red Lion* the Court ruled: "A license permits broadcasting, but the licensee has no constitutional right to be the one who holds the license or to monopolize a radio frequency to the exclusion of his fellow citizens. There is nothing in the First Amendment which prevents the Government from requiring a licensee to share his frequency with others....It is the right of the viewers and listeners, not the right of the broadcasters, which is paramount." So because it regulated frequencies, the government snatched the right to regulate content?

Then came FCC Chairman Mark S. Fowler. He was a communications attorney who had served on Ronald Reagan's presidential campaign staff in 1976 and 1980. Fowler was appointed by President Reagan to head the FCC. Under Fowler, the FCC soon began to repeal parts of the Fairness Doctrine. Fowler said the doctrine hurt the public interest by violating free speech rights guaranteed by the First Amendment. In 1987, the FCC abolished the doctrine by a 4–0 vote; known as the Syracuse Peace Council decision, the FCC stated: "The intrusion by government into the content of programming occasioned by the enforcement of [the Fairness Doctrine] restricts the journalistic freedom of broadcasters ... [and] actually inhibits the presentation of controversial issues of public importance to the detriment of the public and the degradation of the editorial prerogative of broadcast journalists."

On February 16, 2009, Fowler told conservative radio talk-show host Mark Levin that his work toward revoking the Fairness Doctrine had been a matter of principle, not partisanship. Fowler said Reagan's White House staff thought repealing the policy would be politically unwise. Fowler said that the White House staff thought the Fairness Doctrine was the "only thing that really protects you [Reagan] from the savageness of the three networks ... and Fowler is proposing to repeal it."[37]

However, instead of doing the politically expedient thing, President Reagan supported Fowler's struggle to repeal the Fairness Doctrine's gag order on free speech. Reagan later even vetoed a Democratic-controlled Congress's effort to make the Fairness Doctrine federal law. While the Fairness Doctrine's stated goal was to expand discourse in the name of the "public interest," Reagan and Fowler saw that the Fairness Doctrine was trampling on the First Amendment.

Many Democrats have long seen it differently. They think government is a fair arbitrator that can neutrally decide when someone can speak, even on a privately owned station; in fact, after the 2006 midterm elections,

Democrats began pushing to allow government regulators to act again as censors by listening to broadcasts and fining those it thinks don't present both sides fairly.

After a Democratic sweep in the 2008 elections, some Democrats decided it was time to require radio networks to air liberal points of view. By forcing networks to give opposing points of view, the government would conversely silence the talk show hosts who would have won that time in a free market of ideas. The threat of fines, and of possibly losing radio licenses, created by a new Fairness Doctrine would prompt many radio station owners to just walk away from politics, as they had previously done. It is not a coincidence that conservative talk radio flowered right after the original Fairness Doctrine was abandoned by the Reagan administration.

Because of the rise of conservative talk radio, in 2009 Senator Tom Harkin (D-IA) said, " … we gotta get the Fairness Doctrine back in law again."[38] Speaker of the House Nancy Pelosi (D-CA) is on the record saying she wants to bring it back.[39] During an appearance on a radio show in February 2009, former president Bill Clinton said, "Well, you either ought to have the Fairness Doctrine or we ought to have more balance on the other side, because essentially there's always been a lot of big money to support the right-wing talk shows."[40]

Also, in December 2010, Democratic FCC commissioner Michael Copps suggested in a speech that broadcasters should be subject to a new "public values test" every four years to determine if they should be allowed to stay on the air. Copps said news outlets should have to prove they are making a meaningful commitment to public affairs. They should have to show they are committed to diversity programming (such as giving women and minorities more air time). He also said they should have to report to the government about which topics they plan to air. Finally, Copps said private media companies using "public" airwaves should be required to make greater disclosures about who funds political ads.[41] Basically, Copps would like the FCC's five-member board to control, and thereby censor, the airwaves.

Despite the Democratic Party's renewed effort to reinstate some version of the Fairness Doctrine and thereby muzzle dissenting speech, President Barack Obama hadn't officially come out in favor of this censorship; however, it appears his regulatory czar, Cass Sunstein, is for it. Sunstein also believes that animals should have the right to file lawsuits, with humans as their attorneys. He also wrote a book titled *Democracy and the Problem of Free Speech*, in which he argued that capitalism has corrupted free speech by giving those with money a louder megaphone than those who don't have the cash to pay for ads. He says this isn't the view of America that James Madison, the "father of the U.S. Constitution," held, even though this is precisely the rubric that Madison lived within. In 1776 they had newspapers, books, and pamphlets, not radio, TV, and the Internet, but even in Madison's time, those with money could afford to buy more ads or print more pamphlets than those without. Madison believed in limiting the federal government to the powers listed in the Constitution. He never argued for taking away the free speech of those with money. Nevertheless, to fix his false premise, Sunstein concluded that the government must muzzle corporations and then decide who gets airtime and how much.

Sunstein said,

> Sites from one point of view agree to provide links to other sites so if you are reading a conservative magazine they would provide a link to a liberal site and vice versa....If we could get voluntary arrangements in that direction it would be great.... But the word "voluntary" is a little complicated. Sometimes people don't do what's best for our society....And the idea would be to have a legal mandate as the last resort and to make sure it's as neutral as possible....[42]

Anyone who doesn't find that logic creepy doesn't believe in freedom of speech.

Next, the Government Tries to Put the Media in Its Left Hip Pocket

With its pursuit of censorship via "fair" regulations underway, in May 2009 the Obama administration's Federal Trade Commission (FTC) announced a "project to consider the challenges faced by journalism in the Internet age." A year later, at the National Press Club on June 15, 2010, the FTC handed out copies of a "Discussion Draft" entitled "Potential Policy Recommendations to Support the Reinvention of Journalism."

Jon Leibowitz, the chairman of the FTC, commissioned the study. One of the FTC's ideas would impose government fees on websites that link to news websites, such as the Drudge Report. Another would place a tax on consumer electronics, such as iPads, Kindles, and BlackBerrys. The FTC said a 5 percent tax on consumer electronics would generate approximately $4 billion annually, and that a 2 percent sales tax on Internet advertising would generate approximately $5 to $6 billion annually. They also thought consumers could pay a 3 percent monthly tax on their ISP-cell phone bills that would generate $6 billion annually. They had many other tax ideas in the report that would all be redistributed to "traditional" media outlets according to a methodology designed and administered by the FTC.

Sound un-American? The FTC doesn't think so. They began the report with the explanation that the "Post Office Act of 1792 provided the first postal subsidies by charging less to recipients of newspapers than that charged to the recipients of letters." So, somehow the government (which had a monopoly on the delivery of the mail) deciding to charge less for mailing newspapers establishes a rationale for government payouts to the media. Are they kidding?

Taxes that exclusively target the media have been found unconstitutional. In *Grosjean* v. *American Press Co.* (1936), the Supreme Court ruled a state tax on newspaper advertising revenues was unconstitutional, as it could be used to punish the media when they criticize the government. Also, taxes that give preferential treatment to the press have been struck down. In *Arkansas Writers' Project* v. *Ragland* (1987), for example, the Court invalidated an Arkansas law that exempted "religious, professional, trade and sports journals" from taxation. The Court's reason was that the law amounted to the regulation of newspaper content. So these taxes would have strong constitutional challenges.

However, the FTC thinks it has a precedent; it said because "newspapers also receive financial support from government public and legal notice requirements," they're already getting subsidies. So, according to the FTC, because the government has to pay for space instead of just taking it, this is a subsidy.

Also, the FTC pointed out: "The Public Broadcasting Act of 1967 created and provided funding for the Corporation for Public Broadcasting (CPB), which oversees both the Public Broadcasting System (PBS) and National Public Radio (NPR)." Therefore, determined the FTC, more government sponsored media is desirable.

President Barack Obama agreed. He requested to increase CPB's funding from $420 million in 2010 to $451 million in 2011. This caused Senator Jim DeMint (R-SC) to comment: "When presidents of government-funded broadcasting are making more than the president of the United States, it's time to get the government out of public broadcasting."[43] According to the 990 tax forms all nonprofits are required to file, PBS President Paula Kerger's annual salary was $632,233 in 2010; the salary now set for U.S. presidents is $400,000. Of course, President Obama doesn't mind increasing the funding of PBS and NPR because these publicly funded news outlets are liberal. The notion that Americans, whether conservative or liberal, should have to fund obviously biased coverage caused Senator DeMint to add, "The politics will be out of public broadcasting as soon as the government gets out of the business of paying for it."

If you think it's absurd that we're paying for news media in an age when people can get their news from an endless number of sources, and if you think NPR has earned its nickname as "National Progressive Radio," then you should know the FTC next pointed out that a poll paid for by CPB found that "more than 75 percent of the public believe PBS addresses key news, public affairs, and social issues 'very/moderately' well." Oh wait, that's PBS, not NPR. This report is written to evade the truth.

The FTC next noted that the federal government handed CPB $409 million in 2009, which is mere pennies compared to what taxpayers in some other countries have to pay. For example, "[I]f the United States spent at the same per capita level as Canada, our federal commitment would be $7.5 billion. Per capita spending by Finland and Denmark is approximately 75 times greater." And they have constitutionally protected free speech there, too ... oh wait, they don't.

The FTC does caution: "Whatever the means, care must be taken to ensure that government support does not result in biased and politicized news coverage." Are they kidding? No government has *ever* published propaganda, right?

The FTC goes on to recommend establishing a "journalism" division of AmeriCorps. AmeriCorps is the federal program that places young people with nonprofits to get training and do public service work. The FTC says, "It strikes us as a win-win; we get more journalists covering our communities, and young journalists have a chance to gain valuable experience." Of course this is predicated on the idea that college graduates don't have these opportunities today, and that for the good of us all the government has to give journalists jobs and to properly instruct them on what to write...

The FTC then suggested we hand more money to public radio and television, which "should be substantially reoriented to provide significant local news reporting." Sound like control and propaganda yet? Get this: the FTC says this would require "urgent action by and reform of the Corporation for Public Broadcasting, increased congressional funding and support for public media news reporting, and changes in mission and leadership for many public stations across the country." Hmm, didn't they say CPB was already the most trusted news organization ever? So why is "urgent action" needed?

Now for the real initiatives to influence the media: the FTC proposed "a national fund for local news." Another idea would "establish citizenship news vouchers." Still another proposal in the report would "provide grants to universities to conduct investigative journalism."

The agenda is clear: as the Obama administration did with major banks and some car manufacturers, it is extending subsidies in its right hand and then throwing a left hook with regulations that empower the government. With the press in its left hip pocket, there would be no limit to what the FTC could do, or which companies it could censor.

Instead of letting the free market decide which news outlets are worth viewing, listening to, or reading, the government would keep its favorites afloat while, as Regulatory Czar Cass Sunstein would say, nudging the reporting in the right direction. Though the government couldn't force people to read or view certain media, such laws and regulations would allow the government to decide what media was available to be read, listened to, or viewed.

Remember that in 2009 former White House communications director Anita Dunn questioned whether FOX News was a news organization or an "arm of the Republican Party." It isn't much of a leap to conclude that government subsidies and regulations for fairness would make news media reluctant to be too partisan or dogmatic, as doing so might endanger their pay–off–er–subsidy. Also, if such subsidies begin enriching news organizations, every newspaper, Website, and network would need the funds to stay competitive. If, for example, CNN got more than FOX News, then FOX would be at a competitive disadvantage. The funds would even be more important to websites, small-town newspapers, and other media outlets that have tight budgets. Also, the political party in power could use these allocations to enrich friends in the media and to defund enemies. Democrats wouldn't like that special-interest game any more than Republicans and, either way, Americans would be less informed.

Indeed, when the libertarian author Ayn Rand, who had fled the Soviet Union, was asked by *Playboy* magazine when, if ever, people should go on strike from the government, as her novel *Atlas Shrugged* had postulated, she said, "When censorship is imposed, that is the sign that men should go on strike intellectually, by which I mean, should not cooperate with the social system in any way whatever."[44]

The FTC's report acknowledged only in passing the fact that the free market is keeping up with new technology and the public's needs for instantaneous information, which is causing newspapers to be replaced in some cases by the Internet, radio, iPad compatible newspapers, and cable news. As proved by the bankruptcy of the liberal answer to conservative talk radio, "Air America," some news organizations simply cannot compete in a free and open marketplace of ideas. Printed newspapers either have to evolve or follow the milkman into oblivion. But Democrats don't want to see their friends at the *New York Times* and the *Los Angeles Times* go on unemployment or move to smaller, more profit-driven enterprises. They need these prestigious newspapers' endorsements before elections.

It isn't hard to foresee where such censorship would lead, as China, Iran, Russia, Venezuela, and other countries all showcase in slightly different ways what happens when the government controls the media. Each of those repressive regimes censors freedom of speech in order to protect government power. The scary thing is that McCain-Feingold censored speech from corporations and associations for this same reason, as did the Fairness Doctrine. The Disclose Act pushed by Democrats in 2010 would have doubled down on the idea that political speech from groups of people and corporations needs to be silenced near elections. This is why R. Bruce Josten, executive vice president for government affairs at the U.S. Chamber of Commerce, called the Disclose Act the "Democratic Incumbent Protection Act." To keep our freedom, we must defeat each of these government attempts to silence their critics.

What Happened to the Freedom of Religion?

George Mason declined to sign the U.S. Constitution because the document didn't contain a bill of rights. Mason knew the importance of securing freedoms from the imperious growth of government. He'd written the Virginia Declaration of Rights in 1776 amidst the fever for American liberty. In the declaration, Mason hadn't neglected religious freedom. He wrote, "[A]ll men are equally entitled to the free exercise of religion, according to the dictates of conscience...." Later, the first Congress drew on Mason's Virginia Declaration of Rights when writing the Bill of Rights. They protected religious freedom from government in the first two clauses of what became the First Amendment by declaring, "Congress shall make no law respecting an establishment of religion, or prohibiting the free exercise thereof."

Mason didn't want to protect religion from the federal government by building a "wall of separation" that pushed all that is holy from public life; he fought for a bill of rights because it assured the people liberty by restricting government power. It isn't plausible that even a minority of statesmen from the founding period thought monuments inscribed with the Ten Commandments should be banned from courthouses. Nor is it conceivable they would even recognize a country that expels public school students for wearing t-shirts that declare such things as, "The Lord is Our Savior."

For context, consider for a moment that George Washington and George Mason together helped to choose the site for the Pohick Episcopal Church because they wanted the church to be within riding distance of both their homes, Mount Vernon and Gunston Hall.

The Pohick Episcopal Church is a brick Colonial-style building finished in 1774 that still stands in Lorton, Virginia. Washington situated the church on a gently rolling hill because he liked the biblical image of a "city set on a hill":

> You are the light of the world. A city set on a hill cannot be hidden. Neither do people light a lamp and put it under a bowl. Instead they put it on its stand, and it gives light to everyone in the house. In the same way, let your light shine before men,

that they may see your good deeds and praise your Father in heaven.[45]

Given the state of the First Amendment's protection of religion from the state, it is fitting that the Pohick Church no longer gives the impression of being on a hill, as the growth of the federal government has sprawled through Northern Virginia's pastures and crop fields creating mazes of sub-developments and office complexes that hem in and overshadow the Pohick Church. Meanwhile, the oaks and cedars surrounding the church have grown thick and tall for over two centuries, as if in a conscious effort to blot out the changes occurring all around its peaceful property.

On Independence Day, Sunday July 4, 2010, the Pohick Church's 8:00 a.m. service began with a deacon ringing bells and the heels of parishioners tramping up the stairs into the historic building. They passed through a doorway surrounded by carvings (mostly initials) left by occupying Union troops during the American Civil War, soldiers who'd used the church as a barracks and only refrained from tearing it down brick by brick to construct parapets, as they had other churches, because George Washington had helped found it.

Prior to the American Civil War, the church had fallen on hard times and, according to Reverend Donald D. Binder,[46] was only saved in the 1830s by Francis Scott Key, the author of the "Star-Spangled Banner," who came to the church's financial assistance.

Inside, the church has box seating, as Episcopalian churches historically separated their pews with short walls with wooden doors. George Washington's box is front and center with his name on a brass plaque in recognition of the money he'd spent to fund the church. George Mason's family pew is just to Washington's right. I sat there next to a woman named Grace who joyously explained the service. These two iconic men certainly didn't bleed and suffer on the battlefield and pray within these walls for a First Amendment designed to strike religion from the American way of life.

We sang the National Anthem—it being the Fourth of July—and while standing in George Mason's pew, the words of the First Amendment rang in my head: "Congress shall make no law respecting an establishment of religion, or prohibiting the free exercise thereof." I just knew it wasn't in the words any more than it was in the character of the people during the founding period to eviscerate religion from the public square. They'd fought for freedom, of religion and otherwise, not for a federal government that would be as tyrannical as King George III.

Actually, nowhere in the first two clauses of the First Amendment does it say "separation of church and state." Nor does the First Amendment refer to a "wall" harshly dividing religion from government.

So where does that phrase come from?

On October 7, 1801, the Baptist Association of Danbury, Connecticut, sent President Thomas Jefferson a letter congratulating him for winning the election for the presidency. They went on to say:

> Our sentiments are uniformly on the side of religious liberty: that religion is at all times and places a matter between God and individuals, that no man ought to suffer in name, person, or effects on account of his religious opinions, [and] that the legitimate power of civil government extends no further than to punish the man who works ill to his neighbor. But sir, our constitution of government is not specific.... [T]herefore what religious privileges we enjoy (as a minor part of the State) we enjoy as favors granted, and not as inalienable rights.[47]

The Danbury Baptists were worried the First Amendment's "free exercise" clause would give the impression that the freedom of religion is government-given (therefore alienable) and not explicitly separated as being beyond the government's power to regulate (unalienable).

Jefferson replied to the Danbury Baptists on January 1, 1802, by saying in part:

> Gentlemen,—The affectionate sentiments of esteem and approbation which you are so good as to express towards me

on behalf of the Danbury Baptist Association give me the highest satisfaction....Believing with you that religion is a matter which lies solely between man and God; that he owes an account to none other for his faith or his worship; that the legislative powers of government reach actions only and not opinions, I contemplate with sovereign reverence that act of the whole American people which declared that their legis-lature should "make no law respecting an establishment of religion or prohibiting the free exercise thereof," thus build-ing a wall of separation between Church and State. Adhering to this expression of the supreme will of the nation in behalf of the rights of conscience, I shall see with sincere satisfaction the progress of those sentiments which tend to restore to man all his natural rights, convinced he has no natural right in opposition to his social duties. I reciprocate your kind prayers for the protection and blessing of the common Father and Creator of man, and tender you for yourselves and your religious association assurances of my high respect and esteem.[48]

Jefferson clearly saw the First Amendment as a limitation on government, not on religion. This wasn't Jefferson's only mention of religion and the state. Jefferson showed on numerous occasions that he shared the Danbury Baptist's worry and viewpoint; in fact, in his Second Inaugural Address in 1805, Jefferson said, "In matter of religion I have considered that its free exercise is placed by the Constitution independent of the powers of the general government."

Even before receiving the Baptist association's letter, Jefferson had often argued that the federal government could not interfere with religion. For example, in 1790 Jefferson sent a letter to Noah Webster, a Federalist writer and thinker who is perhaps most remembered for the Merriam-Webster dictionary, in which Jefferson said in part:

It had become an universal and almost uncontroverted position in the several States that the purposes of society do not
require a surrender of all our rights to our ordinary governors
… and which experience has nevertheless proved [the federal
government] will be constantly encroaching on if submitted to
them; that there are also certain fences which experience has
proved peculiarly efficacious against wrong and rarely obstruc-
tive of right, which yet the governing powers have ever shown
a disposition to weaken and remove. Of the first kind, for
instance, is freedom of religion.[49]

Jefferson was a libertarian who understood that the First Amendment's
establishment and exercise clauses ("Congress shall make no law respecting an establishment of religion, or prohibiting the free exercise thereof")
simply meant what they said, that the federal government could not create
a preferred state religion, and that people have the right to exercise their
particular faith or lack thereof.

When considered within the full context of his views, it is clear that
Jefferson saw the First Amendment as a check on the federal government
from establishing a state religion or treading on the peoples' free exercise
of religion, a view held also by George Mason. Religion was not treated
as separate from the state during the founding period or well into the
twentieth century; even the Liberty Bell is inscribed with a quotation from
the Bible: "Proclaim liberty throughout all the land unto all the inhabitants
thereof."[50]

Despite these obvious historical facts, on February 10, 1947, Supreme
Court Justice Hugo Black, a Democrat who served as a U.S. senator from
1927 to 1937 and a former Ku Klux Klan member, cited Jefferson's phrase
"wall of separation between Church and State" in *Everson* v. *Board of Education* (1947) to justify a major shift in Supreme Court jurisprudence that
set in motion a whitewashing of religion from federal and even state
governments. Justice Black didn't cite even as much of the letter as is

printed in these pages; instead, he chose to pull one phrase—just eight words—that was convenient to his progressive viewpoint. He then used that phrase in an out-of-context fashion to press his worldview upon all Americans.

Black was nominated for the Supreme Court by President Franklin D. Roosevelt. FDR fingered Black because he was certain Black would rule that the progressive legislation he was pushing was constitutional. The high court had been thwarting FDR by striking down the government's power to set prices and to prevent employers from laying off workers. By turning the government against religion, Black's majority opinion in *Everson* was designed to completely cut religion from government—meaning schools, public lands, courthouses, inaugurations, and so on. Progressives saw religion as an obstacle because religion relies on moral absolutism—rules for justice that act as a check on government authority.

In his majority opinion in *Everson*, Black wrote:

> The "establishment of religion" clause of the First Amendment means at least this: Neither a state nor the Federal Government can set up a church. Neither can pass laws which aid one religion, aid all religions or prefer one religion over another. Neither can force nor influence a person to go to or to remain away from church against his will or force him to profess a belief or disbelief in any religion. No person can be punished for entertaining or professing religious beliefs or disbeliefs, for church attendance or non-attendance. No tax in any amount, large or small, can be levied to support any religious activities or institutions, whatever they may be called, or whatever form they may adopt to teach or practice religion. Neither a state nor the Federal Government can, openly or secretly, participate in the affairs of any religious organizations or groups and vice versa. In the words of Jefferson, the clause against establishment of religion by law was intended to erect "a wall of separation between Church and State."

Prior to this decision, the First Amendment's declaration that "Congress shall make no law respecting an establishment of religion, or prohibiting the free exercise thereof" was interpreted to impose limits only on the federal government; it was not ruled as applying to state governments. *Everson* changed that. This case was also used to incorporate the "establishment clause" of the First Amendment as binding to the states through the "due process clause" of the Fourteenth Amendment, meaning that state and local governments must also adhere to its limitations. This included, of course, the First Amendment's new definition that Black's majority opinion wrung from eight out-of-context words from one Founding Father.

Before the Supreme Court's 1947 *Everson* ruling, the high court had referred to Jefferson's 1802 letter to the Danbury Baptists only once, in 1878 (*Reynolds* v. *United States*). Unlike post-1947 courts, which typically publish just the eight out-of-context words from *Everson*, in *Reynolds* the Court published a long excerpt from Jefferson's letter and then decided: "Coming as this does from an acknowledged leader of the advocates of the measure, [Jefferson's letter to the Danbury Baptists] may be accepted almost as an authoritative declaration of the scope and effect of the Amendment thus secured. Congress was deprived of all legislative power over mere opinion, but was left free to reach actions which were in violation of social duties or subversive good order."[51] The Court then went on to rule, "[T]he rightful purposes of civil government are for its officers to interfere when principles break out into overt acts against peace and good order. In th[is] ... is found the true distinction between what properly belongs to the Church and to the State."

In 1878, the Court didn't think Jefferson's letter, or any other evidence, required the government to separate itself completely from churches; however, since *Everson*, the "wall of separation" theory has been used to remove Ten Commandment monuments from courtrooms, to prevent children from sharing a moment of silence in public schools, to stop students in public schools from wearing t-shirts with Biblical references, and to fundamentally attack religion in every facet of public life.

Jefferson never argued for any such interpretation. In 1776, Jefferson had written in the Declaration of Independence: "We hold these truths to be self-evident, that all men are created equal, that they are endowed by their Creator with certain unalienable rights." Jefferson believed that unalienable rights cannot be taken away by any government. He believed the government shouldn't attack religion either by endorsing a state religion or by attacking religion in the public square. Jefferson once even asked, "Can the liberties of a nation be thought secure if we have lost the only firm basis, a conviction in the minds of the people that these liberties are the gifts of God? That they are not to be violated but with his wrath?"[52] (Today, however, President Barack Obama has been leaving "by their Creator" out of the Declaration while quoting it during speeches.)[53]

Justice Black stood against precedent and against what the Founders of America had envisioned and created. Until 1947, the "establishment clause" simply meant that Congress couldn't pick one faith over all other faiths (including atheism), and the "free-exercise clause" meant the federal government had to leave citizens' faith alone. But after Justice Black got through with these two clauses, they meant that the federal government, as well as every other state and local government, had to separate from all that is holy.

Despite this clear evidence that Justice Black and the Supreme Court got it wrong, liberal-progressive justices still invoke the 1947 ruling that "neither a state nor the Federal Government can, openly or secretly, participate in the affairs of any religious organizations or groups and vice versa."

Liberals in the twenty-first century like to invoke *stare decisis* with regards to this made-up wall separating church and state (as in other cases such as a woman's so-called Fourth Amendment right of privacy to abort a child), but they don't have trouble disregarding precedents that don't fit into their worldview, such as the way the courts interpreted the First Amendment's establishment clause for over 150 years. *Stare decisis* originates from the Latin phrase "*Stare decisis et non quieta movere*" ("Stand by decisions and do not disturb the undisturbed"). During the confirmation process to the Supreme Court, Democratic senators demanded that both of President George W. Bush's nominees, Chief Justice John Roberts and Justice Samuel Alito, say they believed *stare decisis* applied to *Roe* v. *Wade* (1973). Conversely, President Barack Obama's liberal-progressive nominees–Justice Sonia Sotomayor and Justice Elana Kagan–were asked by Republicans if they believed *stare decisis* applied to *Heller* v. *D.C.* (2008), a ruling that determined the Second Amendment is an individual right. (Though Justice Sotomayor said *Heller* had become a precedent, she voted against the fact that the Second Amendment is an individual right the first chance she got, in *McDonald* v. *City of Chicago* (2010).)

Despite this liberal doublespeak, an honest, constitutionally bound judge has to rule that precedents that simply got it wrong must be overturned. Two such examples of cases that should have been overturned were *Dred Scott* v. *Sanford* (1857), which found that the federal government couldn't prohibit slavery in new territories and that slaves, as property, were not protected by the Constitution, and *Korematsu* v. *United States* (1944), an opinion that held that FDR's Executive Order 9066, which sent thousands of Americans of Japanese ancestry to internment camps, was constitutional. Dredd Scott was overturned via constitutional amendment after the American Civil War, and the Supreme Court still has not readdressed *Korematsu*.

More recently, the Court has ruled inconsistently on whether the government must be hostile to religion in the public square, as there has been judicial disagreement on this segment of the First Amendment. For example, in *Sherbert* v. *Verner* (1963), the Warren Court applied the strict scrutiny standard of review to this clause, holding that a state must demonstrate a compelling interest in restricting religious activities. But then in *Employment Division* v. *Smith* (1990), the Supreme Court retreated from this standard, permitting governmental actions that were neutral regarding religion. Then in 1994, in *Board of Education of Kiryas Joel Village School District* v. *Grumet,* Justice David Souter, writing for the majority, concluded that "government should not prefer one religion to another, or religion to irreligion."

Meanwhile, in *Anderson* v. *Salt Lake City Corp.* (1973), the Supreme Court ruled that it is constitutional for the Ten Commandments to be displayed on public property, but then and in *Stone* v. *Graham* (1980), the Court ruled it is unconstitutional to allow students to see them. Later, in *Harvey* v. *Cobb* (1993), the Court found it was unconstitutional to display the Ten Commandments at a courthouse. Meanwhile, in *Bogen* v. *Doty* (1979), the Court found it is constitutional to begin public meetings with religious invocations, but it ruled in *Lee* v. *Weisman* (1992) and *Harris* v. *Joint School District* (1994) that it is unconstitutional for students to hear them. In fact, the Court said it was constitutional to display a nativity scene in *Lynch* v. *Donnelly* (1984), but then ruled it was unconstitutional in *County of Allegheny* v. *ACLU* (1989).

Congress attempted to restore order to this incongruous debate by passing the Religious Freedom Restoration Act, but subsequently, in *City of Boerne* v. *Flores* (1997), the Supreme Court held that Congress' attempt to nullify *Everson* was unconstitutional regarding state and local government actions (though permissible regarding federal actions). As a result, at present there is no consistent line of reasoning with regards to the freedom of religion as conservatives wrestle with progressives over different cases and as the Court's make-up slowly shifts between left and right.

The liberal lie that the First Amendment requires the government to chase religion from public life has not been the only systematic attack on religion from our burgeoning federal government. Next, the federal government began using IRS bureaucrats to censor religious speech.

How the Nonprofit Status Silenced Religious Figures

Many of the Framers of America's founding documents had likely studied the writings of the French political philosopher Baron de Montesquieu (1689–1755), who wrote:

A more certain way to attack religion is by favor, by the comforts of life, by the hope of wealth; not by what reminds one of it, but by what makes one forget it; not by what makes one indignant, but by what makes men lukewarm, when other passions act on our souls, and those which religion inspires are silent. In the matter of changing religion, State favors are stronger than penalties.[54]

Despite the fact that the Bill of Rights was designed to restrict the federal government, not the people, today the IRS has succeeded in gagging churches by requiring them to stay out of politics. If they talk politics, they risk losing their nonprofit tax status. The Founders may have thought they'd avoided Montesquieu's warning by ratifying the First Amendment's "establishment clause," but the U.S. government, through the IRS, has shackled religion to state favors backed by a severe financial penalty–the IRS tax code, a document that's now longer than the Bible.

This battle over free expression of religion in politics was actually debated by the founders. For example, John Witherspoon (1723–1794), who was a minister, a president of Princeton University, and a signer of the Declaration of Independence, and had served on over 100 committees in Congress, made a habit of confronting politicians who said religion should be barred from politics. For instance, in 1777, when the Georgia legislature was preparing its state constitution, it included a stipulation that prevented "clergym[e]n of any denomination" from holding "a seat in the legislature," Witherspoon sent them a letter:

Sir,

In your paper of Saturday last, you have given us the new Constitution of Georgia, in which I find the following resolution, "No clergyman of any denomination shall be a member of the General Assembly." I would be very well satisfied that some of the gentlemen who have made that an essential article of this constitution, or who have inserted and approve it in other constitutions, would be pleased to explain a little the principles, as well as to ascertain the meaning of it.

Perhaps we understand pretty generally, what is meant by a clergyman, viz. a person regularly called and set apart to the ministry of the gospel, and authorized to preach and administer the sacraments of the Christian religion. Now suffer me to ask this question: Before any man among us was ordained a minister, was he not a citizen of the United States, and if being in Georgia, a citizen of the state of Georgia? Had he not then a right to be elected a member of the assembly, if qualified in point of property? How then has he lost, or why is he deprived of this right? Is it by offence or disqualification? Is it a sin against the public to become a minister? Does it merit that the person, who is guilty of it should be immediately deprived of one of his most important rights as a citizen? Is not this inflicting a penalty which always supposes an offence? Is a minister then disqualified for the office of a senator or representative? Does this calling and profession render him stupid or ignorant? I am inclined to form a very high opinion of the natural understanding of the freemen and freeholders of the state of Georgia, as well as of their improvement and culture by education, and yet I am not able to conceive, but that some of those equally qualified, may enter into the clerical order: and then it must not be unfitness, but some other reason that produces the exclusion. Perhaps it may be thought that they are excluded from civil authority, that they may be more fully and constantly employed in their spiritual functions. If this had been the ground of it, how much more properly would it have appeared, as an order of an ecclesiastical body with respect to their own members. In that case I should not only have forgiven but approved and justified it; but in the way in which it now stands, it is evidently a punishment by loss of privilege, inflicted on those, who go into the office of the ministry; for which, perhaps, the gentlemen of Georgia may have good reasons, though I have not been able to discover them.[55]

When Georgia wrote its third constitution in 1798, it no longer prevented people of the cloth from holding public office. Across the new nation, the debate over churches' roles in politics had fallen on the side of religious freedom.

Today, David Barton, an author, minister, and the founder and president of WallBuilders, a group "dedicated to presenting America's forgotten history and heroes, with an emphasis on the moral, religious, and constitutional foundation on which America was built," explained,

> A debate over religion and its relationship to politics occurred in many of the states in the Founding Era, with the consensus coming down decisively for the freedom of religion, hence our First Amendment protection that "Congress shall make no law respecting an establishment of religion, or prohibiting the free exercise thereof." In fact, nine of the original 13 states had official state religions. Also, the first U.S. Congress printed an official Bible that was sent to schools in every state. They clearly believed that religion has a place in public and political life.[56]

Barton pointed out that the law banning tax-exempt organizations, including churches, from politics didn't come from the Founding Era. It was actually engineered in 1954 by then-Senate Minority Leader Lyndon B. Johnson (1908–1973). Johnson wanted to silence two non-profit organizations in Texas that had opposed his reelection, so he pushed the bill through. It wasn't controversial because Johnson passed it off as a favor to churches. The legislation passed as an amendment to another bill via an up-or-down voice vote in the U.S. Senate.

Most churches in America have since organized themselves as 501(c)(3) tax-exempt religious organizations–501(c)(3) churches are prohibited from addressing, in any tangible way, the vital issues of the day. Most churches now stay out of politics. However, in 1995, for the first time in history, the IRS revoked the tax-exempt status of a church for engaging in political activity. The Branch Ministries, Inc., doing business as the Church at Pierce Creek in upstate New York, ran a newspaper ad just before the 1992 presidential election saying that Bill Clinton's position on abortion ran counter to the Bible. The ad asked, "How, then, can we vote for Bill Clinton?" After Clinton won the election, Americans United for Separation of Church and State wrote a letter to the IRS saying that the church had violated its tax-exempt status. After an investigation, in 1995, the IRS revoked Branch Ministries, Inc.'s tax-exempt status. On appeal to the United States District Court for the District Of Columbia (*Branch Ministries* v. *Rossotti*), the court ruled the IRS had not exceeded its authority when revoking the tax-exempt status. Conservatives then pointed out that many inner-city, Democratic-leaning churches had endorsed Bill Clinton, yet these churches were not investigated.

To prevent political parties from continuing to wield the IRS against church opinions they don't favor, Representative Walter Jones (R-NC) introduced the Houses of Worship Political Speech Protection Act (H.R. 2357) in 2002. Representative Jones wanted to give churches, mosques, and synagogues the freedom they had for over 150 years to speak out on political issues. Despite having 133 cosponsors, the bill didn't pass. Just after it failed, Representative Jones said, "We have fought to see this legislation brought to the floor. I was encouraged to finally see a debate on this legislation ... it has been 48 years since Senator Johnson slipped an amendment in a bill that passed by voice vote. This debate was long overdue....This legislation goes beyond party lines and theological debates. We must not allow a government institution to have this kind of chilling effect over America's churches."[57]

Nevertheless, religious figures are increasingly trying to get their First Amendment rights back. To publicly challenge the IRS's authority to censor people of the cloth, the Alliance Defense Fund (ADF), a conservative Christian nonprofit group, and Wallbuilders have been encouraging priests, rabbis, and other clergy to endorse candidates and/or to talk about politics, from a moral perspective, from the pulpit. In 2009, the ADF said thirty-three churches participated in its "Pulpit Initiative." Barton said, as of late 2010, more than 200 priests, reverends, and rabbis were also enrolled in the Black Robe Regiment, a movement looking to force the IRS to take them to court. Barton said, "We have over 100,000 documents from before 1812 that support priests' right to political speech. As long as we get honest judges, we'll have no trouble winning this First Amendment case."

Barton, however, says they've had trouble goading the IRS into court. The IRS did push a case after the 2008 election against Warroad Community Church. Its pastor, Gus Booth, endorsed Senator John McCain for president. The IRS investigated but later suspended its investigation citing "a pending issue regarding the procedure used to initiate the case." The inept bureaucracy had thwarted its own investigation. In 1984, Congress passed the Church Audit Procedures Act that said for an IRS official to make a case against nonprofit groups on grounds of electioneering, the official must hold a rank "no lower than that of a principal Internal Revenue officer for an internal revenue region." But then, in 1998, Congress passed the Internal Revenue Service Restructuring and Reform Act, which abolished the IRS's regional commissioner position. The IRS then gave the authority to audit churches to officials lower down the chain; as a result, the court ruled the IRS official didn't have the authority to audit Warroad Community Church. The government had tripped itself up and, as of this writing, was trying to rectify the disparity so it could enforce the law.

The Alliance Defense Fund's Eric Stanley agrees with Barton. He says the campaign "is really part of a long, sustained campaign" to get a court challenge to IRS laws governing electioneering. "We feel very confident that when we do, it will not take long for a federal judge to strike down this unconstitutional restriction on churches' [First Amendment] rights."[58]

On the left side of this First Amendment issue is Americans United for the Separation of Church and State, a group founded in 1947 that aims to wipe religion out of public life. It has submitted reports to the IRS detailing accounts of church leaders who mention politics from the pulpit. The organization has even encouraged its members to monitor churches so it can report illegal politicking to the IRS. The group argues it has to turn fellow citizens into the government because the IRS cannot launch an investigation in to a church unless it receives a complaint. IRS spokeswoman Nancy Mathis said, "It's not like we're sitting in the pews. It's the honor system plus some third-party oversight."[59]

Rob Boston, communications director of Americans United for the Separation of Church and State, wrote on his blog, "Far from rolling over, it looks to me like the IRS is girding for battle. Churches that choose to follow the Alliance Defense Fund down this misguided path can't say they weren't warned."[60]

Boston may be a little tattletale who is trying to infringe churches' constitutional rights, but he may also be correct about the IRS. As this book was being written, the IRS seemed to be getting its regulations in order so that it can continue to silence priests, pastors, and reverends.

Barton's Black Robe Regiment, meanwhile, has been girding for battle. Wallbuilders says it wants to bring church leaders together to uphold "our biblical responsibility to stand up for our Lord and Savior and to protect the freedoms and liberties granted to a moral people in the divinely inspired U.S. Constitution." The Regiment had its historical beginnings during the Revolutionary War, when pastors from across the colonies led their congregations into the battle for freedom. Unlike today, churches during the American Revolutionary period served as places for political debates. The Black Robe Regiment now says, "Today's church leaders have all but lost that concept of leading their congregations in a Godly manner in all aspects of their worldly existence and are afraid to speak out against the progressive agenda that has dominated our political system for the past century."

When or if these two sides enter the courtroom, the government will have to explain why it feels it necessary to intrude into churches to silence people of the cloth. If anything, the churches' diverse parishioners would act to moderate what religious leaders say from the pulpit. If people don't agree, they'll send complaints through their church's hierarchy, they'll find another church to go to, or they'll leave the church altogether, as is their right. That is the freedom of religion Americans have.

Church leaders have historically spoken their minds to the American public. Outspoken religious figures include George Whitfield (1714–1770), an Anglican minister who helped spread the "Great Awakening" in the American colonies, and Father Charles Edward Coughlin (1891–1979), a politically controversial Roman Catholic priest who had more than 40 million listeners tuned to his weekly broadcasts during the 1930s, and Reverend Jerry Falwell (1933–2007), a Baptist pastor and conservative commentator. Religious figures have always been involved in political debates in America, at least until Lyndon B. Johnson changed the rules in 1954 to prevent nonprofit groups from using the freedom of speech to influence voters.

The freedom of religion needs to be re-won; after all, the last four lines of Francis Scott Key's "Star-Spangled Banner," our national anthem, demand as much:

> Then conquer we must, when our cause it is just,
> And this be our motto: "In God is our trust."
> And the star-spangled banner in triumph shall wave
> O'er the land of the free and the home of the brave!

AMENDMENT II

*A well regulated Militia, being necessary to the security
of a free State, the right of the people to keep and bear Arms,
shall not be infringed.*

"Those who were fearful that the new Federal Government would infringe traditional rights such as the right to keep and bear arms insisted on the adoption of the Bill of Rights as a condition for ratification of the Constitution."[1]
–McDonald v. *Chicago*

The right to keep and bear arms has not only been infringed, it has been violated, taken away, and sometimes turned into a crime. One victim of the destruction of this constitutional right is New Jersey resident Brian Aitken. He was arrested in 2009 after he consented to a search of his vehicle. The police found two handguns Aitken had purchased in Colorado. Aitken was certain he hadn't done anything wrong, as he'd even called the New Jersey State Police before moving from Colorado to see what he had to do to comply with the law.

Aitken, however, didn't foresee New Jersey Superior Court Judge James Morley refusing to let a jury hear about exceptions in New Jersey's firearms laws that allow possession of handguns without a state license when a person is moving.[2] Aitken didn't imagine that his judge wouldn't even care that he had a clean record. But what Aitken really didn't see coming was Judge Morley giving him seven years in prison. But the judge did all that. Seven years, even though Aitken had bought the guns legally after passing a federal background check. Seven years, even though Aitken hadn't broken the law.

Mercifully, just before Christmas in 2010, New Jersey Governor Chris Christie commuted Aitken's sentence, setting him free after about four months in prison. However, as a convicted felon, Aitken will have to win an appeal or get a pardon to be allowed to own a gun in the United States again.

Ward Bird, a resident of New Hampshire, wasn't as fortunate. He spent Christmas 2010 in jail. He got three to six years for yelling at a trespasser on his 60-acre property. Bird says he was wearing his handgun at the time, but that he didn't take it out of its holster. The trespasser, Christine Harris, says he did. In this he-said-she-said case, Bird got three-to-six. The judge said his hands were tied by sentencing guidelines. The prosecution did offer Bird a deal that would have spared him the years in prison, but pleading guilty wouldn't only have been lying, says Bird, it also would have required that he give up his Second Amendment right to own firearms for life.[3]

Of course, as Chris Liu, a California commercial airline pilot can testify, there isn't much of a Second Amendment right left in some states. In December 2010, Liu posted a video online showing that airline employees at San Francisco International Airport could enter restricted areas by only swiping a card, thereby making airport security a farce. Three days after he posted the video clips he'd recorded with a cell phone camera, four federal air marshals and two sheriff's deputies arrived at his residence. The authorities confiscated Liu's federally issued firearm, a gun he'd passed a course to carry in the cockpit so he could fight off terrorists. The pilot recorded this gun confiscation and handed the video to News10. While the marshals took his firearm, a state deputy sheriff made him surrender his state-issued permit to carry a concealed weapon in California.[4] They took away his constitutional rights without even a court hearing.

This book could be filled with accounts of people losing their Second Amendment rights at the whim of government. This is why it's no coincidence that the two men whose life stories so recently helped shape Second Amendment precedents in the U.S. Supreme Court—Dick Anthony Heller and Otis McDonald—spent their lives in Democrat-controlled inner cities, in areas where law-abiding citizens have been restricted from carrying firearms to fend off muggers and rapists.

Threats to their lives taught both men a very human fact, a fundamental truth Americans in 1776 thought was common sense: unarmed people are easy victims for foreign powers, tyrannical governments, and thugs. Thus George Mason, long remembered as the "Father of the U.S. Bill of Rights," once said, "[T]o disarm the people, that was the best and most effectual way to enslave them."[5]

Both Heller and MacDonald found through life experience that self-defense is a human necessity; that the Second Amendment is the individual right that protects all the other rights; and that the right to self-defense is a basic human need, a fact so fundamental even cavemen must have grasped it. After all, the stronger guy gets his way until some smarter, though weaker, individual sharpens a stick.

Indeed, anyone who lives in an inner city "gun-free zone" sooner or later learns that trusting the state to be on the scene to stop a rapist, robber, and/or murderer—however diligent and brave the police might be—is only a workable view for those who get police escorts. In fact, it is hypocritical for those who can afford not to take the responsibility to protect themselves to then tell the rest of the free populace that they must be unarmed prey for criminals.

After all, when we are awoken by the sound of glass breaking, even the softest metro-sexual dandy among us would rather have a gun than a telephone. In such hair-raising moments, people learn that Colonel Samuel Colt wasn't joking when he ran ads declaring, "God made man, but Samuel Colt made them equal." People learn in one terrifying moment that though 911 is an important lifeline, 911 is no more real than good intentions until the police actually arrive. Also, no matter what the law says, the weaker sex learns that gun rights are a necessary ingredient to bring about true equal rights.

Such an experience forever changed Sandra Froman, a Jewish-American woman born in San Francisco who rose to be a president of the National Rifle Association. She said,

> Let me tell you how a girl raised in the San Francisco Bay area,
> who studied in Cambridge's liberal halls at Harvard, became
> a gun owner and a vocal defender of our Second Amendment.

When I was 32 years old and working as an attorney in California, a man tried to break into my house. He was working on my front door's lock with a screwdriver. I was scared. I banged loudly to let him know someone was home. He stopped, but then started again. I called my neighbors, but they didn't answer their phones—at three in the morning, who could blame them? I frantically called the police. I was suddenly aware that if this man got in my home before the police arrived there was nothing I could really do. I didn't own a gun. I'd never even shot a gun before. The man finally gave up and the police finally arrived, missing the would-be intruder by minutes.

The next day I went to a gun store. I told the man behind the counter, "I want to buy a gun." "What kind of gun," he asked. "Any kind," I said. "What do you want it for?" he questioned. I told him what happened and he recommended an NRA gun safety course. I took the class that weekend and soon after bought my first firearm, a .45-caliber handgun.

Such are the experiences that push back on politicians who pass laws to weaken peoples' ability to defend themselves. Such life-and-death encounters are why Heller and McDonald lent their names and life stories to two cases that revitalized the Second Amendment's restrictions on government regulation. Both men live in areas run by anti-gun-rights liberals. Both were tired of being told they either had to be unarmed victims or armed criminals. Both wanted their Bill of Rights back.

Dick Anthony Heller was a security guard who was required to carry a firearm when protecting a federal building by day, but wasn't permitted to have a gun at his District of Columbia residence to protect himself or his loved ones at night. Heller was the last plaintiff standing in a case that went all the way to the Supreme Court. This case, which became known as *District of Columbia* v. *Heller* (2008), was the first case in U.S. history to fundamentally answer whether the Second Amendment is an individual right.

Moments after the court heard *District of Columbia* v. *Heller* in March 2008, the steps of the Supreme Court were obscured by a chaotic crowd of lawyers in classy business suits, law-school students in Banana Republic outfits, and print and television reporters in dark suit jackets, white shirts, and bright ties. At the bottom of the court's marble steps, in the center of the melee, were eight anti-gun rights protesters all holding signs saying, "We Want Reasonable Gun Control," "Stop the Gun Violence," and "Guns Kill."

A television producer was herding the anti-gun-freedom protesters together like a wedding photographer preparing a group shot. She clearly wanted a tight camera angle so the eight activists might look like a small portion of a hundred on network news that evening.

In real life they just looked farcical.

Up on the steps above the protesters, I was interviewing Dick Heller for the National Rifle Association when an AP reporter pushed a tape recorder toward Heller while accusing more than asking, "Mr. Heller, how can you justify letting criminals have handguns on the streets of this dangerous city?"

Heller shifted his brown eyes over to her and replied easily, as he had so many times before: "It's immoral and unconstitutional for the government to tell me it's okay to have a gun during my work hours, when I'm protecting government officials, but that it's illegal for me to have a gun when I'm home, protecting myself and my family."

She shook her head, pursed her lips, and asked in a tone etched with indignation, "But what about [D.C.] Mayor Adrian Fenty's point that the district's ban on handguns is necessary to reduce violent crime?"

Just as Heller was about to point out that the city's crime rate rose after firearms were prohibited, as if on cue, Mayor Adrian M. Fenty finished his remarks to a television reporter and began to scurry away down the sidewalk beneath us. It was hard to see Fenty, even from above, as he was surrounded by a detachment of police officers.

Heller seized the moment. He pointed at Mayor Fenty and said, "Look at that, see all those cops around the mayor? Taxpayers are paying for

Mayor Fenty's protection, yet we the people are not allowed to defend ourselves in the District. That's the hypocrisy we are here today to defeat."

The AP reporter clicked off her tape recorder and without even a "thank you for your time" tossed her nose in the air, spun around, and strode back into the fervent scene.

Minutes earlier, during the Supreme Court hearing, Justice Anthony Kennedy—who was widely regarded as the "swing" vote on the issue—strongly hinted that he believed the Second Amendment protects an individual right. Justice Kennedy's tell came as much from his tone as from his words. Justice Kennedy asked D.C.'s attorney, Walter Dellinger, a 1966 Yale Law School graduate who was acting solicitor general under President Bill Clinton, whether "the second clause [of the Second Amendment], the operative clause ['the right of the people to keep and bear Arms, shall not be infringed'], is related to something other than the militia." And then he pressed further by asking incredulously, "It had nothing to do with the concern of the remote settler to defend himself and his family against hostile Indian tribes and outlaws, wolves and bears and grizzlies and things like that?"

After Justice Kennedy uttered those loaded words, a journalist seated beside me in the press box, a reporter from one of those mainstream networks, hissed, "Oh no." It seemed freedom had at least five out of nine votes.

After the hearing, and back on the steps of the Supreme Court, Justice Kennedy's perceived position was being broadcast by television reporters from the steps of the Court. Gun owners all over America were breathing a cautious sigh of relief.

This was never a foregone conclusion. The high court was so closely divided between judges who endeavor to blindly administer the law and those who find ways to read their own views into the law that at the time even the National Rifle Association (NRA) had serious doubts about bringing the *Heller* case before the Court. Wayne LaPierre, the NRA's executive vice president, even said as much: "There was a real dispute on our side among the constitutional scholars about whether there was a majority of justices on the Supreme Court who would support the Constitution as written."

Nevertheless, Robert A. Levy, an attorney and entrepreneur who'd financed the lawsuit, pushed on, and the NRA eventually threw its muscle behind the effort. Levy now says he didn't have any idea how Justice Kennedy would vote, but that because of decades of scholarship by the NRA on the origins of the Second Amendment the issue had evolved to the extent that there was a consensus even among liberal scholars that the Second Amendment protects an individual right.

Levy served as a co-counsel and hired Alan Gura, a graduate of Georgetown and a self-described Libertarian, to be the lead attorney. Then Levy, with his handpicked legal team, began recruiting plaintiffs for the planned Second Amendment lawsuit against the District of Columbia in 2002. Although Levy had never owned a gun himself, he was interested in the issue because he believed in individual rights. He teamed up with Clark M. Neily III from the Institute for Justice, a conservative group, and began finding and vetting District residents who wanted a gun for self-defense at home. They eventually settled on six residents: Shelly Parker, Tom Palmer, Gillian St. Lawrence, Tracey Ambeau, George Lyon, and Dick Anthony Heller. They tried to select a diverse group, and ended with men and women, black and white, and a variety of income levels.

The lawsuit was filed in 2003 as *Parker* v. *District of Columbia.* The appeals court knocked five of the six plaintiffs out of the case, saying they did not have standing to file a lawsuit because they had never tried to register a gun in D.C.

Levy called that ruling a "Catch-22." He said, "If you want to apply for a license or permit for a handgun, you have to prove ownership of a handgun. Where do you get one? You can't buy a handgun in Washington, D.C., and federal law says you can't buy a handgun in any state except where you reside."

After several reversals and appeals, the case made it to the Supreme Court as *District of Columbia* v. *Heller.* To help with the appeal to the Supreme Court, the NRA submitted an amicus brief and gave legal support to Levy's team, support Levy later said was instrumental in helping to win the case for freedom-loving Americans.

Chris Cox, executive director of the NRA's Institute for Legislative Action, said, "Losing this case would have undermined a fundamental individual right. To prepare for this legal battle we held mock courts for the attorneys, we rallied our membership, and we got fifty-eight U.S. senators, two hundred and fifty-one members of the House of Representatives, and Vice President Dick Cheney to sign on to our amicus brief petitioning the Court to rule in favor of the facts by finding that the Second Amendment is an individual right."

So, after decades of battles and hundreds of books and articles in legal journals on the Second Amendment, the Supreme Court presented the legal question to be resolved this way: "Whether provisions of the D.C. firearms code violate the Second Amendment rights of individuals who are not affiliated with any state-regulated militia, but who wish to keep handguns and other firearms for private use in their homes?" The wording "are not affiliated with any state-regulated militia" was added to directly answer the liberal assertion that the Second Amendment only gave state-sanctioned militia members the right to own and to carry firearms.

During the Supreme Court hearing on *Heller*, the government's attorney, Walter Dellinger, argued that Americans don't have the right to own handguns or to keep functional firearms in their homes because the Second Amendment signifies nothing more than expired words that once regulated now defunct state militias. Dellinger, and other anti-gun liberals, have long tried, and with some notable success, to twist the Second Amendment into meaning it only protected militias, and not, as it says, the people. They claim the amendment's first clause modifies the rest and somehow expunges "the people" from the 27-word amendment.

Dellinger discounted the fact that George Mason said, "I ask, sir, what is the militia? It is the whole people, except for few public officials."[6] Dellinger ignored the sentiments of the views of the entire founding generation and the fact that the Second Amendment wasn't controversial until the progressive era in the late nineteenth and early twentieth century, because it was clearly understood to be an individual right. More than just ignoring the Founding Fathers, Dellinger even disregarded the dictionary.

Noah Webster (1758–1843), whose name has become synonymous with "dictionary" because he compiled the modern Merriam-Webster dictionary (first published in 1828 as *An American Dictionary of English Language*), argued that a constitutional republic must have real and constant definitions for the words within its laws and constitution. Making certain words have definitions that can be looked up is the only way to keep laws and constitutions from being semantically rewritten without the consent of the people. Webster's 1828 dictionary was subsequently adopted by the U.S. Congress as the American standard. Each of the words found in the Second Amendment is defined in Webster's dictionary.

Webster defined "militia" as "…able bodied men organized into companies, regiments and brigades, with officers of all grades, and required by law to attend military exercises on certain days only, but at other times left to pursue their usual occupations."[7] So, at the very least, people "left to pursue their usual occupations" included all able-bodied men from adolescence to senility. Also, the fact that they were "organized into companies" doesn't alter the definition of the word "militia," as there is no historical evidence to suggest that the gradual end of the practice of having volunteer militias changed the definition of the word "militia." Arguing that the militia isn't "the people" because some semantically altered modern definition of "militia" means something else is counter to history and dishonest to the core. Such thinking would mean any word or phrase in the Constitution can simply be taken away by bureaucrats as they rewrite dictionaries in an Orwellian attempt to control the populace.

Webster defined "people" as "the commonality, as distinct from men of rank." Therefore, in the language of Webster's time, "the people" meant average citizens. His dictionary defined "right" as "just claim; immunity; privilege." And "keep" as "to hold; to retain one's power or possession; not to lose or part with; to have in custody for security or preservation." And "bear" was "to carry" or "to wear; name; to bear arms in a coat." (Notice that this definition includes concealed carry.) And "arms" were defined as "weapons of offense, or armor for defense and protection of the body." Now also realize that only civilians would "bear arms in a coat," as soldiers carried firearms in their hands or in a holster. So all of this clearly means that individual citizens have the right to pack a firearm, concealed or otherwise. And therefore Webster defined the words "keep and bear arms" to literally mean a right to hand-held arms that a person could "bear," such as muskets, pistols, and swords, but not artillery pieces and so on that an individual could not carry.

How about the Second Amendment's clause stating the right of the people to "keep and bear Arms shall not be infringed"? Webster defined "infringe" as "to violate, either positively by contravention, or negatively by non-fulfillment or neglect of performance." That's pretty clear. The government can't ban handguns or long guns.

So even by their own logic, Dellinger and his cronies are wrong. But they know that; what bothers them is they didn't get one more progressive justice on the Supreme Court who would go along with their big fat lie.

Progressives need Clintonian room to debate the definition of even the word "is." Dictionary definitions are a solution to their semantics, as there is no room to obfuscate. In fact, on September 20, 2009, on ABC's *This Week,* George Stephanopoulos cited the Merriam-Webster dictionary's definition of "tax" to President Barack Obama to point out that the health-care bill passed in 2010 has tax increases. President Obama still wouldn't admit Stephanopoulos was clearly right and simply answered with an accusation: "George, the fact that you looked up Merriam's dictionary, the definition of tax increase, indicates to me that you're stretching a little bit right now. Otherwise, you wouldn't have gone to the dictionary to check on the definition."[8]

No, citing a dictionary prevents someone from stretching the truth.

Five justices on the Court didn't have a problem with a clear, honest definition. On June 26, 2008, the Supreme Court ruled 5–4 that the Second Amendment is indeed an individual right. The Court upheld the federal appeals court ruling, thereby striking down D.C.'s gun law, which outlawed handguns altogether and barred operable rifles or shotguns in residents' homes. Justice Antonin Scalia, writing for the majority, held, "In sum, we hold that the District's ban on handgun possession in the home violates the Second Amendment, as does its prohibition against rendering any lawful firearm in the home operable for the purpose of immediate self-defense."

Though all the historical evidence—and even the dictionary—shows that the Second Amendment is clearly an individual right, four out of nine justices still voted to expunge the Second Amendment from the Bill of Rights. Given this attack on American freedom, it's worth noting that if Al Gore had beaten George W. Bush for the presidency in 2000, then Gore would have gotten at least one Supreme Court pick—Bush got two. With just one more anti-gun rights vote on the Court, this constitutional right won by Americans taking up arms against tyranny would have been lost. In fact, Darren LaSorte, now the National Rifle Association's manager of hunting policy, said,

> In 2000 I was the state liaison for the NRA in Gore's home state of Tennessee. After Gore lost the election and with it Tennessee, even former President Bill Clinton said Gore lost his home state and likely the election because guns were the issue in Tennessee and were made a major issue by Gore across the nation. Virtually every state legislator—Democrat and Republican alike—and I agreed that Americans saw that their individual freedom was in the balance so they voted for Bush. Without that win Samuel Alito and John Roberts wouldn't now be Supreme Court justices. This shows us just how fragile this hard-won freedom still is.

The majority in this 5–4 decision ruled that the Second Amendment is an individual right that can be regulated, just as any other right can be fairly regulated. Justice Scalia wrote, "It is not a right to keep and carry any weapon whatsoever in any manner whatsoever and for whatever purpose." Justice Scalia went on to say the Court's decision "should not be taken to cast doubt on many existing restrictions against gun possession, including handgun possession by felons and the mentally ill, possession in schools and government buildings and rules governing commercial arms sale. But outright bans on the Second Amendment right, like the First Amendment's free speech, are not constitutional."

As this was a conservative ruling, the Court used judicial restraint. They didn't want to write legislation from the bench. They left it up to the people's elected officials and to future Court rulings to define *reasonable* restrictions on the individual right.

The Brady Campaign, however, was quick to claim the *Heller* ruling protects "reasonable" gun restrictions from litigation that the individual right ruling would undoubtedly trigger—*reasonable* according to the Brady Campaign, of course, includes complete gun bans. For example, the Brady Campaign supported D.C. and Chicago's bans on handguns. "The ruling gives a constitutional green light to a wide range of gun restrictions," announced Dennis Henigan, vice president for law and policy at the Brady Center to Prevent Gun Violence.

Specifically in *Heller*, the Supreme Court ruled that the operative clause of the Second Amendment ("the right of the people to keep and bear Arms, shall not be infringed") is controlling and therefore refers to a pre-existing right of individuals to possess and carry firearms for self-defense. The right of the people to bear arms clearly indicates that the Framers believed the right already existed and therefore they were simply recognizing it formally with the Second Amendment. After all, before the Bill of Rights was written and ratified, the people certainly had the inherent right to own and carry firearms in the American Colonies. To solidify this point, the Court based this ruling on the bare meaning of the words in the clause, along with the usage of "the people" elsewhere in the Constitution and historical materials that explain the clause's original meaning.

The majority also ruled that the prefatory clause of the Second Amendment, which says that a "well regulated Militia, being necessary to the security of a free State," refers to a well-trained citizen militia, which at the time "comprised all males physically capable of acting in concert for the common defense." The Court noted historical materials supporting this interpretation, including "analogous arms-bearing rights in state constitutions."

This is why during most of American history an exhaustive analysis of the Second Amendment wasn't necessary, as the meaning of each word in the Second Amendment was too obvious to question—again those pesky dictionaries were too straightforward to twist semantically. The Second Amendment wasn't even debated until the progressive era in the late nineteenth century and not really disputed until well into the twentieth century. This is why the fundamental constitutional question wasn't answered by the high court until 2008—some 217 years after the Bill of Rights was ratified by the states.

The individual rights decision gave those who dislike this freedom conniptions.

For example, Richard Posner, a judge for the United States Court of Appeals for the Seventh Circuit in Chicago, said,

> The text of the [Second Amendment], whether viewed alone or in light of the concerns that actuated its adoption, creates no right to the private possession of guns for hunting or other sport, or for the defense of person or property. It is doubtful that the amendment could even be thought to require that members of state militias be allowed to keep weapons in their homes, since that would reduce the militias' effectiveness. Suppose part of a state's militia was engaged in combat and needed additional weaponry. Would the militia's commander have to collect the weapons from the homes of militiamen who had not been mobilized, as opposed to obtaining them from a storage facility? Since the purpose of the Second Amendment, judging from its language and background, was to assure the effectiveness of state militias, an interpretation that undermined their effectiveness by preventing states from making efficient arrangements for the storage and distribution of military weapons would not make sense.[9]

Of course, there is zero historical evidence to back up Posner's claim that militia members–nearly the entire male adult population–had to keep their firearms in some barracks miles from their homes There would have been no convenient reason to do so, what with Indian attack a real possibility in some locales, and frontier crime a viable threat. Besides these practical reasons for having guns in their homes, there's the simple fact that, at that time, many muskets were of varied calibers and different makes and models. No hunter or soldier wants to go into the field with a firearm he isn't familiar with and likely doesn't have ammunition for. Posner's entire unhistorical argument is based on how he views the state, not the actual wording of the Constitution, nor the practical needs of the people.

J. Harvie Wilkinson III, chief judge of the United States Court of Appeals for the Fourth Circuit, also weighed in. He said *Heller* "encourages Americans to do what conservative jurists warned for years they should not do: bypass the ballot and seek to press their political agenda in the courts."[10]

No, sorry Wilkinson III, conservatives say the Constitution says what it means and means what it says, which is and was the will of the people. If a majority wants to change the Constitution, they can push for a new amendment.

And Jeffrey M. Shaman, a law professor at DePaul University, said,

> Justice Scalia's extreme version of originalism is based on the misguided belief that the original meaning of the Constitution is fixed in history and can be objectively determined by searching historical records. It is incorrect to believe that the Constitution can be interpreted simply by reference to the original understanding of the document....Justice Scalia's brand of originalism is dysfunctional, an instance of cultural lag whereby the meaning of the Constitution is left dormant while the world changes around it.[11]

It seems that Shaman also needs to be reintroduced to the dictionary. And, again, the Constitution can be changed if the people desire it to be altered.

Such are the convoluted views of the liberal-progressive justices who would rip a freedom first won by the English in 1689 from the American people. (The English Bill of Rights of 1689 included: "That the Subjects which are Protestants may have Arms for their Defence suitable to their Conditions and as allowed by Law.") One more vote from such a liberal justice would have torn the right to bear arms from the Bill of Rights, and it still can. Many interpretive rulings have been revisited and reversed. Indeed, in one of two dissenting opinions, Justice John Paul Stevens called Scalia's argument that the Second Amendment is an individual right "strained and unpersuasive." "Until today, it has been understood that legislatures may regulate the civilian use and misuse of firearms so long as they do not interfere with the preservation of a well-regulated militia," Stevens wrote. "The Court's announcement of a new constitutional right to own and use firearms for private purposes upsets that settled understanding."

No, Justice Stevens, the government can't regulate Americans' right to own and carry firearms as long as it doesn't "interfere with the preservation of a well-regulated militia." That has never been the law of the land. The facts are quite clear: constitutional scholar Stephen Halbrook has noted that there is no evidence that anyone associated with drafting, debating, or ratifying the Second Amendment considered it to protect anything other than an entirely individual right. In fact, James Madison, who introduced the Bill of Rights in Congress, wrote in *The Federalist Papers* (No. 46) that the federal government would not be able to tyrannize the people "with arms in their hands, officered by men chosen from among themselves, fighting for their common liberties, and united and conducted by [state] governments possessing their affections and confidence." Also, in *The Federalist Papers* (No. 29), Alexander Hamilton wrote, "If circumstances should at any time oblige the government to form an army of any magnitude that army can never be formidable to the liberties of the people while there is a large body of citizens, little, if at all, inferior to them in discipline and the use of arms, who stand ready to defend their own rights and those of their fellow-citizens." Such is the history progressives have been trying to delete from the history books.

This battle for your rights is hardly in the past tense. Next came the nationwide battle.

The Battle over "Reasonable" Gun Control

Though the *Heller* decision declared that the Second Amendment is an individual right, before the ink was dry on the decision, the NRA filed a lawsuit to challenge the city of Chicago's gun ban. In fact, in the months after *Heller*, nearly 100 lawsuits challenging gun-control laws under the Second Amendment made it to federal court. The NRA filed five federal lawsuits requesting that the Second Amendment be applied to state and local governments via the Fourteenth Amendment. Four of those lawsuits were dropped following the repeal of the local gun restrictions at issue in those cases. The fifth, *NRA* v. *Chicago*, was appealed to the Supreme Court. On September 29, 2009, the Supreme Court discussed whether to review *NRA* v. *Chicago*. The Court instead decided to review *McDonald* v. *Chicago*, a case that closely paralleled *NRA* v. *Chicago*, but since the outcome of *McDonald* v. *Chicago* would also decide the fate of the NRA case, the Court also made the NRA a party to the *McDonald* case.

Otis McDonald, who gave this case its name, is the second man who wanted to wrestle his Second Amendment rights back from the government. In April 2008, McDonald, a retired maintenance engineer, agreed to serve as the lead plaintiff in a lawsuit challenging Chicago's handgun ban. Though McDonald keeps two shotguns in his house, he says those firearms are unwieldy inside his home. He wanted to have a handgun by his bedside to protect his wife and family. So to challenge the unconstitutional restriction, McDonald walked into the Chicago Police Department and applied for a .22-caliber Beretta pistol, which he knew he'd be denied, thus setting the lawsuit in motion.

McDonald is the child of black Louisiana sharecroppers. He was seventeen years old when he borrowed $18 from his mother and set off for Chicago in 1951. He was just one of millions of African Americans who fled the South during the "Great Migration." McDonald settled in

Chicago's Morgan Park neighborhood. At the time, the neighborhood was bustling and relatively safe. In the ensuing years he got married, had and raised eight children, and spent his career working at the University of Chicago, where he started as a janitor and worked his way up to become a maintenance engineer. But by the time he'd retired, in 1997, Morgan Park had been lost to gangs. McDonald told the *Chicago Tribune*, "I know every day that I come out in the streets, the youngsters will shoot me as quick as they will a policeman."[12]

McDonald decided to become involved in the gun-rights movement in 2005, when Mayor Richard Daley was pushing a statewide ban on "assault weapons." McDonald was concerned that his shotgun might be outlawed under the proposed ban, so McDonald started attending gun rights rallies. The connections he made at those events led to his inclusion in the class-action lawsuit against the city of Chicago.

McDonald and three co-plaintiffs were carefully recruited by the same legal team, behind Robert A. Levy, who had put together the *Heller* case. McDonald, a Democrat and longtime hunter had by then been a married, law-abiding resident of Chicago for over fifty years. He was the perfect person to be the face of this case. He'd spent almost forty years in a two-story house in Morgan Park, an increasingly rough Chicago neighborhood, and he only wanted to keep his family and his property safe. McDonald explained, "I was feeling the poor blacks who years ago had their guns taken away from them and were killed as someone wished. That was a long time ago, but I feel their spirit. That's what I was feeling in the courtroom....This lawsuit, I hope, will allow me to bring my handgun into the city legally. I only want a handgun in my house for my protection."[13]

Levy, who is now the chairman of the Cato Institute, said, "We wanted to be able to present the best face not just to the court but also to the media. We didn't want some Montana militia man as the poster boy for the Second Amendment."

He chose well. McDonald is hardly a rural, conservative redneck—the type the media characterize as being 99 percent of the nation's gun owners.

According to the *Chicago Tribune*: "Photos of McDonald's children, smiling in their graduation caps and gowns, hang on the walls next portraits of Barack Obama and Bill and Hillary Clinton. A large Bible rests on the coffee table next to a crystal bowl of peppermints."[14]

And he has been a victim of crimes. According to police reports, McDonald's house was burglarized three times in the 1980s and early 1990s; in fact, on one occasion, three young men surrounded McDonald's car and threatened to "off" him. McDonald is living proof that to remain truly free, we must be armed and capable of defending ourselves.

Levy says the strategy of attacking an immoral and unconstitutional regulation by finding compelling victims was partly inspired by the civil rights-era cases that challenged racial segregation in the 1940s and 1950s. The NAACP's winning method in those cases became the template for other reform movements, such as women's rights in the 1970s and conservative challenges to affirmative action in the 1980s.

Levy and his team stepped into the legal system knowing the lower courts were only preliminary bouts. The main event would be at the U.S. Supreme Court. The first trial court entered judgment in favor of the City of Chicago on December 18, 2008. The decision was appealed to the Seventh Circuit Court of Appeals and combined with a similar case, *NRA v. Chicago*. The oral argument occurred on May 26, 2009, and the court issued its opinion on June 2, 2009, affirming the trial court's decision that the Chicago and Oak Park gun regulations were constitutional. Levy says they knew they wouldn't get a fair reading of the Constitution in lower courts that were stacked with progressives. He was waiting for the Supreme Court's final word.

They appealed, and the Supreme Court agreed to take their case in March 2010, with the NRA as a party in support of *McDonald*. The court also granted the NRA time to participate in oral argument. This enabled the NRA's legal team—the constitutional scholars who'd researched and published much of what we know about the origins of the Second Amendment—to add their expertise to the hearing.

Justice David Souter, who had voted against ruling that the Second Amendment is an individual right, had since retired. President Barack Obama had replaced him with Justice Sonia Sotomayor. During her confirmation hearings in the U.S. Senate she said the *Heller* case was "settled law." According to the philosophy of *stare decisis,* she said she would respect the decision.

The Supreme Court heard *McDonald* v. *Chicago* and delivered its decision on June 28, 2010. It turned out to be another 5–4 close-call ruling. Justice Sotomayor went back on her word under oath. During her U.S. Senate confirmation hearing on July 16, 2009, she had this conversation with Senator Lindsey Graham (R-SC):

> GRAHAM: Well, that's groundbreaking precedent in the sense that just until a few months ago, or last year I guess, that was not the case. But it is today. It is the law of the land by the Supreme Court that the Second Amendment is an individual right. And you acknowledge that, that's correct?
>
> SOTOMAYOR: That was …
>
> GRAHAM: The Heller case.
>
> SOTOMAYOR: … the decision. And it is what the court has held, and so it is unquestionably an individual right.

Despite agreeing the Second Amendment is an individual right, she voted against "settled law" and decided the Second Amendment is not an individual right after all. This poses the question: what else would she renege on? Indeed, what has happened to our country when a confirmation process to put someone in judgment of our Constitution for life allows and even rewards their lies under oath?

Perhaps it is time the U.S. Congress flexed its muscles just a little bit by threatening to impeach a justice who so clearly fibbed during the confirmation process. That would be entirely constitutional.

So *McDonald* was another 5–4 close call for freedom. The Court determined the Second Amendment also applies to state and local governments via the Fourteenth Amendment's "due process" clause. Over nearly a century of cases, the Court has extended to the states the restrictions on government from the Bill of Rights, including part or all of the First, Third, Fourth, Fifth, Sixth, and Eighth Amendments. As a result, it would have been peculiar and intellectually inconsistent for the high court not to incorporate the Second Amendment.

Justice Alito used "substantive due process" under the Fourteenth Amendment to cement the majority decision. This is the logic that liberals have long used to apply the other segments of the Bill of Rights to the states—objections to using the Fourteenth Amendment to selectively decide which amendments in the Bill of Rights also restrict the state have historically come from conservatives. Indeed, the practice of "selective incorporation" evolved over time and was primarily pushed by progressive judges; as a result, Justice Antonin Scalia mentioned his own "misgivings about Substantive Due Process" as a matter of original constitutional interpretation in his concurring opinion. But he said he "acquiesced" in this decision "because it is both long established and narrowly limited."

Justice Alito's majority opinion was also careful to define the reach of substantive due process, saying it should apply only to those rights that are "fundamental to our scheme of ordered liberty." *Heller* had decided that basic question, Justice Alito wrote, and thus to decide not to apply it to the states would "treat the right recognized in *Heller* as a second-class right, subject to an entirely different body of rules than the other Bill of Rights guarantees that we have held to be incorporated into the Due Process Clause."

All the legal wrangling of incorporation aside, *McDonald*'s majority opinion didn't pull its punches: "Founding-era legal commentators confirmed the importance of the right to early Americans. St. George Tucker, for example, described the right to keep and bear arms as 'the true palladium of liberty' and explained that prohibitions on the right would place liberty 'on the brink of destruction.'"[15]

The majority opinion did leave room for state and local gun regulation, as did the *Heller* decision; in fact, the liberals on the Court could have joined the majority to help shape the opinion and to allow for even more state and local latitude, if they were so open minded. They chose not to; they instead came out in vociferous dissent and refused to accept even the basic finding in *Heller* and the fundamental right to self-defense. In fact, in a flip-flop of intellectual consistency that should make the liberal justices blush, Justice Stephen Breyer, Justice Sonia Sotomayor, and Justice Ruth Bader Ginsburg even suddenly became states' rights advocates. They argued that incorporation would curtail the ability of states to craft their own gun laws, which is a bold lie, as every tenet of the Bill of Rights that has been applied to this is regulated to some extent by state laws. Even the Fifth Amendment's last clause ("nor shall private property be taken for public use, without just compensation") is regulated by the states, a fact that led to laws being passed by states to strengthen property rights after *Kelo* v. *The City of New London* (2005) ripped property rights from private citizens (which will be discussed further when we get to the Fifth Amendment).

This obvious use of a legal principle they've traditionally stood in opposition to didn't seemed to bother Justice Breyer or the other liberals when they overturned state laws based on a "right to privacy" that, unlike the Second Amendment's "right of the people to keep and bear Arms," isn't mentioned in the text of the Constitution. Actually, their willingness to be opportunistic suggests that the liberals are biding their time as they wait for a majority so they can overturn both *Heller* and *McDonald* and thereby take away this constitutional freedom. This means that the matter of Second Amendment rights is far from settled and that the National Rifle Association and all freedom-loving gun owners had better not get complacent if they want their rights upheld.

Also, McDonald's battle with the city of Chicago didn't end with the ruling. To sidestep the Supreme Court decision, Chicago quickly passed a new ordinance. City officials called the new law "the strictest in the nation." As it turns out, it is perhaps the stupidest. As of late 2010, the measure prohibited gun stores from opening in Chicago, and it prevented gun owners from so much as stepping outside their homes with a handgun. It even prevented citizens from using a firearm on their porches or in their garages. That's right, the law actually explained where you could and couldn't defend your life. Though precisely what a "porch" is under the law will have to be answered later. Does screened-in count? What if it has windows with an air conditioner?

After the *Heller* ruling, the District of Columbia started the same mad dash to see just how far they could push the constitutional right to self-defense by making it nearly impossible for Dick Heller to register a handgun in Washington, D.C. Such is the battle now being waged across the country to determine what constitutes "reasonable" gun control.

However, the *McDonald* decision dug into another moral/human-rights point that anti-gun liberals would rather not discuss: when the liberals who form the core of the Democratic Party use every semantic twist to slay the Second Amendment, they are actually being true to their party's history. It was Democrats from whom people such as Otis McDonald fled in the South in the mid-twentieth century. It was Democrats who used state laws to disarm free blacks after the American Civil War. And it is Democrats who are still trying to keep minorities disarmed and helpless.

In *McDonald,* Justice Samuel Alito's majority opinion noted that after the Civil War, many of the over 180,000 African Americans who served in the Union Army returned to the States of the old Confederacy, where systematic efforts were made to disarm them and other blacks. The laws of some States formally prohibited African Americans from possessing firearms. "For example, a Mississippi law provided that "no freedman, free negro or mulatto, not in the military service of the United States government, and not licensed so to do by the board of police of his or her county, shall keep or carry fire-arms of any kind, or any ammunition, dirk or bowie knife...."

In fact, wrote Justice Alito:

> Throughout the South, armed parties, often consisting of ex-Confederate soldiers serving in the state militias, forcibly took firearms from newly freed slaves. In the first session of the 39th

Congress, Senator Wilson told his colleagues: "In Mississippi rebel State forces, men who were in the rebel armies, are traversing the State, visiting the freedmen, disarming them, perpetrating murders and outrages upon them; and the same things are done in other sections of the country."

Justice Alito explained that during this period the most explicit evidence of the Congress' view was articulated in the Second Freedmen's Bureau Act of 1866, which provided that "the right ... to have full and equal benefit of all laws and proceedings concerning personal liberty, personal security, and the acquisition, enjoyment, and disposition of estate, real and personal, including the constitutional right to bear arms, shall be secured to and enjoyed by all the citizens ... without respect to race or color, or previous condition of slavery."

The Second Freedmen's Bureau Act of 1866 thus explicitly guaranteed that "all the citizens," black, white, or green, have "the constitutional right to bear arms." Also, the Civil Rights Act of 1866, which was considered at the same time as the Second Freedmen's Bureau Act, similarly sought to protect the right of all citizens to keep and bear arms. Section 1 of the Civil Rights Act guaranteed the "full and equal benefit of all laws and proceedings for the security of person and property, as is enjoyed by white citizens."

The Court's conclusion was that the Civil Rights Act, like the Freedmen's Bureau Act, aimed to protect "the constitutional right to bear arms" and not simply to prohibit discrimination. In *McDonald*, the Court noted that one of the "core purposes of the Civil Rights Act of 1866 and of the Fourteenth Amendment was to redress the grievances" of freedmen who had been stripped of their arms and to "affirm the full and equal right of every citizen to self-defense."

After the Civil War, Congress ultimately found these legislative remedies to be insufficient, so they decided that a constitutional amendment was necessary to provide full protection of rights for blacks. "Today, it is generally accepted that the Fourteenth Amendment was understood to provide a constitutional basis for protecting the rights set out in the Civil Rights Act of 1866," ruled the Court in *McDonald*.

In fact, when debating the Fourteenth Amendment, Senator Samuel Pomeroy said, "Every man … should have the right to bear arms for the defense of himself and family and his homestead. And if the cabin door of the freedman is broken open and the intruder enters for purposes as vile as were known to slavery, then should a well-loaded musket be in the hand of the occupant to send the polluted wretch to another world, where his wretchedness will forever remain complete."

The right to keep and bear arms was also widely protected by state constitutions in 1868; in fact, at the time some twenty-two of the thirty-seven states had constitutional provisions explicitly protecting the right to keep and bear arms. The majority in *McDonald* noted this fact and went on to rule:

> While of the Fourteenth Amendment contains "an antidis-crimination rule," namely, the Equal Protection Clause, munic-ipal respondents can hardly mean that it does no more than prohibit discrimination. If that were so, then the First Amend-ment, as applied to the States, would not prohibit nondis-criminatory abridgments of the rights to freedom of speech or freedom of religion; the Fourth Amendment, as applied to the States, would not prohibit all unreasonable searches and sei-zures but only discriminatory searches and seizures–and so on. We assume that this is not municipal respondents' view, so what they must mean is that the Second Amendment should be singled out for special–and specially unfavorable–treat-ment. We reject that suggestion.

Justice Alito, writing for the majority, additionally determined:

> Municipal respondents, in effect, ask us to treat the right rec-ognized in *Heller* as a second-class right, subject to an entirely

different body of rules than the other Bill of Rights guarantees that we incorporated into the Due Process Clause. Municipal respondents' main argument is nothing less than a plea to disregard 50 years of incorporation precedent and return (presumably for this case only) to a by-gone era.

Actually, the liberal justices contended that the Fourteenth Amendment doesn't protect a fundamental right to bear arms because countries such as England, Canada, Australia, and Japan either ban or severely limit handgun ownership. Perhaps, given their life-long appointments, the liberal justices don't care when they are called "activist judges" for trying to use world opinion and laws to usurp the Constitution. But it was still bold of them to use the laws of other nations to condone taking away a constitutional freedom from Americans.

The conservative justices, thankfully, smacked down the liberal justices' attempt to use other countries' laws to take away an American constitutional freedom: "If our understanding of the right to a jury trial, the right against self-incrimination, and the right to counsel were necessary attributes of any civilized country, it would follow that the United States is the only civilized Nation in the world." Juxtaposing America's constitutional rights against other nations' freedoms shows how much folly was in the liberal argument that, because other civilized countries disarmed their citizens, the U.S. government has the power to disarm law-abiding Americans.

Aside from world opinion, the liberal justices didn't even have a majority of Americans on their side. For example, an amicus brief submitted by 58 members of the U.S. Senate and 251 members of the U.S. House of Representatives—clear majorities in both houses of Congress—urged the Court to hold that the right to keep and bear arms is a fundamental and individual right.

After tearing apart the dissenting justices on legal grounds, the conservative justices morally indicted the liberals' utopian attempts to expunge the world of crime by taking away peoples' ability to defend themselves. The majority opinion noted:

[The] number of Chicago homicide victims during the current year equaled the number of American soldiers killed during that same period in Afghanistan and Iraq ... 80 percent of the Chicago victims were black....If, as petitioners believe, their safety and the safety of other law-abiding members of the community would be enhanced by the possession of handguns in the home for self-defense, then the Second Amendment right protects the rights of minorities and other residents of high-crime areas whose needs are not being met by elected public officials.

Indeed, despite their state-centric ideology, any anti-gun liberal can comprehend the Founders' point of view by simply imagining asking an African American living in the South just after the American Civil War if he or she had a right to use a gun to fight off a lynch mob. White southern Democrats often used "Black Codes" to bar African Americans from owning firearms. These laws prohibited black freedmen from exercising the right to bear arms because it's easier for lynch mobs to hang unarmed men and for racists to enforce poll taxes and Jim Crow laws on an unarmed minority. A provision preventing blacks from owning guns in Mississippi read that no freedman "shall keep or carry fire-arms of any kind, or any ammunition."[16] In fact, in the late nineteenth century, under the Mississippi law, a person informing the government about illegal arms possession of a freed slave was entitled to receive the confiscated firearm, a powerful incentive to disarm blacks.

Understanding this period of history makes you realize how appalling it is that today's inner-city and largely black neighborhoods, which often have the highest murder rates, have some of the strictest gun-control laws in the nation. Honest people in those neighborhoods are barred from defending themselves just as southern blacks once were. And the same political party is doing it to them. Thus, after his Supreme Court victory, Otis McDonald couldn't wait to register a handgun so that he could more effectively protect his family.

Between the Lines of the Constitutional Battles

Like Otis McDonald, Patty Konie, a grandmother living in New Orleans, found out what a government can do to individual rights. She stayed in her New Orleans home during the flooding after Hurricane Katrina. She was on dry ground and had plenty of food. She had dogs and wanted to make sure they were safe. The police showed up at her house days after they'd let the city go wild. They came into her home. They told her she had to leave. Patty said she had a handgun to protect herself with and that she'd be fine. She pointed to cupboards full of canned foods. The cops asked to see her gun. Patty showed them her revolver and several cops immediately tackled her. A news camera caught the attack. She didn't resist arrest. Nevertheless, they bruised her face and broke her collarbone as they forcibly arrested her for utilizing her constitutional rights. They took her handgun away and she never got it back again. Her dogs have not been seen since. (To see the footage of this event, log on to http://www.youtube.com/watch?v=-taU9d26wT4).

Many other people had their guns taken away when they needed them most by overzealous law enforcement during the aftermath of Katrina. They were treated like criminals. Police lost control of the city and then treated law-abiding citizens like they were armed thugs.

New Orleans Police Superintendent P. Edwin Compass said at the time, "No one will be able to be armed. Guns will be taken. Only law enforcement will be allowed to have guns."[17]

The order to evacuate the city had come from Mayor Ray Nagin, who is a long-time opponent of lawful gun ownership.

Calls started coming into the NRA about law-abiding citizens' guns being confiscated in and around New Orleans. These people were then left helpless. Chris Cox, executive director of the NRA's Institute for Legislative Action, said the stories were hard to believe. What American city would so blatantly step on constitutional rights? To see what was going on, the NRA literally put lawyers into cars (as flights weren't going into the area) and drove down from Virginia to see for themselves. They soon found that the stories were true. The local government authorities were illegally disarming citizens.

The National Rifle Association and the Second Amendment Foundation filed suit to stop the unconstitutional gun confiscations. The gun-rights groups won an injunction against the city. According to the terms of the permanent injunction against New Orleans, issued in October 2008, the city had to "make an aggressive attempt to return any and all firearms which may have been confiscated during the period August 29 to December 31, 2005." Nevertheless, many of the firearms were ruined by severe rust as they sat in the city's storage units. Most of the firearms were never returned, nor were records kept during the gun confiscation. This event is a horrific example of what a statist mentality can do to free Americans in the throes of a crisis. However, the NRA has fought for and passed laws around the United States designed to prevent something like this from ever happening again.

Other assaults on Second Amendment rights continue from all fronts. In the spring of 2010, Attorney General Eric Holder and then-White House Chief of Staff Rahm Emanuel pushed the idea of allowing the FBI's National Instant Criminal Background Check System (NICS), a mandatory federal background check done on anyone purchasing a gun, to reject people whose names appear on secret FBI watch lists, such as the no-fly list. The obvious problem with this unconstitutional idea is that you can find yourself on one of these lists by having the same name as a suspected criminal or terrorist, and if you are on a list, you may not be able to determine which one you are on, much less get yourself removed. Basically, such a power would have given the federal government the ability to make secret lists that could be used to take away constitutionally protected rights from anyone it chose. Ironically, even the late anti-gun Senator Ted Kennedy once ended up on a "no-fly list" for reasons that have not been made public.

When the NRA resisted this frightening usurpation of individual rights, they were demonized. The bill (S. 1317) was written by Senator Frank Lautenberg (D-N.J) and was named the "Denying Firearms and

Explosives to Dangerous Terrorists Act." In a letter asking other senators to co-sponsor the bill, Senator Lautenberg claimed the bill would only "permit the Attorney General to deny firearms and firearms and explosive licenses to known and suspected terrorists."

On the contrary, Lautenberg's bill would also have prohibited the possession of firearms by people who had been improperly placed on the FBI's secret Terrorist Screening Database. The bill would also have allowed the attorney general to revoke a person's Federal Firearm License on the same basis. The bill was stopped thanks to lobbying by the NRA.

The truth about the Second Amendment is that it is a right that is easy to lose. You might think only murderers and rapists get their firearms taken away, as convicted felons are not allowed to own firearms. Well, think again. Here are just a few things that could lead to the confiscation of your personal-defense gun: drag racing in Pennsylvania (it's a felony in the Keystone State); becoming a fugitive from justice (not showing up for traffic court counts); having a protection order placed against you (a shouting match with your spouse can result in one of these); and getting convicted in any court of a misdemeanor crime of domestic violence (a fist fight with your brother qualifies).

Basically, if you plead guilty to or are convicted of any federal law that can be punished by one year or more in jail, the government has the right to confiscate your .30-06. Likewise, if you plead guilty to or are convicted of a state misdemeanor that is punishable by two years in prison, the state can take your Winchester.

Still feel invulnerable? So did Donald G. Arnold, a private investigator who was named a "citizen of the year" in Maryland in 2000 for his work helping the police stop drug dealers in Baltimore. Arnold went to renew his handgun carry permit in Maryland and was denied, because in 1969, after returning from Vietnam, he got into a scuffle with a college student who called him a "baby killer." Arnold had gone to court without a lawyer and received a 60-day suspended sentence and unsupervised probation.

What Arnold didn't know was that thirty years later, the Maryland Attorney General J. Joseph Curran Jr. would issue a 63-page report titled

"A Farewell To Arms: The Solution To Gun Violence In America." In this report, Curran would claim that a 1996 decision by the Maryland Court of Appeals allowed the state to disqualify a person from possessing firearms based on the sentence he or she *could have received.* Arnold eventually won the battle for his rights and Curran left public office, but the incident shows the lengths some go to in order to take away individual rights they don't like.

So before you plead guilty to any criminal violation, get the facts. (In some states, public exposure—tinkling on the rose bushes, for example— carries a one- to five-year sentence.) It's all the more critical to be aware now, according to Chris Cox, executive director of the National Rifle Association's Institute for Legislative Action, because we've entered the third and most important phase of Second Amendment jurisprudence: the period where the bounds of the Second Amendment right will be defined. Every right safeguarded in the Bill of Rights, including the First Amendment, can be fairly regulated. So in the coming decades, the courts and legislatures will decide whether the Second Amendment protects rights such as concealed carry, the citizenry's right to own semi-automatic handguns, "gun-free zones" in municipalities, and so much more.

Liberals on the court and in the legislatures believe they can enact any gun regulation they think is reasonable, including bans on gun ownership. Thus the struggle to protect our Second Amendment rights is still necessary.

AMENDMENT III

*No Soldier shall, in time of peace be quartered
in any house, without the consent of the Owner, nor in time
of war, but in a manner to be prescribed by law.*

"The 1947 House and Rent Act ... is and always was the incuba-
tor and hatchery of swarms of bureaucrats to be quartered as storm
troopers upon the people in violation of Amendment III...." [1]
–United States v. *Valenzuala*

I n 1984, Jerrold and Ellen Ziman moved from Los Angeles to Manhattan's Greenwich Village and looked for a property to buy, not to
rent, as they had the old-fashioned American dream of raising their
two children–then ages two and seven–between their own walls, even in
the city that doesn't sleep.

They found a charming 2,400-square-foot brick townhouse on Minetta
Street, a curving, tree-lined oasis tucked away from the bustle of the city's
byways, and they thought themselves lucky. They plunked down $280,000
for the property, including a mortgage and savings.

The Zimans' new Manhattan home had been split into six one-room
apartments and one two-room apartment. At that time renters occupied
three of the units. All of the first floor and most of the second and fourth
floors were occupied, leaving the Ziman family just 450 square feet on the
third floor to live in; however, before the Zimans bought the brick townhouse, their attorney and the seller assured them that, as owner-occupants,
the state and city rent-control laws allowed them to evict the tenants in
the coming months so they could convert the building back into the single-
family residence it was originally designed to be.

The real-estate attorney and the seller were right, at the time.

Soon after the Zimans moved into the vacant apartment in the
Greenwich Village townhouse, they filed paperwork to evict the building's

tenants. But, just a few weeks after they'd filed the paperwork, the bureaucracy changed the rules. The state's legislature altered the rent-control laws by banning owner-occupants from evicting tenants who had lived in an apartment for twenty years or more, those who are sixty-two years of age or older, and those who are handicapped. The law was effective immediately and overrode all pending eviction applications. All three of the Zimans' tenants were either covered by the changes to the law or would be in the immediate future. In other words, three strangers had the legal right to occupy 80 percent of the Zimans' home for the rest of their lives.

The Zimans were dumbfounded. They'd given their life savings to live in a tiny portion of their own home? How can such an injustice be legal in the land of the free?

Besides, aren't ex post facto (retroactive) laws unconstitutional? (The federal government is prohibited from passing ex post facto laws by clause 3 of Article 1, section 9 of the U.S. Constitution, and the states are prohibited from the same by clause 1 of Article 1, section 10.) New York City bureaucrats replied that, as they hadn't gotten around to acting on the Zimans' request, they didn't consider it be an ex post facto action. When another citizen curbs your rights, you can turn to the government, but when the government does, you're left helpless, said Jerrold Ziman.[2]

The Zimans began to read the laws. They found that the system had been rigged in favor of tenants, that landlords were the *bourgeoisie* the laws were written to keep in line. They found they weren't as free as they'd thought.

As they digested the complex rent-control laws and fathomed the depth of the bureaucracy, they gave more money to their attorneys to find a way out of the mess. They were then cooking, sleeping, and reading the Constitution in one room with an adjoining bathroom. They could have rented a lot more space in Manhattan for a lot less than $280,000. Could New York City really demand they become landlords or sell their property at a major loss? Could the laws constitutionally force them to take up and to stay in an occupation by mandating that they become landlords?

Though the Zimans had plunked down $280,000 for the property, one tenant was paying just $148 a month, another $179.98, and the third $113 for a total of $440.98 per month. If the Zimans had borrowed $250,000 with an interest rate of 6.5 percent (in 1984 interest rates were closer to 12 percent) and an average property tax rate of 1.5 percent, their monthly payment would be $1,840.59. Even with the three apartments rented in the rent-controlled building, the Zimans were still footing $1,399.61 per month to live in 20 percent of their own home; meanwhile, their life-long tenants individually paid not even a quarter as much. And tourists wonder why so many abandoned buildings fringe Manhattan, a city with some of the highest (and lowest) rental rates in the country.

The Zimans' attorneys noted that the Fifth Amendment said, "No person shall … be deprived of life, liberty, or property, without due process of law; nor shall private property be taken for public use, without just compensation." The Zimans had certainly been deprived of their property.

They also noted that the Third Amendment said, "No Soldier shall, in time of peace be quartered in any house, without the consent of the Owner, nor in time of war, but in a manner to be prescribed by law." In this time of peace, weren't tenants whom the state gives the right to stay in a private residence for life then de facto agents of the state?

Two years before the Zimans had purchased their Greenwich Village townhouse, another New York case gave them a Third Amendment precedent. The court decision was actually the first time the Third Amendment was used to decide a major case. The case was *Engblom* v. *Carey* (1982) and was decided by the U.S. Court of Appeals for the Second Circuit. The case was initiated by a 1979 strike by New York State correction officers. While the officers were on strike, the U.S. National Guard performed some of the prison guards' duties. At New York's Mid-Orange Correctional Facility (and other facilities), striking employees were evicted from employee housing that was then used to house some of the National Guard troops. Two of the evicted officers at Mid-Orange C.F., Marianne E. Engblom and Charles E. Palmer, subsequently filed suit against the state of New York and its governor, Hugh L. Carey.

In *Engblom* v. *Carey*, the Court established that the National Guardsmen legally qualify as soldiers under the Third Amendment. Using the modern theory of selective incorporation for the amendment in the Bill of Rights, the Court next determined that the amendment applies to the states as well as the federal government under the Fourteenth Amendment. The court also found that the Third Amendment has a more general significance: referring to the Supreme Court's use of the Third Amendment in *Griswold* v. *Connecticut* (1965), the court maintained that "the Third Amendment was designed to assure a fundamental right to privacy."[3] Next, realizing that the U.S. Supreme Court has rejected rigid definitions of "ownership" when applying Fourth Amendment's protections against unreasonable search and seizure,[4] in *Engblom* the U.S. Court of Appeals for the Second Circuit applied a similar analysis to the Third Amendment by holding that "property-based privacy interests protected by the Third Amendment ... extend to those recognized and permitted by society as founded on lawful occupation or possession with a legal right to exclude others."

The majority opinion in *Engblom* stated that the officers' occupancy in the rooms was covered under the legal rules of "tenancy" and was protected under the Third Amendment. So the Court found that the National Guard troops were in fact agents of the state, and therefore the state had no right to evict the prison guards and then to house the troops in their place.

Though this case gave the Zimans some hope, as it handed them the "legal right to exclude others" from their private residence, constitutional questions take years of appeals and deep pockets to keep the appeals moving, even if they do find justices along the way who believe the Constitution says what it means and means what it says. Besides, the city had much deeper pockets than the Zimans, and no case had ever found rent control to be in violation of the Third Amendment.

Also, regardless of *Engblom*'s effects on Third Amendment theory, it failed to specify the remedies available to victims of quartering. Equitable remedies were inappropriate under the facts of the case, and the Court neglected to set guidelines for monetary damages. So though *Engblom* presented a constitutional path forward—it seems possible that homeowners trapped in rent control could prevail on claims of illegal peacetime quartering and thereby receive something for their troubles—fighting the bureaucracy is never so clear cut.

So the Zimans' attorneys reviewed the rent-control laws and found another way through. There was a provision that allowed property owners to cease renting if they permanently removed the premises from the rental market, and if they could show the inability to make a minimum return from their property; in this case, if owners could show they weren't getting at least an 8.5 percent return on their rental property, they could make a claim of "financial hardship." Such provisions are often placed in rent-control laws so a state or city attorney can say, "Judge, just look at the language of the law, it doesn't violate the Fifth Amendment's 'takings clause' because it explicitly *says* owners are allowed to attain a reasonable profit."

To win this way, the Zimans had to show all their tax returns, savings accounts, and investments, as well as their monthly bills, to a court in a belittling effort to beg relief from bureaucrats.

The Zimans swallowed their pride and did so.

"After a lot of hearings the Zimans did succeed in proving that giving eighty percent of their house for a few hundred dollars a month was a financial hardship," said Sam Kazman, general counsel for the Competitive Enterprise Institute, who worked pro-bono on the Ziman's case. Kazman explained that the Zimans actually went through two different accounting audits by the New York State Division of Housing and Community Renewal (DHCR), and after three years, a hearing officer deemed that they did show a financial hardship. But at that point the agency that had been conducting the audits concluded: Wait a minute! You're using the avenue of financial hardship, but we know your real reason to evict these tenants isn't that you're suffering financial hardship, but that you want to live there yourself. You've got an illegitimate motive, and even though you've satisfied the requirements for financial hardship, that's not what's really driving you here.

Subsequently, the Zimans brought a lawsuit against the DHCR, arguing that the agency's determination had been arbitrary and capricious. The New York State Supreme Court then rubber-stamped the DHCR without stating a rationale, and ruled the Zimans couldn't evict the tenants, at least not so they could occupy all the rooms of their own home. Of course, they couldn't evict the tenants so they could rent it to other tenants or lease it to a retail enterprise or for any other reason either. So, though there was technically a path for homeowners to follow so they could take control of their property, a Catch-22 was calculated into the law to stop them.

Then another constitutional question came up. Under the Constitution, the inability to earn a just return on one's capital is quite often considered a denial of due process or a takings, a Fifth Amendment infringement. The New York Court of Appeals even recognized the fundamental unfairness of denying a property owner the right to earn a just profit. In *Fred F. French Investing Co.* v. *City of New York* (1976) the court found that "the ultimate evil of a deprivation of property ... under the guise of an exercise of the police power is that it forces the owner to assume the cost of providing a benefit to the public without recoupment."

Kazman explained,

> The problem with takings suits, such as the one we filed for the Zimans, is that those sorts of challenges have almost always bogged down in the fact that the rent-control statute says that the landlord shall earn a just return and the rent shall be regulated. But the problem is that showing that you've been deprived of a just return is basically impossible. They simply bury you between funny accounting methods and the discretion the courts give to agencies to put together their own numbers.

If you're now scratching your head as to how all this is possible in America, you probably live in a freer part of the country than Manhattan. Understanding New York City's rent-control bureaucracy and its proletariat's damn-the-bourgeoisie mindset takes a Russian's cynical view of a state that decides what's good for the people, whether they like it or not. Indeed, to comprehend what the Zimans were battling, you must first realize that property rights have fundamentally disappeared into a web of tenants' rights in the land of rent control. Owners, known derisively as "those [expletive] landlords," are a popularly reviled class in New York City. As Kazman explained, "We were actually told when we brought this into New York City's Housing Court that the court was set up to protect tenants." Translation: The case was weighted against the Zimans from the start.

Rent control's progressive shackles on property rights were clamped in place in 1942 when Franklin D. Roosevelt signed the Emergency Price Control Act into law. FDR thought he could halt inflation by government dictum. Subsequently, in November 1943, the Office of Price Administration froze New York's rents at their March 1, 1943, levels. Later, when the Emergency Price Control Act was allowed to expire, Congress passed the Federal Housing and Rent Act of 1947 and thereby exempted construction done after February 1, 1947, from rent controls (though New York's "Rent Stabilization Law of 1969" brought rent control to units built after 1947). Since the early 1940s, there have been many more tweaks and power struggles between rent-control advocates and property owners. The short of it was that the Zimans' home was covered by the complex rent-control usurpation of property.[5]

Since FDR's mad attempt to freeze inflation began, economists have almost unanimously concluded that rent control is counterintuitive; in fact, the conservative economist Friedrich Hayek and his ideological rival, the Swedish leftist Gunnar Myrdal, both agreed that rent control creates shadow markets, severe housing shortages, and an immobilized tenantry, and that rent control destroys incentives to upgrade or even to maintain rent-controlled housing.

"In fact," said Kazman, "there is a book on rent control put out by the Fraser Institute of Canada that has photographs of areas in cities that were destroyed during World War II bombing raids and areas that have been destroyed by rent control. The book challenges you to tell which photo is which, as the answers follow only later. Rent control has a real physical consequence."

Some even joke that "Nelson's Third Law," the contention by the late-economist Arthur Nelson that the worse a government regulation is, the harder it is to get rid of it, explains why rent-control laws in New York City have lasted since being enacted as emergency measures during World War II. Nelson's Third Law stipulates that whatever governmental distortions a regulation creates, some people will adjust to the warped rules and actually find a way to profit from them. In this case the people benefiting, and then lobbying to keep the status quo, are the millions who have way-below-market rental rates. In fact, the courts, the HPD (housing enforcement) and DHCR, the building department bureaucracy, zoning enforcers, architects, plumbers, electricians, attorneys, large landlords ... all depend upon and perpetuate all of the detailed requirements of rent-control ordinances.

Without firsthand experience, says Jerold Ziman, it is hard to imagine how these cooperating players suck all of the benefits of private property ownership out of the city's system. The city gets its taxes either way, but the rent-controlled tenants suffer as much as the owners because "quality" is constantly being sacrificed to greed and scarcity, and everyone's humanity is diminished in the fray. So it's not just the tenants benefiting from below-market rents, it's the whole symbiotic system. Because this interest group is a tenant population that forms a near majority, the chances that rent control will be abolished by elected officials is infinitesimal.

So though the battle over rent control is routinely portrayed as a contest of "tenants versus landlords," in fact, the situation is far more convoluted. Even in New York, which has some of the strictest rent control in the country, only 1.1 million of the city's 1.7 million apartments–about 63 percent–are regulated by rent control, meaning that many tenants benefit, while others pay above-market rates to fund the lucky ones who have rent-controlled units.[6] This is nothing more than a redistribution of wealth, only it isn't necessarily going from the wealthy to the poor; it is more often going from the lucky or the connected (those with a friend or a relative sub-leasing a rent-controlled apartment to them) to the newcomers in town.

Such was the twisted system the Zimans had bought into in the Orwellian year of 1984. But then, a few years after the Zimans learned the city wouldn't let them get strangers out of their home, in 1987, one of the tenants passed away, which freed up an upstairs apartment. As the two other tenants, both of whom were males, were staying put, the family then had to pass through a common area to go to the free apartment. The Zimans' decided their oldest son, who was then ten years old, could sleep in the upstairs apartment. Because drug paraphernalia were occasionally found in the hall, the Zimans began a nightly ritual of walking their son by rooms in their own home that were occupied for life by disgruntled men, one of whom the Zimans were certain was a drug user. They then made sure their son locked his door before they returned to the other portion of their home that was then under their control.

Though the Third Amendment was drafted after the British government had forced homeowners to house soldiers, the Third Amendment was ratified to stop the federal government from doing the same thing. And *Engblom* v. *Carey* had incorporated the Third Amendment, meaning it restricted all state and local governments from housing people in people's private residences as well.

The Third Amendment was written just a few years after British soldiers—many of whom were Hessians (Germans) who may or may not have spoken English—were permitted by the English king to move into colonialists' homes as they pleased. These soldiers often raided the homeowners' pantries and perhaps pinched the bottoms of ladies who'd not yet dreamed of a women's suffrage movement. During this period, farmers commonly hid their daughters in barns to keep them from the advances of soldiers who were an ocean away from their wives and sweethearts.

The quartering of troops in private residences became an issue after Lieutenant-General Thomas Gage, commander-in-chief of the forces, and other British officers who'd fought in the French and Indian War found it hard to persuade colonial assemblies to pay for the quartering and provisioning of troops. Gage asked the English Parliament to do something about the problem. The result was the Quartering Act of 1765. The colonies disputed the legality of this Act since it violated the English Bill of Rights of 1689, which forbade taxation without representation and the raising or keeping of a standing army without the consent of Parliament. Subsequently, this became one of the rallying cries for American independence.

The Quartering Act of 1765 allowed England to house its soldiers in American barracks and public houses, but if its soldiers outnumbered the housing available, it allowed them to quarter soldiers "in inns, livery stables, ale houses, victualing houses, and the houses of sellers of wine and houses of persons selling of rum, brandy, strong water, cider or metheglin [mead]." If numbers required, soldiers could also be housed in "uninhabited houses, outhouses, barns, or other buildings." Colonial authorities were required to pay the cost of housing and feeding these troops. The Quartering Act expired on March 24, 1767, but a second Quartering Act was passed on June 2, 1774, as part of a group of laws that were deemed the "Intolerable Acts."

In the two-plus centuries since the ratification of the Bill of Rights, the Third Amendment has been among the least cited sections of the Constitution. Tom W. Bell, in *The Third Amendment: Forgotten but Not Gone,* noted that this amendment lacks respect when he joked, "Few people would giggle about the Third Amendment if they had to tiptoe around slumbering G.I.s on the way to breakfast each morning."

Some Supreme Court justices have invoked the Third Amendment when seeking to establish a base for the right to privacy. For example, the opinion of the high court by Justice William O. Douglas in *Griswold* v. *Connecticut* (1965) cites the amendment as implying a belief that an individual's home should be free from agents of the state.

The tactic of using the Third Amendment to prevent bureaucrats from telling us what light bulbs we can use, what kind of paint we can slather on our walls, how many people we can have in our homes, or to block a myriad of other mandates and regulations is appealing, but the courts haven't bought this constitutional overreach.

The Zimans appealed the denial of their application in the state Supreme Court to the Appellate Division where they prevailed, albeit in a non-unanimous decision. This prompted another appeal to the Court of Appeals, New York State's court of last resort.

Finally, nearly a decade after the fight for their property rights had begun, the New York Court of Appeals handed the Zimans a unanimous victory on the grounds of financial hardship. This wasn't the constitutional victory they'd hoped for. It was simply decided on the grounds that they had satisfied the technical requirements of financial hardship after all. Unfortunately, the tenants, who had been permitted to intervene, delayed by making a motion to reargue. That application was denied, and the Zimans were eventually issued certificates of eviction by the DHCR.

Kazman has another view: "One of the reasons the Zimans were given a financial hardship win, I think, is because we had some very strong constitutional arguments with regards to the Third and Fifth Amendments. And this ruling was one way of avoiding rulings that would have shown rent control to be unconstitutional."

After the victory, in 1990, another two years dragged by until the Zimans were finally able to obtain warrants of eviction in the Housing Court and get the two tenants out. So after eight years of battling to have their home free of agents of the state, during which time their oldest son went from the age of seven to fifteen, the Zimans finally had a home to raise their children in.

Though they won, Kazman argues, "It was still a temporary taking of property, which meant that they were still entitled to monetary compensation." The Supreme Court case *First English Evangelical Lutheran Church* v. *Los Angeles County* (1987) found that even if there's a temporary taking of property that comes to an end, you're still entitled to compensation. There's a good reason for this legal doctrine. One common scheme among government planners is to pass a regulation knowing it really doesn't matter if it gets knocked off in five or ten years, because when that happens they can just pass another regulation. Therefore, the only remedy is not only to rule the illegal law unconstitutional, but also to penalize the government monetarily to make them think twice before wiping their heels on the Constitution.

Kazman figured he had a good chance of getting the Zimans compensated for eight years of financial hardship under the Fifth Amendment's "takings" clause; after all, in *Loretto* v. *Teleprompter Manhattan CATV Corp.* (1982) the Supreme Court held that even an intrusion as small as that inflicted by an unwelcome video cable could constitute a taking of private property under the Fifth Amendment.[7] However, after more years of appeals the Zimans lost the case. The court system decided the Zimans didn't qualify.

Despite the loss, Kazman said,

> The Zimans were very lucky, they succeeded because they showed financial hardship. We represented another woman who owned a brownstone in Harlem that she also purchased with the intention of turning it into a single-family home. As with the Zimans, the changes to the law were passed just after she'd bought the property, so she found she was stuck with tenants. And, by the way, to be stuck with unwanted tenants in a place like Harlem, with people who know you want them out, results in a lot of destruction. This woman had strangers barging in to her daughter's bedroom claiming they thought it was the bathroom down the hall. This woman did not succeed in showing financial hardship. She ended up having to pay her tenants to leave. Unfortunately, she paid them in the midst of our appeal of her case, to the N.Y. Court of Appeals, and as a result the Court of Appeals threw the case out as moot, despite the fact that it wasn't moot. The fact that she had suffered for ten years before she raised the money to get her tenants to move out was once again a temporary taking, for which she was entitled compensation.

In 2007, one case did begin to show weakness in the constitutionality of rent control. In *Pultz* v. *Economakis,* New York Supreme Court justice Faviola A. Soto decided that an owner does not require DHCR approval to seek possession of all rent-stabilized units in a building for use by the owner and/or the owner's immediate family as their primary residence within the City of New York.

Kazman, general counsel for the Competitive Enterprise Institute who was working free-of-charge for the Zimans, only used the Third Amendment argument in a footnote in the Zimans' legal arguments. But perhaps it's time attorneys representing owners in rent-controlled areas took their noses out of the DHCR's regulations and made a constitutional challenge with regards to the Third Amendment. The Supreme Court might just reach down and snag the case to adjudicate an area of law that has not yet been defined. After all, even if justices decide against tearing down the private property burdens of rent control, a case in the high court would at least bring the injustice of the laws to the awareness of the American public.

Roughly 80 percent of the Zimans' home was taken by the state for about eight years, yet the Zimans weren't compensated for the takings. If the government can force us, as it did the Zimans, to keep people in our homes against our will, then private property will cease to exist. Colonial Americans fought and bled to free themselves from a government that could control even who they have in their private homes. We need to make sure what they won isn't lost to a statist bureaucracy.

AMENDMENT IV

*The right of the people to be secure in their persons,
houses, papers, and effects, against unreasonable searches and
seizures, shall not be violated, and no Warrants shall issue,
but upon probable cause, supported by Oath or affirmation,
and particularly describing the place to be searched, and the
persons or things to be seized.*

*"Civilization is the progress toward a society of privacy.
The savage's whole existence is public, ruled by the laws of his
tribe. Civilization is the process of setting man free from men."[1]
–Ayn Rand*

Supreme Court Justice Stephen Breyer thinks technology has out-paced freedom. He is certain the Fourth Amendment's restriction on government intrusion is outdated. He articulated this liberal-progressive view on December 12, 2010, when he boldly told FOX News' Chris Wallace: "The Founders didn't know that commerce included air-planes. They didn't know about the Internet or even television. And so the difficult job in open cases where there is no clear answer is to take those values in this document, which all Americans hold, which do not change, and to apply them to a world that is ever changing."[2]

While it's true that in 1791, the year the Bill of Rights was ratified, the Internet was nearly two centuries from being invented, this doesn't give judges the right to ignore the Fourth Amendment protection of our "per-sons, houses, papers, and effects, against unreasonable searches and sei-zures." The Founders might not have foreseen the Internet, but they did outlaw warrantless invasions of our privacy. The Framers certainly foresaw the possibility of a centralized federal government infringing on basic human liberties; this is why they protected our privacy in the Bill of Rights.

Justice Breyer claims "there is no clear answer" to what the Fourth Amendment protects because he likes having the power to make it up as he goes along. Justice Breyer feels he can argue this aloud because people scratch their heads and say, "Oh yeah, George Washington didn't know there would be an Internet." Instead of falling for this deception, people need to realize that, while it's true that today our papers are more often digital (something unfathomable in 1776), this doesn't end their constitutional protections. After all, no one argues the First Amendment protection of free speech ends when our voices go digital over the Internet or on television. So how is it that liberals can say the Fourth Amendment doesn't cover cell phones, computers, digitized documents, and websites? Just because our "papers" appear on a screen shouldn't mean the Fourth Amendment doesn't protect them from warrantless searches.

Incredibly, some historians say that a duplicitous attempt in the first U.S. Congress to make the Fourth Amendment's wording stronger actually made the undermining of these rights feasible. During the first session of Congress James Madison defined the Fourth Amendment as: "The rights of the people to be secured ... from all unreasonable searches and seizures, shall not be violated by warrants issued without probable cause supported by oath or affirmation."[3] But the Fourth Amendment didn't come to us in Madison's clean prose. Representative Egbert Benson of New York thought Madison's wording was weak. He thought that "by warrants issued without probable cause" should be changed to "and no warrants shall issue, but upon probable cause." The U.S. House of Representatives subsequently rejected Benson's proposed change to the text; however some claim that Benson, who was the chairman of a committee appointed to arrange the amendments and send them to the U.S. Senate, sent the Senate his wording, not Madison's. According to this theory, no one caught the change. Benson's wording was subsequently approved by the Senate and later ratified by the states.[4]

However it happened, this small change, which Benson thought strengthened the Fourth Amendment, actually weakened it. By breaking the direct linkage between the probable cause standard and the protection from unreasonable searches and seizures with the word "but," Benson's change created an ambiguity—and progressives can fit anything they desire into an ambiguity. The altered text could be interpreted by a creative attorney or judge to mean probable cause is only necessary in cases that involve warrants. Now at the time the Bill of Rights was ratified, a warrant was always necessary because a person's private residence or person had to be physically searched. This is no longer true.

Today's technological developments, such as the telephone and the Internet, have made it possible to search a computer from the other side of the planet. Now phones can be tapped, computers hacked, and listening devices can eavesdrop on private conversations in peoples' homes by measuring the vibrations from a home's windowpanes; as a result, this fractured wording has made it possible for liberal judges to weaken the probable cause standard for all but physical searches, and as you'll see, they've created exceptions to the need for warrants in even physical searches.

Historically, probable cause required more than just suspicion—someone couldn't be stopped on the street and searched simply because they fit a certain profile. The traditional definition says probable cause for a search exists only when information thought to be reliable indicates that evidence of a crime will be found where authorities wish to search. Probable cause is a subjective measure, but it is supposed to be weighed according to real evidence that someone swears to by "oath or affirmation," meaning an individual has to officially swear they think there is probable cause. This person can later be held accountable in a court of law.

All that was well and good until the Supreme Court undermined the probable cause standard by establishing the "special needs doctrine," which, if certain factors make getting a warrant problematic, now allows the Court to apply a balancing test to determine whether a search and/or seizure is reasonable without a warrant. This exception holds that the government may conduct a search without a warrant or probable cause "when special needs, beyond the normal need for law enforcement, make the warrant and probable-cause requirement impracticable."[5]

So once again the Supreme Court put itself into a position to judge when individual rights can be ignored. The Court found that if the needs of law enforcement *outweigh* the liberty of the person, then law enforcement needn't get a warrant. This purely subjective test gives the judiciary the ability to decide when the Fourth Amendment can flatly be disregarded.

As any cop knows, attempting to explain a bold-faced lie with more lies gets complex and often contradictory in a hurry. As a result, the Supreme Court hasn't been able to find the "special needs doctrine" to be comprehensible or even logical. In fact, the Court has determined that not every special needs search is constitutional. If the special needs doctrine exception applies, the Court must then balance the nature of the privacy interest, the character of the intrusion, and the nature of the government's concern all to determine whether the search is reasonable.

The special needs doctrine most often comes into play when a government agency wants to justify random drug searches of students, state employees, or patients at a state-operated hospital. (As the Fourth Amendment is only a restriction on the government, it does not apply to private drug screenings or databases.) For example, in 1995 the Supreme Court ruled in *Vernonia School District* v. *Acton* that requiring urine tests for student athletes was constitutional. The Court found that the state's need to prevent student athletes from making illegal drugs seem cool outweighed the Fourth Amendment's privacy protections of the students. But then a Tenth Circuit case, *Earls* v. *Board of Education* (2001), held that mandatory drug testing of all students who participate in any extracurricular activities in Tecumseh High School was a violation of the Fourth Amendment. How could a lower court break from a Supreme Court precedent? The Tenth Circuit distinguished this case from *Vernonia* by ruling that Tecumseh High School didn't have a drug problem. They noted that data showed that only two of the nearly 500 students who participated in extracurricular activities at Tecumseh High School tested positive for drugs in the 1998–1999 academic year; as a result, the court didn't think the special needs doctrine was necessary.

So instead of clearly applying the Fourth Amendment's restrictions on the government, the courts began looking at data to legislate from the bench. This makes any reasonable person wonder: by this new and vague standard, what percentage of students using illegal narcotics gives the state the right to ignore the Fourth Amendment? Would it be five students? How about fifty? Obviously this is a policy debate that is supposed to be waged by elected legislators who are accountable to voters, not by Supreme Court justices with lifetime appointments.

This arbitrary wielding of justice with regards to privacy doesn't only effect those who find themselves in public institutions. In 2000, Congress enacted the DNA Analysis Backlog Elimination Act, which requires convicted sex offenders and other felons to submit DNA samples to the Combined DNA Index System (CODIS), a national database used to identify DNA evidence found at crime scenes. The CODIS database has been vastly expanded since 2000. Currently all fifty states have mandatory DNA collection from certain felony offenses, such as sexual assault and homicide, and forty-seven states collect DNA from all convicted felons. Other states now collect DNA samples from juveniles and all suspects arrested, whether they were subsequently convicted or not. For example, in California, as a result of Proposition 69 (passed in 2004), all suspects arrested for a felony, as well as some individuals convicted of misdemeanors, have their DNA collected and kept on file.

As of this writing, two federal district courts had applied the Supreme Court's special needs doctrine to determine whether the collection of samples from felons under the DNA Act violates the Fourth Amendment: *United States* v. *Miles* (2002) and *United States* v. *Reynard* (2007). The *Miles* and *Reynard* courts agreed that the blood-sample extractions mandated by the Act are warrantless searches lacking probable cause, and therefore would be constitutional only if they fell under the "special needs" exception to the warrant requirement developed by the Supreme Court.

In both *Miles* and *Reynard,* the government tried to slip DNA databases past the Fourth Amendment by arguing that the primary purpose of the searches was to set up an accurate DNA database for public protection that would help law enforcement solve crimes. Ruling on the *Miles* case, a court concluded that the DNA database was "indistinguishable from the government's basic interest in enforcing the law." However, when deciding *Reynard* a few years later, a court found that "the creation of a more accurate criminal justice system" was a rationale that surpassed "the normal need for law enforcement." In both cases the debate over the constitutionality of the DNA Act searches came down to a semantic disagreement over the meaning of "law enforcement purposes"; it was never discussed whether the Fourth Amendment permitted these warrantless searches in the first place.

If you're confused, it's because the justices are, too. The Supreme Court created a subjective test based on a loophole that isn't clearly definable; as a result, the courts are not being consistent and your rights are being lost in the process.

When ruling on the constitutionality of DNA Act searches, the courts in both *Miles* and *Reynard* relied on *Ferguson* v. *City of Charleston* (2001), a Supreme Court case that found that the Medical University of South Carolina couldn't involuntarily test pregnant women for illegal drug use. In *Ferguson,* a hospital had required pregnant women to undergo urinalyses when certain symptoms were present. Although the purpose of the Medical University of South Carolina's use of these tests was to get the women into drug-treatment programs, the hospital was doing the tests in cooperation with the police. If a woman tested positive, then she was told if she didn't agree to undergo drug-rehabilitation treatment she would be prosecuted. Because the drug users were being threatened with prosecution, the Supreme Court held that this drug test was in violation of the Fourth Amendment.

So basically, when determining whether a warrantless search falls under the special needs exception to the Fourth Amendment, the Court now asks, "What is the primary purpose to which the government intends to put the results of the search?" If the answer is "to generate evidence for law enforcement purposes," then the special needs exception hasn't typically been ruled to apply. If, however, the government can plausibly argue it needs the search results primarily for something other than criminal prosecution, then the Court has more often ruled that the special needs exception it created can apply.

To navigate through this nuanced and subjective judicially manufactured loophole in the Fourth Amendment, the government's attorneys now tweak laws and their justifications for invasions of privacy to suit the views of the current majority on the Court. Also, when applying the special needs doctrine, lower courts faced with special needs arguments now have to determine whether a given primary purpose is non-law-enforcement-related. But, no matter how you spin it, this question doesn't determine whether warrantless searches are reasonable according to the Fourth Amendment. For starters, why does the Court think that searches conducted primarily for non-law-enforcement purposes are more reasonable than law-enforcement searches? Put another way, why is it the Supreme Court thinks the individual and his or her private property are only fully protected by the Fourth Amendment when the individual is suspected of criminal behavior?

Because of this false premise, the courts in both *Miles* and *Reynard* never questioned whether the federal government could have a DNA database—it thought that question superfluous. Instead the Court dove into the details of the legislation. Then it saw that the database couldn't be achieved without warrantless searches, so the Court decided the government could create a database cataloging everything about individual Americans just so as long as the searches weren't being done primarily to toss an individual behind bars.

This entire judicial mess could be cleaned up if the Supreme Court would simply apply the Fourth Amendment as it is written by striking down these warrantless searches. However, because the Supreme Court has historically been reluctant to give up a newfound power, perhaps voters need to compel Congress to act.

Redefining the Word "Search"

The Supreme Court's boldest attack on the Fourth Amendment, however, came when it redefined the word "search." For more than a century and a half, a search was a physical trespass. Today, however, the Court more often says law enforcement needn't get a warrant unless a person has a "reasonable expectation of privacy." Thus, when an officer enters a driveway or uses a binocular to peer into private property from a roadway, the Court says there hasn't been a search.

The "reasonable expectation of privacy" standard was used in *Terry* v. *Ohio* (1968). In this case the Court determined the police could stop a person in a public place and give them a "pat down" for weapons regardless of whether the police had probable cause; all the authorities needed was a "reasonable suspicion" the person was about to commit a crime. The Court reasoned this was necessary for the officer's safety, and few would argue that cops shouldn't be able to search someone they think is about to go on a murder spree; as a result, few Americans were bothered that the Court had lowered the standard from probable cause (when someone swears by "oath or affirmation" that so-and-so has done something or is about to do something illegal) to suspicion (when a cop simply has a hunch). This reinterpretation, however, next allowed the government to toss out any verifiable justification whatsoever.

The case that most clearly ignored the Fourth Amendment's protections was *United States* v. *Martinez-Fuerte* (1976). This case allowed authorities to set up a checkpoint near the Mexican border and to detain anyone of Mexican ancestry to nab illegal immigrants. As a result of *Martinez-Fuerte*, it is now permissible for the police to put up roadblocks so they can decide whether they are suspicious that someone might be up to no good.

Though many today are okay with police roadblocks, pat downs, and "crime cameras" that may utilize facial-recognition programs, many may not like that in 2010 the Obama administration urged the U.S. Court of Appeals for the District of Columbia to allow the government, without a court warrant, to affix GPS devices to suspects' vehicles so they could track the movements of anyone. The U.S. Justice Department did this by asking the federal appeals court to rehear a case in which it reversed the conviction of an alleged cocaine dealer whose Jeep was tracked with a GPS for a month. The government had not bothered to get a warrant to put the tracking device on the Jeep. The authorities, however, later obtained warrants for various residences and found drugs in the locations where the defendant, Antoine Jones, had stopped.

Assistant U.S. Attorney Peter Smith wrote the court in the government's petition for rehearing and said, "The panel's conclusion that Jones had a reasonable expectation of privacy in the public movements of his Jeep rested on the premise that an individual has a reasonable expectation of privacy in the totality of his or her movements in public places." The U.S. Justice Department was taking the position that everything we do in public is their business.

GPS devices have become a common tool in crime fighting. An officer can now shoot a moving vehicle with a GPS dart. But, as of this writing, they couldn't do that without a warrant in the District of Columbia. Across the country some states require a warrant for this, while others don't. This legal question centers on a 1983 Supreme Court decision (*U.S. v. Knotts*) in which a tracking beacon was affixed to a container (without a court warrant) and used to track a motorist to a cabin. The government wanted to use this precedent to nullify all rights to privacy outside our homes.

The appeals court, however, said *Knotts* did not apply to today's GPS monitoring because the beacon tracked a person "from one place to another," whereas the GPS device monitored Jones's "movements 24 hours a day for 28 days." The government argued that the appellate court's decision "offers no guidance as to when monitoring becomes so efficient or 'prolonged' as to constitute a search triggering the requirements of the Fourth Amendment." However, the circuit court countered that a person "who knows all of another's travels can deduce whether he is a weekly churchgoer, a heavy drinker, a regular at the gym, an unfaithful husband, an outpatient receiving medical treatment, an associate of particular individuals or political groups—and not just one such fact about a person, but all such facts."

This court got it right. Others have not; for example, the U.S. Court of Appeals for the Ninth Circuit decided the government can monitor you with a GPS virtually anytime it wants and with no need for a search warrant. This case began in 2007 when Drug Enforcement Administration (DEA) agents decided to monitor Juan Pineda-Moreno, an Oregon resident whom they suspected was growing marijuana. They snuck onto his property at night and found his auto in his driveway, a few feet from his trailer home. They attached a GPS tracking device to the vehicle's underside.

Later in court, when Pineda-Moreno challenged the DEA's actions, a three-judge panel of the Ninth Circuit ruled it was perfectly legal for the police to attach a GPS to his private vehicle without a warrant. The court didn't care that the government violated Pineda-Moreno's privacy rights by entering his driveway. The courts have long held that people have a reasonable expectation of privacy in their homes and in the "curtilage," a legal term for the area around a residence. The government's intrusion on property just a few feet away was certainly in this zone of privacy. The judges argued, however, that Pineda-Moreno's driveway was open to strangers, such as delivery people, so it was not a private location, even though it was on private property.

Chief Judge Alex Kozinski, who dissented in the decision, pointed out that the court's ruling means that people who protect their homes with electric gates, fences, and security guards have a larger zone of privacy around their homes than people who can't afford such barriers. Justice Kozinski's argument is poignant: how can the rich have more property rights than the poor in a country founded on equal rights and justice under law?

Why the Left Attacked the Exclusionary Rule

The exclusionary rule has been popularly demonized in court dramas and on network news for decades as an unfair exception that allows the guilty to go free.

The exclusionary rule simply declares that evidence obtained by law enforcement illegally cannot be used to convict a person. The reason for this rule is simple: if law enforcement can use illegally obtained evidence in court then the police can simply ignore the Fourth Amendment's protections. Without the exclusionary rule, the Fourth Amendment is moot. But liberals don't like this impediment to government power. And some conservatives are uncomfortable with the idea that some criminals may go free because of a Fourth Amendment "technicality."

The Supreme Court first barred evidence that was obtained in violation of the Fourth Amendment in 1886. In *Boyd* v. *United States*, the Court threw out a verdict of guilty as an "unconstitutional proceeding" because illegally obtained evidence had been used to convict. Decades later, in *Weeks* v. *United States* (1913), the Court found:

> If letters and private documents can be seized [illegally] and used in evidence against a citizen accused of an offense, the protection of the Fourth Amendment ... is of no value, and ... might as well be stricken from the Constitution. The efforts of the courts and their officials to bring the guilty to punishment, praiseworthy as they are, are not to be aided by the sacrifice of those great principles established by years of endeavor and suffering which have resulted in their embodiment in the fundamental law of the land.

In 1920, the Supreme Court adopted the "fruit of the poisonous tree" doctrine in *Silverthorne Lumber Co.* v. *United States*, which stated that allowing illegally gathered evidence into court "reduces the Fourth Amendment to a form of words." The "fruit of the poisonous tree" doctrine is a legal metaphor used to describe evidence obtained illegally; if the evidence (the tree) is tainted, then anything taken from it (the fruit) is as well. Nevertheless, the Fourth Amendment didn't apply the "exclusionary rule" to state and local governments until *Mapp* v. *Ohio* (1961) incorporated this fundamental individual protection via the Fourteenth Amendment's due-process clause.

Before 1961 only about half the states had adopted the exclusionary rule on their own; as a result, Robert B. Traynor, chief justice of the California Supreme Court, wrote, "My misgivings ... grew as I observed ... a steady course of illegal police procedures that deliberately and fragrantly violated the Constitution....It had become too obvious that unconstitutional police methods of obtaining evidence were not being deterred...."[6]

The exclusionary rule is a necessary device to keep the government within the bounds of the law, but critics say it increases the crime rate by letting guilty people go free, even though studies have shown this not to be the case. A comprehensive study published in the *American Bar Foundation Research Journal* found that only 1.77 percent of criminal cases are lost because of the exclusionary rule.[7] This is because the rule is rarely used, since law enforcement agencies adhere to the law, and even when it is used to squelch evidence, people are often still found guilty based on legally obtained evidence.

However, since 1961 the Supreme Court has been busy shooting holes in the exclusionary rule. For example, illegally obtained evidence today isn't barred from grand jury proceedings where people get indicted and forced to stand trial; also, this rule doesn't apply to deportation cases. And then there is the "good-faith exception," which holds that as long as law enforcement reasonably relied on a search warrant, evidence seized is admissible in court. With the good-faith exception the Court put itself in the position to decide when the police acted "reasonably." So once again the Court grew its power with another exception to a formally firm constitutional limit.

Specifically, the exclusionary rule was weakened by two companion cases decided by the Supreme Court in 1984: *United States* v. *Leon* and *Massachusetts* v. *Sheppard.* The rule was judged to permit the courts to consider the mental state of the police officer and to judge whether the officer(s) had reason to believe their actions were legal, as per the "reasonable person test." The reasonable person standard holds that each person owes a duty to behave as a reasonable person would under the same or a similar situation. These rules give the courts yet more wiggle room—which equates to an ability to circumnavigate the Constitution—when determining each case.

Any "reasonable person" can surely understand that more crimes could be solved if police could simply go wherever they chose without a warrant. But is such a police state a society that any reasonable person wants to live in? An all-powerful state certainly wasn't the society the Framers of the Constitution endeavored to create. Once the reasonable Americans understand this, they next realize there is a balance point that needs to be found between privacy and police power. This balance was originally struck by requiring the state to obtain a warrant based "upon probable cause" and "supported by oath or affirmation," meaning someone had to swear that someone else committed a crime or was about to do something illegal. To save the Fourth Amendment from the government, this restriction needs to be put clearly back in place.

As Daniel Webster said, "The first object of a free people is the preservation of their liberty. The spirit of liberty ... demands checks; it seeks guards ... it insists on securities....This is the nature of constitutional liberty, and this is our liberty, if we will rightly understand and preserve it."[8]

Why Liberals Don't Want the Fourth Amendment to Apply to New Technology

Technology began to baffle the Court as early as its 1928 decision *Olmstead* v. *United States*. In *Olmstead*, the Supreme Court held that the use of a wiretap to listen to a private telephone conversation was not a "search" protected against by the Fourth Amendment. The Court ruled there had been no physical intrusion into the person's home, so there was no search. Under *Olmstead's* narrow view, the Fourth Amendment would become irrelevant as technology bloomed.

This disturbing ruling was rectified in *Katz* v. *United States* (1967). This case began when Charles Katz used a public payphone to illegally place bets. The FBI secretly recorded his conversations and later used the evidence to convict Katz. Katz fought the wiretap by arguing that the recordings were obtained in violation of his Fourth Amendment rights. A lower court sided with the government because there was no physical intrusion into the phone booth itself, but the U.S. Supreme Court reversed and ruled in favor of Katz's Fourth Amendment rights to privacy. As a result, in *Katz*, the Supreme Court rejected *Olmstead*'s "trespass" doctrine by ruling that the Fourth Amendment protects people's privacy, not just places:

> *What a person knowingly exposes to the public*, even in his own home or office, is not a subject of Fourth Amendment protection. But what he seeks to preserve as private, even in an area accessible to the public, may be constitutionally protected.

So, although the Government's activities in *Katz* involved no physical intrusion, they nevertheless were found to have violated the Fourth Amendment.

In 1968, just one year after *Katz*, Congress passed Title III of the Omnibus Crime Control and Safe Streets Act authorizing microphone surveillance or wiretapping for law enforcement purposes; to stay within the reestablished scope of the Fourth Amendment, the Act required a warrant, based on probable cause, prior to such surveillance or wiretapping.

Subsequently, the Court developed a two-pronged test to determine if an individual had a reasonable expectation of privacy against intrusions by the government that triggered Fourth Amendment restrictions. First, an individual had to believe a given communication is private; and second, a disinterested observer (a court) had to agree that the individual's expectation of privacy was indeed reasonable. If these two factors are satisfied, then the government must comply with the Fourth Amendment—of course, except when the Court thinks the "special needs doctrine" applies.

As expressed by the Court in *Kyllo* v. *United States* (2001): "[A] Fourth Amendment search occurs when the government violates a subjective expectation of privacy that society recognizes as reasonable." Conversely, "a Fourth Amendment search does not occur–even in the explicitly protected location of a house–unless the individual manifested a subjective expectation of privacy in the object of the challenged search, and society [is] willing to recognize that expectation as reasonable."

The two-part test guides the courts, but interpreting such a vague standard has left room for judges to assert their will upon the public. The first requirement–the "subjective expectation" of privacy–has long since been eroded. As Justice Harlan concluded in *United States* v. *White* (1971): "[O]ur expectations, and the risks we assume, are in large part reflections of laws that translate into rules the customs and values of the past and present." Basically, courts have ignored the simple ruling established by *Katz* and now weigh our Fourth Amendment rights based upon assumptions about privacy "expectations," which gives the Court a lot of room to do as it pleases.

So though the Court's reversal from the *Olmstead* decision with the *Katz* ruling was welcome, the test Justice Harlan suggested about privacy "expectations" has proven to be subjective and weak. For example, a dozen years after the *Katz* ruling, the Supreme Court, in *Smith* v. *Maryland* (1979), held that the installation and use of a "pen register" (phone tap) was not a "search" within the meaning of the Fourth Amendment and therefore a warrant wasn't required. The tap on the phone was done on telephone company property so, in the majority opinion, Justice Harry Blackmun rejected the idea that the phone tap constituted a violation of the "legitimate expectation of privacy," because the numbers would be available to and recorded by the phone company. This disturbing view of the Fourth Amendment could give the government the right to open a UPS package or review emails taken from Google without first getting a warrant.

The *Smith* v. *Maryland* ruling means there is no search when officers monitor what phone numbers an individual dials, although Congress has enacted laws that restrict such monitoring. The Supreme Court has also ruled that there is no objectively reasonable expectation of privacy (and thus no search) when officers hovering in a helicopter 400 feet above a suspect's house conduct surveillance.[9]

So according to the government and the high court, anything visible from the air or your driveway might be fair game for a warrantless search. Also, anything that can be taken from a third party, such as a bank, social-networking website, or shipping company, might be viewed without a warrant. The government and liberals on the Supreme Court have shot holes all through the Fourth Amendment. They've even sold the argument that technology is great, but it does come with a natural reduction in privacy. They're lying. Technology does not mean privacy is dead—as so many claim it does today—the government just deemed it so. Technology can also safeguard every segment of privacy that has been stripped.

The Supreme Court, however, drew the line with thermal imagery. In *Kyllo* v. *United States* (2001), the Court made it illegal for the government to use a thermal-imaging device to see inside a private home without first getting a warrant. The rule devised by the Court in *Kyllo* limits police use of new technology that can "shrink the realm of guaranteed privacy." The ruling found that "obtaining by sense-enhancing technology any information regarding the interior of the home that could not otherwise have been obtained without physical 'intrusion into a constitutionally protected area' … constitutes a search, at least where the technology in question is not in general public use."

So, when thermal imagery becomes commercially available to the public, you'll lose this piece of your privacy, too.

Now, if police using thermal imaging to see into homes sounds a little too sci-fi to be real, you're behind the times. Privacy-conscious travelers may fret when they see full-body scanners at airports, but few are aware that the same technology, capable of seeing through walls and clothes, has also been driving down U.S. avenues. American Science & Engineering (AS&E), a company based in Billerica, Massachusetts, has sold the United States and foreign government agencies more than 500 backscatter X-ray scanners. These devices are mounted in vans that can be driven alongside vehicles or cargo containers to snoop into their contents. Though the biggest buyer of these mobile devices has been the Department of Defense for operations in Afghanistan and Iraq, the company says law enforcement agencies are using them domestically. "This product is now the largest-selling cargo and vehicle-inspection system ever," says Joseph Reiss, AS&E's vice president of marketing.

These rolling X-ray machines look like plain white vans. Officers sit in the back of the panel van operating X-ray machines to scan passing vehicles. Most Americans wouldn't mind if they're used on the U.S. border to nab drugs runners or illegal immigrants, but how many people want the government to use one of these X-ray vans in their neighborhood?

Emerging technologies make the Fourth Amendment particularly relevant today. This is why the Supreme Court precedents matter regarding how this 200-plus-year-old amendment is applied to new technologies. It is a big deal for the Court to decide whether someone has a "legitimate" expectation of privacy that society finds "reasonable."

Decisions such as *Rakas* v. *Illinois* (1978) have found that property rights by themselves assume a certain level of privacy. In *Rakas* the Court ruled: "One of the main rights attaching to property is the right to exclude others ... and one who owns or lawfully possesses or controls property will, in all likelihood, have a legitimate expectation of privacy by virtue of this right to exclude."

In *Rakas*, the Court cited *Alderman* v. *United States* (1969), a Supreme Court case that held that individuals' property interest in their own homes is so great that they could object to electronic surveillance of conversations that might emanate from their home. These strong private-property rulings are the backbone the Fourth Amendment needs to survive.

This is why the protection of the home is at the apex of Fourth Amendment rights. However, the ownership of other things, such as automobiles, have not received a similar degree of protection. The police don't necessarily need a warrant to search your car's trunk or to pat you down, but they do to use an X-ray scanner to see inside your home. Because the

Supreme Court hasn't applied the Fourth Amendment equally, or even consistently, it has created a confusing and convoluted list of rulings.

The government has seen opportunities in this uncertainty. For example, in 2010 the Obama administration argued that cell phones offer no reasonable expectation of privacy. U.S. Department of Justice lawyers said, "[A] customer's Fourth Amendment rights are not violated when the phone company reveals to the government its own records."[10] Though the left fringe of the Democratic Party spent years screaming about the loss of liberty from the Patriot Act, this move by Obama's Justice Department to listen in on Americans'–not foreign terrorists'–cell phone conversations received little attention from the *Huffington Post*/MoveOn.org crowd.

The government can maintain this position because of the "third-party doctrine," which was created by a pair of cases in the early 1970s in which the Supreme Court found there weren't Fourth Amendment restrictions when the government requires service providers to maintain records about their customers–records the government can later demand. The third-party doctrine has grown more onerous as technology has evolved; for example, cellular telephone networks now pinpoint customers' locations all day long, and Internet service providers (ISPs) maintain copies of huge amounts of private information–data that are often tied to customer identifiers. Google maintains records, as do retailers. These records are windows into each individual's activities, nature, and political affiliations. The government ought to be required to get a warrant to see this private information–as these data are the modern equivalent of our "papers and effects," which are explicitly protected by the Fourth Amendment–but they aren't.

If individuals are acting in a private manner, whether online or not, their records, photos, and documents should enjoy Fourth Amendment protections from the government. Because the Fourth Amendment, as well as the rest of the Bill of Rights, is a restriction on the government, not on other private citizens and entities, the government shouldn't just be able to demand companies' records because such documents are no longer in the control of the person who created them. Once the courts realize it is the reasonableness of the government's actions that is in question, not the reasonableness of the individual's "expectations," the Fourth Amendment will be back on the strong footing it held for well over its first century.

Just because we have a new way of communicating shouldn't allow the government to decide the Constitution doesn't cover it.

The Fourth Amendment's Internet Troubles

Currently, records stored on computers do not necessarily have the same protections as those in a home desk. Today banks must report our transfers and transactions. Unbeknownst to us, Yahoo!, Google, AOL, and other Internet service providers give in to government subpoenas and hand over our emails and search results. Also, in these digital times, online marketing companies can legally imbed spyware into home computers that may later be subpoenaed without a warrant. These days digital records, especially those held by a third parties–Time Warner, Bank of America, Chase–have not, as yet, been afforded the same protections as those in our home offices. Welcome to the post-private age, where people are even beginning to think a lack of privacy is a necessary result of technology. It's not.

Every facet of personal privacy that has been eroded by technology can also be protected with technology. Also, a commonsense enforcement of the Fourth Amendment protections by admitting the Fourth Amendment covers new technologies just as much as good old handwritten letters would end this entire, complex, and often semantic debate.

The government doesn't want you to know that. They've created exceptions and loopholes in every segment of Fourth Amendment rights and have systematically fought technology designed to protect our homes, papers, and effects. For example, when Phil Zimmermann created the first version of "Pretty Good Privacy" (PGP) encryption in 1991, he quickly ran into opposition from the National Security Agency (NSA), which viewed encryption as a state secret.

Zimmermann's PGP used a symmetric-key algorithm that protected the privacy of emails and other data. Pretty Good Privacy soon found its way onto the Internet and began to be used by political dissidents in totalitarian countries. As a result, in February 1993, Zimmermann became the formal target of a criminal investigation by the U.S. Government for "munitions export without a license."

Cryptosystems using keys larger than 40 bits were then considered to be "munitions." PGP has never used keys smaller than 128 bits, so it qualified at that time. The NSA wanted to keep the technology for the government, but as the Internet grew and a real need for the protection of financial and other transactions became apparent, the NSA's attempt to keep encryption off the market lost in Congress. So, after several years, the investigation of Zimmermann was dropped.

Zimmermann challenged the laws designed to keep the private economy in the dark ages by publishing the entire source code of Pretty Good Privacy in a hardback book.[11] Anyone who wished to build their own copy of PGP could buy the book, cut off the covers, separate the pages, and scan them using an OCR program, which would create a set of source code text files. A savvy person could then build the application using the freely available "GNU Compiler Collection." As it was in a book, it had strong First Amendment protections from the government–the First Amendment has fared better over time than the Fourth Amendment. This First Amendment question was never tested in court. Two federal appeals courts, however, established the rule that cryptographic software source code is speech protected by the First Amendment.

For example, *Bernstein* v. *United States*, a set of court cases brought by Daniel J. Bernstein, challenged restrictions on the export of encryption software. In 1995 Bernstein was a student at the University of California at Berkeley. He wanted to publish a paper and associated source code for his encryption system. The federal government wanted to stop him. After four years he won a landmark decision from the Ninth Circuit Court of Appeals that determined that software source code is speech protected by the First Amendment.[12]

The government then substantially loosened the regulations again. Subsequently, in 2000, a Sixth Circuit Court of Appeals case, *Junger* v. *Daley*, also found that software source code is protected by the First Amendment. Today, PGP encryption no longer meets the definition of a non-exportable weapon, and the government has turned its attention to getting our private papers and effects in other ways, such as keeping the Fourth Amendment's protections weak.

As the Fourth Amendment is simply a restriction on government intrusion, there is no Fourth Amendment infringement when a private company, unbeknownst to us, places a "cookie" on our hard drive that then tracks our movements over the Internet. This company may then later sell this information to Web advertisers or even to the government. Some argue that you can avoid these privacy intrusions by simply disallowing your browser's acceptance of "cookies." But try turning the cookies off on your browser to find out if this is really an option. Unless you are very computer savvy, you'll probably have to call in expert. When you do, disallowing cookies will affect your navigation on the Net.

In 2010, the U.S. Court of Appeals for the Eleventh Circuit ruled, in *Rehberg* v. *Paulk*, that a person does not have a reasonable expectation of privacy in an email once any copy of the communication is delivered to a third party. Of course, every email sent over the Internet goes through third parties, so the Court was saying no email sent through an Internet service provider (ISP) is private.

This deterioration of our rights took another twist in 2010 with the Federal Communications Commission's (FCC) "National Broadband Plan." Under the Obama administration, the FCC began trying to insert itself into the Internet business by supplying Internet services to poorer communities. The trouble with this is that if the government begins supplying Internet service, it will have the ability to ignore the Fourth Amendment and thereby see and record without a warrant whatever passes over the Internet to these people.

If you don't think the government would snoop on these private communications, consider that in 2010 the Obama administration declassified part of its "Cybersecurity Plan."[13] The declassified part details how "EIN-STEIN 2" and "EINSTEIN 3" systems are "designed to inspect Internet traffic entering government networks." If the government is supplying your ability to search Google and to buy stocks on eTrade, then the bits and bytes coming and going from your computer are "entering a government network." And though classified, reports suggest EINSTEIN 3 can read the contents of emails and other messages.[14]

Meanwhile, in 2010, Democrats united to pass a financial regulatory bill (the Dodd–Frank Wall Street Reform and Consumer Protection Act) that allows the government to collect data on any person operating in financial markets at any level, including the collection of personal transaction records from local banks. The Act created the Bureau of Consumer Financial Protection and empowered it to "gather information and activities of persons operating in consumer financial markets," including the names and addresses of account holders, ATM and other transaction records, and the amount of money kept in each customer's account. The new unaccountable bureaucracy was then allowed to "use the data on branches and [individual and personal] deposit accounts ... for any purpose," and it may keep all records on file for at least three years and these can be made publicly available upon request.[15]

All of these intrusions begin to make sense when you realize that in September 2010, the *New York Times* reported that broad new regulations being drafted by the Obama administration would make it easier for law enforcement and national security officials to eavesdrop on Internet and email communications.[16] Essentially, officials want Congress to require all services that enable communications, including encrypted devices like iPhones, social-networking sites such as Facebook, and software that allows direct peer-to-peer messaging like Skype, to be technically capable of complying with a wiretap. The mandate would allow the government to intercept and unscramble encrypted messages.

Depending upon how the legislation might be written, the government could then view Internet activity without a warrant; also, the mandate that all Internet service providers (ISPs) and software have backdoors programmed in for the government would give foreign governments, such as China, Russia, and Iran, an easy way to view communications and to punish people who organize protests. The consequences of this statist approach to government regulations would likely get people killed in Iran and other countries and would silence speech all over the world, yet the liberals who lambasted the Patriot Act have been mute?

In 1928 Justice Louis Brandeis prophetically wrote in his dissent in the first Supreme Court wiretapping case (a case that held a wiretap was not a Fourth Amendment search), *Olmstead v. United States*, that

> [d]iscovery and invention have made it possible for the government, with means far more effective than stretching upon the rack, to obtain disclosure in court of what is whispered in the closet....The progress of science in furnishing the Government with means of espionage (on American citizens) is not likely to stop with wiretapping....Ways may some day be developed by which the government, without removing papers from secret drawers, can reproduce them in court.

The Age Brandeis Prophesied Has Arrived

Despite all of these government moves to find that the Fourth Amendment doesn't apply to new technologies, the Fourth Amendment was certainly written to protect the privacy of our "persons, houses, papers, and effects," and, like other amendments, those protections should translate to new mediums. No one argues that the First Amendment's right to free speech fails to apply to someone texting a message, so why do statists think the Fourth Amendment becomes irrelevant when a document goes digital?

The purpose of the protection is the same. The Fourth Amendment was written to restrict the government from "unreasonable searches and seizures" because the British had used "writs of assistance" against the colonists. Writs of assistance gave British authorities the right to search anywhere they wanted so that they could enforce tariffs on trade goods—incidentally, these writs were not legal in England even as they were used to invade the privacy of English colonists.

The British regulations were so onerous and the taxes so high that some colonists thought it moral to avoid the tariffs. In the years leading up to the American Revolution, well-known patriots either smuggled or defended smugglers; for example, Boston businessman John Hancock, who later signed the Declaration of Independence, was defended in 1769 by a future president, John Adams, on charges stemming from the importation of French wine in violation of the Townshend Acts. Hancock's ship, the *Liberty*, had been boarded and the wine seized pursuant to a writ of assistance.

When the writs expired following the death of King George II in 1760, a group of merchants went to court in an attempt to block new ones. James Otis resigned his position as advocate general of the Admiralty to represent the merchants pro bono. Although the court decided against Otis and the merchants, John Adams, who'd attended the court hearing, said, "Every man … appeared to me to go away, as I did, ready to take up Arms against Writs of Assistance. Then and there the child of independence was born."[17]

After the Revolution, the Founders didn't forget about those invasive writs of assistance, hence our Fourth Amendment protections. The Bill of Rights was written and ratified as "negative liberties," restrictions on the government. The colonists learned from their experiences with British rule that government isn't the protector of rights—government is what people need to be protected from.

The Politically Incorrect Truth about the USA Patriot Act

The Left demonized the USA Patriot Act, as they claimed to be the true defenders of First and Fourth Amendment rights. But were they being honest or even intellectually consistent? In the weeks after the terrorist attacks on September 11, 2001, Democratic congressmen added their amendments to the Patriot Act and largely voted for it. The Patriot Act passed 357 to 66 in the U.S. House of Representatives (with 145 Democratic votes) and 98 to 1 in the U.S. Senate.

However, the Act wasn't simply speedily written in the weeks after 9/11, as is popularly thought. The Patriot Act is actually a massive conglomeration of previously written bills. A large portion of the Patriot Act was taken from the "Omnibus Counterterrorism Act of 1995," a bill sponsored by then Senator Joe Biden (D-DE)[18] after the Oklahoma City bombing. The bill had failed to make it to President Bill Clinton's desk, even though Clinton supported it.

Democrats have not been honest to the public about the Patriot Act.

The title of the Patriot Act is an Orwellian-style acronym, which stands for "Uniting and Strengthening America by Providing Appropriate Tools Required to Intercept and Obstruct Terrorism Act of 2001." The Act reduced restrictions on law enforcement agencies' ability to search telephone, email, medical, financial, and even library records; the Act loosened restrictions on foreign intelligence gathering within the United States; it expanded the Secretary of the Treasury's authority to regulate financial transactions, especially those involving foreign individuals and entities; and it allowed immigration authorities to detain and/or deport immigrants suspected of terrorism. The act also expanded the definition of terrorism to include domestic terrorism, which greatly enlarged the Patriot Act's law enforcement powers.

Though the Patriot Act has been amended many times since 2001, critics are correct when they say the bill was passed too fast. Bipartisanism isn't necessarily a good thing when people are panicking. Though, to be fair, this was a reason why many of the elements of the act had sunset clauses.

Michael Moore, a leftist film producer and pundit, included a scene in his film *Fahrenheit 9/11* in which Congressman Jim McDermott alleges that no senator had read the bill, and Congressman John Conyers Jr. says,

"We don't really read most of the bills. Do you know what that would entail if we read every bill that we passed?" Moore also hired an ice cream truck and drove around Washington, D.C., with a loud speaker, reading the Act out loud to people on the street. Though Moore didn't seem to mind later when senators neglected to read President Barack Obama's "Patient Protection and Affordable Care Act," the criticism is sound.

However, since 2001, many of the unconstitutional provisions in the Patriot Act have been struck down by courts, and various revisions of the bill have addressed controversial issues. Still, problems with the Patriot Act start with its definitions; for example, the Act never defines "terrorist" or "terrorism," which has given the government an open-ended definition it can apply to nearly anyone or anything.

The Patriot Act also does a lot more than allow wiretaps. The Act, to pull one example from its 243 original pages, even makes it illegal to open a bank account via a post office box. If you try, according to law, the financial institution is legally required to decline your request while citing the money-laundering provisions in the Patriot Act.

Other provisions of the Act require the financial institution to report suspicious activity; for example, in section 351, the Patriot Act says:

> If a financial institution or any director, officer, employee, or agent of any financial institution, voluntarily or pursuant to this section or any other authority, reports a suspicious transaction to a government agency … the financial institution, director, officer, employee, or agent may not notify any person involved in the transaction that the transaction has been reported;
>
> … no officer or employee of the Federal Government or of any State, local, tribal, or territorial government within the United States, who has any knowledge that such report was made may disclose to any person involved in the transaction that the transaction has been reported, other than as necessary to fulfill the official duties of such officer or employee.

We'll just call this the "Federal Gag Order Snitch Clause." Not only does it give the government the ability to see private financial information without a warrant, it also allows the government to do so in secret. This infringes on the right of financial institutions to utilize their First Amendment protected free speech, as it forbids banks from telling their customers that their private information has been given to the government. However, since the Sixteenth Amendment made the income tax constitutional in 1913, the American people have systematically lost the ability to keep their finances private; as a result, this latest loss of freedom wasn't all that controversial.

Meanwhile, the Act's roving wiretaps were controversial. Roving wiretaps are worrisome because the government, in its quest to nab domestic terrorists, will inevitably intercept law-abiding American citizens' communications without the warrant required by the Fourth Amendment. Because sophisticated terrorists could evade law enforcement by switching cell phones or by randomly using pay phones, the government thought it necessary to tie warrants to people rather than to telephone numbers. This could include a legal wiretapping of a public pay phone. As a result, anyone using a public phone a terrorist may be using could have their conversation recorded by the government.

As this seems to be a reasonable power to grant the government in very specific cases, Professor David D. Cole, a liberal who works for the Georgetown University Law Center, has argued that though roving wiretaps come at a cost to privacy, they're a sensible measure.[19] And Paul Rosenzweig, a conservative who is a senior legal research fellow in the Center for Legal and Judicial Studies at the Heritage Foundation, has contended that roving wiretaps are simply a sensible response to rapidly changing communications technology.[20]

Allowing roving wiretaps in very specific cases makes sense; after all, electronic surveillance laws were originally written to cover phones that were fixed in one place and linked to a network via a copper wire. Today phones can be taken across state and international boundaries and are not physically connected to networks. In response to these changes in technology, in 1986 Congress authorized roving wiretaps for the investigation of drug offenses. Under the modified law, the authority to intercept an individual's electronic communication was simply attached to the individual who was the suspect of criminal activity. In 1998, Congress altered the standards somewhat to permit use of a roving wiretap when the target's conduct in changing telephones or facilities had the effect of thwarting the surveillance. Prior to September 11, 2001, it was not clear that these authorities could be used to track terrorists. To clarify the law, section 206 of the Patriot Act authorized similar techniques for foreign intelligence investigations.

The Patriot Act's expansion of court jurisdiction to allow the nationwide service of search warrants also became controversial, as it theoretically allowed agencies to "shop" for friendly judges. This could reduce the likelihood that smaller Internet Service Providers (ISPs) or phone companies would try to protect the privacy of their clients by challenging a warrant in court. For example, a small Atlanta ISP served with such a warrant is unlikely to have the resources to appear before a court in Los Angeles. Also, only the ISP, and not the individual being investigated, is typically able to challenge the warrant—many warrants are issued *ex parte*, meaning that the target of the order is not present when the order is issued. These provisions were originally set to sunset on December 31, 2005, but were reauthorized.

For a time, the Act allowed agents to undertake "sneak-and-peek" searches in which the American citizen being searched didn't have to be informed of the sneak-and-peek search for an unspecified amount of time. In 2004, FBI agents used this provision to search and secretly examine the home of Brandon Mayfield, who was wrongfully jailed for two weeks on suspicion of involvement in the Madrid train bombings. The U.S. Government publicly apologized to Mayfield.[21] Nevertheless, Mayfield took the government to court. On September 26, 2007, Judge Ann Aiken found the law unconstitutional according to the Fourth Amendment.

Secret Administrative Subpoenas?

Perhaps one of the biggest controversies has involved the use of National Security Letters (NSLs) by the FBI. An NSL is a form of administrative subpoena used by the FBI and reportedly by other federal agencies including the Central Intelligence Agency (CIA). It is a "demand letter" issued to a particular entity or organization to turn over various records pertaining to individuals. NSLs require no probable cause or judicial oversight. From 2003 to 2006 the bureau issued 192,499 national security letter requests.[22] Section 505 of the Patriot Act allowed NSLs to be used to investigate U.S. citizens even if they are not suspects in a criminal investigation.

NSLs are still controversial. On February 15, 2011, Senator Rand Paul (R-KY) sent a "Dear Colleague" letter to his fellow U.S. senators regarding the renewal of the USA Patriot Act in which he said:

> My main objection to the PATRIOT Act is that searches that should require a judge's warrant are performed with a letter from an FBI agent–a National Security Letter ("NSL"). I object to these warrantless searches being performed on United States citizens. I object to the 200,000 NSL searches that have been performed without a judge's warrant. I object to over 2 million searches of bank records, called Suspicious Activity Reports, performed on U.S. citizens without a judge's warrant.

NSLs used to be even more problematic. They originally contained a gag order preventing the recipient of the letter from disclosing that the letter was issued; however, the gag order was ruled unconstitutional as an infringement of free speech in *Doe* v. *Ashcroft* (2004),[23] because the recipient of the subpoena could not challenge the NSL in court. Congress later tried to remedy this legal dispute in a reauthorization act, but because they did not remove the non-disclosure provision, a federal court again found the gag order to be unconstitutional.[24]

Why Even Librarians Lost Their Tempers

The Patriot Act even ticked off librarians. Section 215 allowed the FBI to apply for an order to produce materials that assist in an investigation to prevent terrorism. The "tangible things" include "books, records, papers, documents, and other items." Supporters of the provision point out that these records are held by "third parties," and therefore according to progressive justices are exempt from a citizen's reasonable expectations of privacy. The American Library Association was so outraged they founded a resolution condemning the Patriot Act and urged members to defend free speech and protect patrons' privacy.[25] Consequently, some librarians reportedly shredded records to avoid having to comply with such orders. In response, Attorney General John Ashcroft released information in 2003 showing that section 215 had never been used.[26] Section 215 was later amended to give greater judicial oversight and review.

Another controversial aspect of the Patriot Act has been the immigration provisions that allow for the indefinite detention of any alien the Attorney General believes may cause a terrorist act. The ACLU said the Act gave the Attorney General "unprecedented new power to determine the fate of immigrants....Worse, if the foreigner does not have a country that will accept them, they can be detained indefinitely without trial."[27]

All of this healthy criticism, mostly from the Left but also from Republicans such as Representative Ron Paul (R-TX)–largely went silent when President Barack Obama took office. Over the last few decades, Fourth Amendment privacy rights have been consistently losing to the needs for law enforcement to keep people safe in a world with nuclear and biological weapons.

Republicans and Democrats have thus given the state massive injections of power to root out crime and terrorism threats. As all criminal activity can be better fought when the public gives up its privacy, the American people need to weigh what they're trading for the perceived increase in safety. Justice William J. Brennan warned that this trend to erase the Fourth Amendment at the expense of individual rights was underway in 1973 when he wrote, "The needs of law enforcement stand in constant tension with the Constitution's protections of the individual.... It is precisely the predictability of these pressures that counsels a resolute loyalty to constitutional safeguards."[28]

Indeed, Americans have long asked how far law enforcement powers should be extended; for example, a quote often attributed to Benjamin Franklin, one repeated in different ways by Thomas Jefferson, is often paraphrased thus: "Those who would give up essential liberty to purchase a little temporary safety, deserve neither liberty nor safety."

So how far we go down the path toward a police state is dependent on the education of the American people. As Thomas Jefferson counseled, "If a nation expects to be ignorant and free in a state of civilization, it expects what never was and never will be."[29]

Why the Left Claims They're for Individual Rights

Despite all the exceptions and loopholes now bleeding the Fourth Amendment into dead letters, the Left has used this amendment's "right to privacy" as cover to claim they are the defenders of individual liberty. To fully understand how today's liberal-progressives can maintain the fallacy that they're individualists, it's necessary to comprehend their modern expansion of the "right to privacy," which can be traced to 1961 when Justice John Marshall Harlan penned his dissent in *Poe* v. *Ullman.*

Planned Parenthood manufactured *Poe* v. *Ullman* by recruiting a group of plaintiffs to challenge a Connecticut law that prohibited the sale and use of contraceptives. The Supreme Court, however, dismissed the case because the 1879 Connecticut law had never been enforced. (It is a basic judicial principle that there has to be an actual legal, not theoretical, dispute to be adjudicated before the Court can act.) Nevertheless, Justice Harlan wrote in his dissent: "I believe that a statute making it a criminal offense for married couples to use contraceptives is an intolerable and unjustifiable invasion of privacy in the conduct of the most intimate concerns of an individual's personal life."

Some historians, such as the conservative radio host and author Mark R. Levin, assert that Justice Harlan derived this newfound right to privacy from Melvin L. Wulf, an attorney for the American Civil Liberties Union (ACLU). Wulf claimed he raised the issue in his friend-of-the-court brief for *Poe* v. *Ullman*; in fact, Wulf later claimed: "Judges dislike breaking entirely new ground. If they are considering adopting a novel principle, they prefer to rest their decision on earlier law if they can."[30] To give the liberal justices legal standing, Wulf said he presented the Court with a means to enact a new privacy right that covered contraceptives, and later abortion, by postulating they were covered by an implied right to privacy.

Before the 1960s, the Supreme Court had consistently ruled that the Framers of the Constitution had left regulations pertaining to drugs, alcohol, abortion, public nudity, profanity in public places, gay marriage, premarital sex, and more up to the people to decide via elected state legislatures or, in some states, with voter initiatives. Nevertheless, even though Justice Harlan's dissenting opinion had no legal effect, his and Wulf's view of privacy would soon be used to rewrite the Constitution.

After *Poe* v. *Ullman* failed, Planned Parenthood manufactured a live case: *Griswold* v. *Connecticut* (1965). They found a cop who would arrest someone for strapping on a condom and then appealed the case to the U.S. Supreme Court.

If the people of Connecticut didn't like this law banning contraceptives—and given that it wasn't being enforced, they likely didn't—they could have petitioned their state legislature to have it repealed democratically. Instead, in *Griswold* v. *Connecticut* liberal justices, by a 7–2 vote, usurped the will of the people in every state by declaring what happens in the bedroom to be a matter of privacy. Though few want the government in their bedrooms giving pointers or wagging their disapproving fingers, this ruling opened the door to a whole new level of judicial activism that has since usurped the will of the voting public.

Before *Griswold* it was understood that in areas where the Constitution is silent, the power to deal with issues touching privacy resided with the states. The state legislators, as represented by the people, could determine what was legally moral or immoral, tolerable or intolerable. Laws thereby reflected the moral sense of the community, as the people in the various states decided what kind of society they wanted to raise their kids in; however, after *Griswold* such laws could no longer reflect the moral sense of the community unless the judges happened to agree with the public.

Justice William O. Douglas wrote for the majority that he'd located the newfound privacy right somewhere in the "penumbras" and "emanations" of other constitutional protections, but exactly where he'd found it he couldn't say. He was obviously making it up. After all, legal dictionaries define "penumbra" as "an area within which distinction or resolution is difficult or uncertain." And the American Heritage dictionary defines "emanation" as "something that issues from a source; an emission." So Douglas was literally saying the privacy right he uncovered had uncertainly, and perhaps with difficulty, issued from a source he presumed was the Constitution.

How did this big, fat lie become possible?

Historically, judges frowned on those who used "unenumerated rights" (rights that don't explicitly appear in the Constitution) to issue rulings. Conservative justices consider not using unenumerated rights, natural rights, and so on, to be a matter of judicial restraint, lest they undermine the will of the people. Liberal justices, however, have decided they simply know better than the voting public. The logic of *Griswold* and its progeny—such as *Roe* v. *Wade* (1973) and *Planned Parenthood of Southeastern Pennsylvania* v. *Casey* (1992)—has given activist judges the ability to tell individuals what kind of society they must live in.

It wasn't supposed to be this way. For example, Alexander Hamilton noted that a "limited constitution ... [is] one which contains certain specified exceptions to the legislative authority; such for instance as that it shall pass no bills of attainder, no ex post facto laws, and the like." Because of such "specified exceptions," Hamilton argued, "the constitution is itself in every rational sense, and to every useful purpose, a BILL OF RIGHTS."[31] The Constitution was designed to restrict the reach of the federal government.

By using unenumerated privacy rights, *Griswold* paved the way for the Court to subsequently decide *Roe* v. *Wade.* In *Roe,* the majority decision, written by Justice Harry Blackmun, asserted that the "right of privacy, whether it be founded in the Fourteenth Amendment's concept of personal liberty and restrictions upon state action, as we feel it is, or, as the District Court determined, in the Ninth Amendment's reservation of rights to the people, is broad enough to encompass a woman's decision whether or not to terminate her pregnancy."

So the liberal Court felt a right to abortion was there, though they couldn't put their finger just where it was, yet they also thought the right is "broad enough" to overrule people who live in a state where a majority might *feel* abortion is a bad thing.

At different points in history, the Court had been tempted to go down the unmarked path toward natural law and unwritten rights; however, such philosophical departures from the law rarely held, until *Griswold.* The reason, as Justice James Iredell explained early on in the republic—in *Calder* v. *Bull* (1798)—was:

> [T]he ideas of natural justice are regulated by no fixed standard: the ablest and purest men have differed on the subject.…
> If, on the other hand, the Legislature of the Union, or the Legislature of any member of the Union, shall pass a law, within the general scope of their constitutional power, the Court cannot pronounce it to be void, merely because it is, in their judgment, contrary to the principles of natural justice.

The first case to begin to bust such a fissure in the Constitution was actually *Dred Scott* v. *Sandford* (1857), in which Chief Justice Roger B. Taney ruled that Congress didn't have the power to prohibit slavery in the territories—

making the Missouri Compromise unconstitutional. As he took a breather from his racist diatribe, Taney ruled that "an act of Congress which deprives a citizen of the United States of his liberty or property in a particular territory of the United States, and who has committed no offense against the laws, could hardly be dignified with the name of due process of law." By linking the idea of vested interests to the due process clause of the Fifth Amendment (by using it to protect the "property" rights of slaveholders) Taney implied that even unenumerated rights that don't explicitly appear in the text of the Constitution were nevertheless protected in the Constitution, and that judges were just the people to create and define these rights.

So the first time a Supreme Court justice made a bold stab at using a right that doesn't explicitly appear in the Constitution was to protect slavery—and Democrats still don't understand why doing this is a bad thing.

At the time, Chief Justice Taney's opinion drew an impassioned dissent from Justice Benjamin Curtis. His dissent is particularly worth noting in this age of judicial activism:

> When a strict interpretation of the Constitution, according to the fixed rules which govern the interpretation of the laws, is abandoned, and the theoretical opinions of individuals are allowed to control its meaning, we have no longer a Constitution; we are under the government of individual men, who for the time being have the power to declare what the Constitution is, according to their own views of what it ought to mean.

The judicial activism that created *Griswold* and *Roe* has grown like a weed. In *Cohen* v. *California* (1971), the Court ruled that a person could wear a jacket in a courthouse that read "Fuck the Draft," as it is covered by a "First and Fourteenth Amendments" right to "freedom of expression." And in *Erznoznik* v. *City of Jacksonville* (1975), the Court struck down a city ordinance that stopped a drive-in movie theater from showing movies that portrayed nudity. The drive-in theater faced a church and two public streets, but the Court said the ban could not "be justified as an exercise of the [city] ... for the protection of the children."

In each of these cases, liberal judges struck down standards of decency on constitutional grounds even though the Constitution had left these, as well as a host of other social and/or moral issues, up to the people through their state legislatures. Conservative justices typically practice judicial restraint by ruling the privacy right simply covers "persons, houses, papers, and effects" because that is what the Constitution says. Liberal justices, on the other hand, have increasingly found ways to read their views into the Constitution.

Liberal-progressives see undermining moral laws and regulations as setting the individual free from the burdens of stodgy morality, propriety, or even the harsh standards of Victorian decency. This belief was most clearly expressed in the 1960s anti-Vietnam war, anti-establishment movement, which is why so many of these rulings came from that period. But though former hippies have largely now become a part of the modern establishment, they still think ending dress codes, or even stopping dressing at all, is what empowers individual expression. Like rebellious teenagers, they are sure nose rings and tattoos are signs of individuality. The problem with their logic is a person with multiple body piercings and a t-shirt that declares "A Friend with Weed is a Friend Indeed" is likely just conforming to a group of potheads.

Sloppy attire, profanity, and body piercings don't necessarily express individual liberty; nor does the lack of them necessarily express a conservative mindset. However, allowing judges to overrule a free polity by declaring that things that don't appear in the Constitution are constitutional rights does inhibit individual freedom.

The Framers left questions of principle to the people and to the states; activist judges have increasingly taken away the ability of the people to decide moral issues at the ballot box, leaving an impotent and often unfulfilled public with no means to democratically protest a newfound right to have an abortion or, in a few cases, for a state to sanction same-sex marriage. In so doing, liberal ideology hasn't empowered the individual, but has shackled the individual to the beliefs of unelected justices who have lifelong job protection. Indeed, it's worth pondering whether abortion would be a hot-button issue today if voters at the state level had been allowed to debate and decide what the law should be. A compromise might have been found, at least one that satisfied the majority of any given state.

For example, when the Supreme Court in 1972 declared the death penalty to be unconstitutional under the Eighth Amendment, controversy raged across the United States about whether capital punishment was constitutional. When the Supreme Court reversed itself in 1976, once again giving the states the ability to decide the issue, according to new guidelines, the controversy lost a lot of its momentum. Today states have different policies, and rarely flares up as a national issue.

All this complexity and judicial rule-making–and even the use of privacy rights not found anywhere in the Constitution–obscures a very simple point liberal-progressives don't want you to realize: the Fourth Amendment is actually a very straightforward list of protections designed to keep the government out of our "persons, houses, papers, and effects," unless they have a lawfully obtained warrant. To retake and save this right of privacy, the voting public must insist that the government apply the Fourth Amendment to new technologies and old.

AMENDMENT V

No person shall be held to answer for a capital, or otherwise infamous crime, unless on a presentment or indictment of a Grand Jury, except in cases arising in the land or naval forces, or in the Militia, when in actual service in time of War or public danger; nor shall any person be subject for the same offense to be twice put in jeopardy of life or limb; nor shall be compelled in any criminal case to be a witness against himself, nor be deprived of life, liberty, or property, without due process of law; nor shall private property be taken for public use, without just compensation.

*"This battle against eminent domain abuse may have started
as a way for me to save my little pink cottage, but it has
rightfully grown into something much larger—the fight to restore
the American Dream and the sacredness and security of each
one of our homes."*
—Susette Kelo

In July 2010, the stone foundation that once held up Susette's Kelo's little pink house lay exposed, a planter for weeds. Corrugated metal fences separated a road from the vacant lot where her dream house once stood. Daffodils and daisies were growing stubbornly between stretches of gravel on the ninety acres of the city of New London, Connecticut, seized via eminent domain. Far below the wasteland that had been a community for more than a century, the Thames River in this quiet corner of New England flowed placidly on to the Atlantic.

What the city of New London had done to the Constitution wasn't so serene. New London officials took a working-class neighborhood from private residents so they could give the real estate to Pfizer, the largest pharmaceutical company in the world. The city's bulldozers had ripped down the homes and readied the earth for Pfizer to build a waterfront hotel and marina, eighty new upscale residences, and an office complex. The New London Development Corporation (NLDC) had greedily estimated Pfizer's expansion along the Thames River would generate between $680,000 and $1,250,000 in new annual tax revenue. Politicians couldn't wait to spend the money. But then Pfizer, after the years of court battles it took for the city to seize the land, announced it was closing its research-and-development headquarters in New London and moving its employees to nearby Groton. The land was left stripped and vacant.

Susette, a registered nurse, didn't find out the city was taking her property from an attorney or even from a visit from a city official. She found out from a notice of eviction nailed to her home's front door on the day before Thanksgiving in 2000. She was horrified. She couldn't believe this could happen in America. Some government stooge had pounded nails through her front door to tell her she had to scat from her land. The hubris of this unconstitutional use of eminent domain pushed Susette and six other homeowners to dig in and fight for their freedom. In seizing Susette's land, the city of New London had underestimated, if not the courts, then at least the American people.

Wilhelmina Dery was another one of the homeowners who decided to stay and fight for her rights. Wilhelmina was born in her home in 1918. Her family had owned the home for more than a century. Her son and family lived in a house next door, on land Wilhelmina gave her son as a wedding present. They were all living the American dream ... until progressives disregarded the Constitution and with it the Bill of Rights and used growing government power to violate these citizens' rights and appropriate their dreams.

To keep their homes, Susette, Wilhelmina, and the other homeowners relied on the Fifth Amendment's takings clause to safeguard their private property. This clause reads, "... nor shall private property be taken for public use, without just compensation." They thought they were on firm constitutional ground; after all, anyone with a dictionary could have told them Pfizer, a private company, couldn't be called a "public use."

They were up against people who thought they could do anything, as long as they deemed it to be for the "public good"–people such as Wesley Horton, the attorney for New London who said ripping down Susette's little pink house so they could give her land to Pfizer "is just as important as eliminating blight." Horton even arrogantly added as he stood in front of news cameras, "It might have been impossible to build the World Trade Center where it was," without eminent domain–as if even the building destroyed by terrorists might have been prevented in the first place by some little old lady who refused to sell her dream house.

The Fifth Amendment's takings clause has been incorporated to include state and local governments under the Fourteenth Amendment, meaning the Fifth Amendment doesn't only apply to the federal government, but also to state and all local governments. Susette, and the other appellants, were simply arguing that an economic development, which was the stated purpose of the taking and subsequent transfer of the land to the New London Development Corporation, did not qualify as a public use. To any non-lawyer, it seems like a simple case and an easy win for Susette and the other homeowners.

Nevertheless, in a 4–3 vote, the Connecticut Supreme Court sided with New London on March 9, 2004. The court said the city was allowed to take the homes so it could give them to someone else who would pay more taxes; of course, every single home in America would produce more jobs and tax revenue if it was an office building, but that logic didn't sway the court.

Susette and the others were flabbergasted. Words still have meanings, don't they? Has the Fifth Amendment become dead words in a bygone document?

Actually, thanks to progressives, words don't mean what they used to. The Fifth Amendment's takings clause does still say "public use," not "private use," and New London did intend to give their property to a private corporation; however, progressives on the U.S. Supreme Court had semantically changed the definition of "public use" to mean "public purpose" in 1954. This seemingly subtle change is not so subtle at all, as it allows the government to define "public purpose" to mean anything it wants. In this case, the city of New London argued, as many progressives have done around the country, that its public purpose was for the greater economic good of the local community.

Susette and the other homeowners appealed. The Supreme Court took the case. Susette says she cried with joy and triumph when she heard the Supreme Court would hear the case, as she thought she'd find justice in its hallowed halls. Her lawyers, however, knew the outcome was far from certain, as progressives on the high court had been weakening the Fifth Amendment since the 1950s.

In 1954 the Supreme Court decided *Berman* v. *Parker*, a case in which Washington, D.C., attempted to use the power of eminent domain to take blocks of private property so the city could hand the properties to other private entities that would redevelop the slum areas for possible sale or lease. Instead of inducing private investment by reducing red tape and taxes, the city decided to take over the private properties, use private developers to rebuild them, and then to lease or sell them to the people it wanted to own them.

The plaintiffs in the case owned a department store that was obviously not a dilapidated ghetto, but the city determined it should be seized nevertheless in order to clear a larger blighted area. The plaintiffs pointed out that their property was not slum housing and that it could not be taken for a project under the management of a private agency. The owners further argued that taking the land with the power of eminent domain and giving it to redevelopers amounted to "a taking from one businessman for the benefit of another businessman" and so was not a public use, thus violating the Fifth Amendment.

Supreme Court Justice William O. Douglas, however, who had been nominated in 1939 by President Franklin D. Roosevelt, wrote for the majority in *Berman* v. *Parker* that "[i]f owner after owner were permitted to resist these redevelopment programs on the ground that his particular property was not being used against the public interest, integrated plans for redevelopment would suffer greatly."

Instead of interpreting the law, as a judge should, Justice Douglas voted for a policy, something legislators are elected to do. Justice Douglas then read the phrase "for public use" right out of the Fifth Amendment by altering it to "public purpose" and gave the city the ability to take the department store.

Today, more than a half century after the *Parker* decision usurped private property rights, anyone who wanders far off Capitol Hill can see for themselves how well the District of Columbia cleaned up its slums. If you go, leave your wallet at home and carry a few dollars with you to pacify the muggers.

Three decades after *Parker*, the Supreme Court heard *Hawaii Housing Authority* v. *Midkiff* (1984). In this case, the Hawaii Housing Authority was attempting to use eminent domain to take land that was overwhelmingly concentrated in the hands of a few private landowners so they could redistribute the property to the wider population of private residents and thereby lower property costs. The local government basically wanted people who had leases for homes to have outright titles, but the move would also force a private landowner to sell to another private landowner.

In deciding *Midkiff*, the Court cited *Parker* as a precedent and allowed the Hawaii Housing Authority to effectively redistribute the land.

This land redistribution was also a failure, as land values on the island didn't fall after the government usurped the residents' property rights, but actually skyrocketed. As the former lessees acquired titles to their homes, the homes became attractive to wealthy Japanese and to other investors who paid outlandish prices for houses largely located in the upscale Kahala and Hawaii Kai neighborhoods. This caused a ripple effect that was blamed for a spike in property values throughout the islands.

Such are some of the unintended consequences that occur when government, with the high court's sanction, wipes it heels on individual rights in its effort to control the economy.

Despite both policy failures, Susette and the other appellants had these progressive precedents waiting to rob them of their Fifth Amendment rights. Not being lawyers, they naïvely thought the Constitution held its original protections of individual rights when the Supreme Court agreed to hear *Kelo* v. *The City of New London* (2005). They didn't know that in the decades since the loss of private property rights after the *Midkiff* decision, states and municipalities had extended their use of eminent domain and had frequently used economic development purposes as an excuse to appropriate private property.

Some forty amicus curiae ("friend of the court") briefs were filed in the *Kelo* case, twenty-five on behalf of the petitioners. Susette's supporters ranged from the libertarian Institute for Justice (the lead lawyers) to the NAACP and the AARP. The latter groups signed an amicus brief arguing that eminent domain has often been used against politically weak com-munities with high concentrations of minorities and the elderly.

After a contentious oral hearing at the Supreme Court and more cameras and reporters, Susette and the other plaintiffs went back to their homes to wait for justice. The neighborhood wasn't the same. Most of the houses around them had been torn down. Pfizer's shadow seemed to have blocked out the sun. The government felt authoritarian.

Months passed, and on June 23, 2005, the Supreme Court ruled 5–4 in favor of the City of New London. The Court allowed the government to take their homes. Susette was crushed. America wasn't the country she thought it was.

Justice John Paul Stevens wrote the majority opinion, joined by Justices Anthony Kennedy, David Souter, Ruth Bader Ginsburg, and Stephen Breyer. Justice Kennedy wrote a concurring opinion setting out a more detailed standard for judicial review of economic development takings than that found in Stevens' majority opinion. In so doing, Justice Kennedy contributed to the Court's trend of turning minimum scrutiny–the idea that government policy need only bear a rational relation to a legitimate government purpose–into a fact-based test the Court can use to determine when a government can take a private property for a public purpose, such as raising more tax revenue. But he still sided with the progressives and upheld *Parker*'s destruction of the Fifth Amendment.

Two 1996 Supreme Court cases had clarified the concept of what could constitute a so-called legitimate government purpose to take someone's private property. In *Romer* v. *Evans*, the Court said the government *purpose* must be "independent and legitimate." And in *United States* v. *Virginia*, the Court said the government *purpose* "must be genuine, not hypothesized or invented post hoc in response to litigation." Thus, the Court made it clear that, in the scrutiny regime established in *West Coast Hotel* v. *Parrish* (1937), government *purpose* is a question of fact for the *Court* to decide. So the Court decided that the Fifth Amendment's provision that "private property [should not] be taken for public use, without just compensation," can be taken for a "public purpose." They based their decision on an overly complex and forced definition that gives municipalities just enough of a gray area to do whatever they want. Meanwhile, the Court, not the U.S. Congress or other legislatures, decided it has absolute authority.

Justice Kennedy explained his convoluted position by writing, "A court confronted with a plausible accusation of impermissible favoritism to private parties should [conduct] … a careful and extensive inquiry into 'whether, in fact, the development plan is of primary benefit to … the developer … and private businesses which may eventually locate in the plan area.'" In so doing, Kennedy ruled that judges must not only define but also decide policies—things that elected legislators are supposed to do, not people in black robes who have lifelong appointments.

In the majority opinion, Justice Stevens wrote that the "Court long ago rejected any literal requirement that condemned property be put into use for the general public." Thus a misguided precedent by FDR's progressive Supreme Court gave justification for a 5–4 decision of the Supreme Court that allows the government to take away anyone's home as it likes, even if the government just wants to give it to someone with better political connections.

Justice Sandra Day O'Connor wrote the principal dissent, joined by Chief Justice William Rehnquist, Justice Antonin Scalia, and Justice Clarence Thomas. Their dissenting opinion said, "Any property may now be taken for the benefit of another private party, but the fallout from this decision will not be random. The beneficiaries are likely to be those citizens with disproportionate influence and power in the political process, including large corporations and development firms."

Justice O'Connor argued that the decision eliminates "any distinction between private and public use of property—and thereby effectively delete[s] the words 'for public use' from the Takings Clause of the Fifth Amendment." As a result, the Fifth Amendment's protection of private property from the government was effectively rubbed out.

Justice Thomas penned a separate dissent in which he argued that the precedents the Court's decision relied on were so flawed that "something has gone seriously awry with this Court's interpretation of the Constitution."

He accused the majority of replacing the Fifth Amendment's "public use" clause with a very different "public purpose" test, saying, "This deferential shift in phraseology enables the Court to hold, against all common sense, that a costly urban-renewal project whose stated purpose is a vague promise of new jobs and increased tax revenue, but which is also suspiciously agreeable to the Pfizer Corporation, is for a 'public use.'"

Thomas also made use of the argument presented in the NAACP/AARP amicus brief on behalf of three low-income residents' groups fighting redevelopment in New Jersey, noting: "Allowing the government to take property solely for public purposes is bad enough, but extending the concept of public purpose to encompass any economically beneficial goal guarantees that these losses will fall disproportionately on poor communities. Those communities are not only systematically less likely to put their lands to the highest and best social use, but are also the least politically powerful."

The day after the ruling, the *New York Times* called the decision "a welcome vindication of cities' ability to act in the public interest."[1] The *New York Times* had actually put its position into action: its current headquarters building was taken via eminent domain for economic redevelopment. The *Washington Post* also liked that the government has taken the right to override the Fifth Amendment when it chooses: "[T]he court's decision was correct….New London's plan, whatever its flaws, is intended to help develop a city that has been in economic decline for many years."[2]

Most of America didn't agree with the liberal newspapers. Outrage from homeowners grew so intense that some citizens in Plainfield, New Hampshire—a town where Justice Stephen Breyer owned a home—began a campaign to use eminent domain to take Justice Breyer's home so they could use the land to make a "Constitutional Park."

Actually, Justice Breyer had not only voted to give the government the power to seize private property so it could give it to people who'd pay more taxes, but he also argued in his book *Active Liberty* that judges should interpret the Constitution in a way that takes the consequences of rulings into account. Breyer thinks an unelected justice should socially engineer a society, not just apply equal justice under law. Plainfield never took Breyer's property, but the New Hampshire legislators did pass a constitutional amendment that limits the state's use of eminent domain to property that will be put to public use, as in a highway or a dam, which is what the Fifth Amendment originally allowed.

After a wave of outage crashed over the nation, many other states also altered their eminent domain laws. Prior to the *Kelo* decision, only eight states specifically prohibited using eminent domain for economic development; however, as this book was being written, forty-three states had amended their eminent domain laws to stop state and local government's from wiping their backsides with the Bill of Rights.[3] About half of those states enacted laws that severely inhibit the takings allowed by the *Kelo* decision, while the rest enacted laws that place some limits on the power of municipalities to invoke eminent domain for economic development.

Some states and cities, however, still don't respect property rights. New York City is the worst offender. In 2010, New York City used eminent domain to seize homes and businesses so that the University of Columbia could expand its campus into West Harlem. Nick Sprayregen, the owner of Tuck-It-Away Self-Storage, and gas station owners Gurnam Singh and Parminder Kaur, fought the city in court and lost. The U.S. Supreme Court declined to hear their appeal in December 2010, which meant a New York State Court of Appeals decision allowing the city to seize these people's private property stands.

So New York City got to level one of the few gas stations in Manhattan in order to give Columbia's privileged students more elbow room. Put another way, taxpayers' private properties and businesses were transferred to a private, non-profit university that will not pay taxes, because the university had more political clout and because the Supreme Court made a bad decision. The city can't even argue this use of eminent domain had the public "purpose" of increasing tax revenue.

Columbia also got rock-bottom prices. Columbia estimates that its endowment value averaged $6.516 billion in 2009–2010.[4] Clearly this wealthy university could have upped its bids until Nick Sprayregen,

Gurnam Singh, and Parminder Kaur agreed to sell. They instead used the government to reduce what they had to pay to the "market values" (figures determined by the city) for the West Harlem properties. The real "market value" of any property is what a buyer will pay, but the value Columbia had to pay was a depressed amount based on what similar properties in the local area were selling for.

Though eminent domain is often referred to as a struggle between the people and the powerful, as this egregious eminent domain case shows, property rights are supposed protect poorer, less-connected people from the wealthy and the well-connected. But statists don't really care about the little guy; what they care about is government power.

The Supreme Court's *Kelo* decision also didn't end Susette's battle with her local government. Soon after the decision, New London's officials said they intended to charge Susette and the other residents who'd stayed in their homes throughout the court fights for back rent for the five years since the city's condemnation procedures began. The city argued that the residents had been on city property for those five years and so they therefore owed tens of thousands of dollars in rent. The city wanted revenge because Susette and the other homeowners had won in the court of public opinion.

Susette's case was finally resolved, however, with the city of New London paying substantial additional compensation to the homeowners. The final cost to the city and state for the purchase and the destruction of the homes was estimated to be $78 million.

Beth Sabilia, New London's mayor at the time of the property-rights battle, later said, "Never, ever delegate the powers of eminent domain.... My lesson is, if the state offers you $70 million, say 'no thank you.' Yes, the city won, but no one in the City of New London really won. In New London we are all connected. I don't care if you live in a lean-to or a 4,000-square-foot house. It's where we all take our babies home."[5]

Sabilia seems to have learned that private property is the basis of a free society. She even said she'd personally received 4,000 email death threats, and that New London still suffers a poor reputation from the episode.

Meanwhile, a local homebuilder, Avner Gregory, came to Susette's rescue. He bought Susette's little pink house for $1 and moved it to 36 Franklin Street in New London. He deeded it to back Susette on the condition the home couldn't be sold for ninety-nine years. Though the circa 1893 home was moved board by board, it's still pink and in the same style, only now there's a monument out front explaining her fight for property rights in what is supposed to be the land of the free.

Seeing Susette's little pink house sitting humbly in its new location brings the classic John Mellencamp song "Pink Houses" to mind: "Ain't that America … home of the free … yeah … little pink houses for you and me.…Because the simple man pays the bills … the bills that kill.…"

Taking Property by Regulation

The Fifth Amendment says, "No person shall be … deprived of life, liberty, or property, without due process of law; nor shall private property be taken for public use, without just compensation." Property includes our homes, autos, and other possessions. The ownership of this property comes with implied rights. We have the right to sell our property, to tell others to get the hell off it, and to treat it well or poorly just as long as someone else's property or property rights aren't harmed in the process. It is this last point that has allowed government during the past century to take private property rights via onerous regulations, as they've twisted and expanded what affects other people's property. In so doing, the government has trampled on individual rights in its quest to engineer communities and expand its own power.

"Regulatory takings" occurs when the government passes laws and/or regulations that diminish a property's value so much that it becomes a Fifth Amendment takings. The government must then theoretically pay just compensation for the value it has taken. For example, if the public wishes to create public-access corridors through private land, to enact open-space laws that will prevent property owners from building an addition so the public can have unspoiled views, or to stop private owners from farming, ranching, or recreating because there may be endangered species on the private land, then the public should pay for what it is taking from the property owner(s).

After all, forcing the government to pay for onerous restrictions or other private property takings is the only way to keep politicians from simply eroding property rights to advance their own political futures. This is fundamental, because if a political party can enrich a large section of the public by taking something from a few individuals, then it becomes politically advantageous for politicians to "spread the wealth around," as President Barack Obama told "Joe the Plumber." Private property rights would soon disappear in such a political climate.

Once it's understood that some regulations can be onerous enough to property owners to require compensation for takings, and that in a just society the public should pay for what it wants, the next question is just when does a regulation become a takings? The courts have long had trouble answering this question.

People who have sued the government over takings from Clean Water Act restrictions, those who have sued over historical-preservation laws, and more have typically lost because the current Supreme Court test to determine whether a takings has occurred starts by asking whether the regulation in question is "rational." This rational test doesn't ask if the legislature had a rational purpose in mind, but just whether any sane adult could find a reason for the policy or rule. This gives progressive justices a free hand because it doesn't force them to rule from a constitutionally grounded view of the law. If they can conjure up a reason for a regulation that they view to be sane, then they can rule against the individual. Worse still, this rational-person test puts the burden of proof on the private property owner, as the regulation is assumed to be rational unless proven otherwise. (To realize how un-American that is, imagine a criminal-justice system that assumes we're guilty until proven innocent.)

Justice Oliver Wendell Holmes Jr. fairly noted in 1922 that "[g]overnment hardly could go on if to some extent values incident to property could not be diminished without paying for every such change in the general law."[6] And he's right, to a point; however, federal, state, and local government regulations have, since 1922, burdened property owners with restrictions that test the imagination.

Today the federal government can tell us what light bulbs we must use, how much water our toilets can flush, and whether the presence of fairy shrimp can prevent us from putting in that pool we've always wanted. State and local governments sometimes get to tell us whether we can cut down a tree in our backyard; they get to dictate how high our fences can be; they can tell us whether the public is permitted to cross our private property; and in California, some local governments tell homeowners they can't cut brush from around their homes despite the very real danger this poses if a forest fire comes their way—as happens every year in California.

This deterioration of private property rights escalated in 1916 when New York City adopted the first zoning regulations that applied citywide. This first zoning law was a reaction to the Equitable Building, a 38-story Manhattan building completed in 1915. People living around this first "skyscraper" complained it blocked out the sun. New York City then passed complex zoning regulations, including floor-area ratio rules and air rights.

The constitutionality of zoning ordinances was subsequently upheld by the Supreme Court in the 1926 case *Village of Euclid, Ohio* v. *Amber Realty Co.* To stop industrial growth, the village of Euclid had passed a complex zoning ordinance based on six classes of use. Amber Realty Co.'s property was thus divided into three of these use classes, thereby preventing Amber Realty Co. from developing the land commercially. Ambler Realty sued the village of Euclid, arguing that the zoning ordinance had substantially devalued its land. The Supreme Court, however, ruled that Ambler Realty Co. was speculating when it claimed the ordinance reduced the value of its property. Speculating? Any realtor would have said, "Hell yeah it's been devalued; that property went from big commission to not worth a damn."

On the day after this unfortunate Supreme Court decision, city planners and housing boards all over the country read the newspapers and realized they could meddle with property rights in just about any way they desired without having to pay for the devaluation of private property. So they began passing restrictions on property rights that before 1926 seemed unimaginable in a free society, all without having to pay for the regulatory takings.

Zoning codes have now evolved to horrifying levels of malfeasance. Urban-planning theory has changed and legal constraints have fluctuated, but zoning is now used throughout the country. *Euclid* v. *Amber Realty Co.* led to "Euclidean zoning codes," which categorizes land uses into specified geographic areas, such as commercial and residential. However, social engineers today don't like the rigidness of Euclidean planning—it gives people zoned residential or commercial too much freedom within their specific designations—so they invented "effects-based planning," "performance zoning," and first implemented in Chicago and New York City, "incentive zoning." These new planning theories have taken the restraints from Euclidean zoning codes and have allowed bureaucrats to socially engineer their every desire by forcing individual property owners to abide by increasingly onerous and often misguided regulations.

Zoning boards and city councils can now strip property owners of their right to use their land, via wetland laws, acreage zoning restrictions, or a myriad of other rationales to enhance the collective good of the community, all without paying a dime. They can even designate areas as "historical" to impose restrictions that they can use to say property values have increased, so they can charge higher property taxes. Such intricate zoning laws work against economic efficiency because they hinder growth and force developers to create cookie-cutter communities with inflexible planning codes and designs.

To see this in your mind's eye, consider the fact that everyone loves communities such as Old Town Alexandria, Virginia, and Brighton, Massachusetts, neighborhoods that grew into eclectic mixes of homes and shops long before zoning was deemed constitutional; however, people don't love planned communities nearly as much, as such communities tend to be static, lackluster, and devoid of the life that the small stores and cafés in the old communities sprout, as such shops are illegal in Euclid-zoned residential areas. And even communities with shops planned in don't get mom-and-pop entrepreneurship, but rather chain stores that won a contract by playing politics. People love the old communities that predate zoning ordinances so much that they pass historical-preservation laws to keep them that way. Can you see people a century from now passing laws to preserve mazes of urban cul-de-sacs?

Today, with nearly a century of zoning ordinances on the books, few people realize why the old communities evolved they way they did, and how the bureaucracy has whitewashed the individuality, the eccentricity, even the Americana out of towns and cities. These zoning regulations also reduced the value of the new planned communities. Jane Jacobs (1916–2006), an editor and writer on architecture in New York City, pointed this out in her book *The Death and Life of Great American Cities* (1961). Jacobs showed that urban diversity and vitality are destructive when city planners create complex zoning regulations and other property restrictions. She argued that zoning laws should be abolished and a free market for land restored. She pointed out that a free market results in dynamic, mixed-use neighborhoods; as an example, she frequently cited New York City's Greenwich Village, which is an unplanned, vibrant urban community that liberals adore, even if they don't know why.

Meanwhile, as zoning has taken hold and diminished private property rights, proving regulatory takings have even occurred has become nearly impossible. The precedent-setting case was *Penn Central Transportation Co. v. New York* (1978). Penn Central Transportation Co. was the owner of Manhattan's Grand Central Station. The station was constructed in 1913. Its original plans included a 20-story office building on top; though the addition was never completed, the structure was designed to support the added weight. As a result, Penn Central thought it had a smart way to make a profit. UGP Properties then offered to pay Penn Central $1 million annually for the right to add to the top of the building and $3 million after construction was completed. The construction wouldn't affect the train service below, only the aesthetics of the building.

But aesthetics was reason enough for the City of New York to butt in. In 1965 the city passed the Landmarks Preservation Law. The law created an 11-member commission to find and protect properties that have "a special character or special historical or aesthetic interest or value as part of the development, heritage, or cultural characteristic of the city, state, or nation." Though having such an historical designation might at first seem appealing, as Penn Central found out, the designation also brings substantial costs, as the law gave the commission the power to approve or deny any proposal to "alter the exterior architectural features of the landmark or to construct any exterior improvement on the landmark site."

The commission denied Penn Central's proposed addition. In doing so, the commission ignored an ancient maxim of common law: "*Cujus est solum, ejus usque al coelum es ad inferos.*" (Whosoever owns the land, owns to the heavens, and to the depths.") Despite this obvious regulatory takings, Penn Central lost several lower courts decisions before it appealed to the U.S. Supreme Court. Penn Central argued that the Fifth and Fourteenth Amendments should uphold their rights and allow for the city's actions to be considered a regulatory takings—the public should pay for the property rights they were taking. Nevertheless, the Supreme Court, like the New York Court of Appeals, found that the city's restrictions on land use for Grand Central Terminal was not a Fifth Amendment takings and therefore did not require just compensation.

Penn Central had lost the right to make a profit on their building. Why? Because the architecture was done so well the city's 11-member commission thought it should be left alone. But though the city thought it was too valuable to alter, the city didn't have to compensate the private property owner for it. Ironically, this ruling created a disincentive for private property owners to construct architecturally interesting or even expensive projects, as doing so might mean a loss of property rights.

The loss of property rights to zoning and other ordinances in *Penn Central Transportation Co.* and other rulings allowed the modern "green" and "wise-use" movements to use pushed Clean Water Act regulations and Endangered Species Act restrictions to control private property owners in ways that wouldn't have been imaginable in the nineteenth century.

Simply devising some reasonable compensation standard when a property value is diminished would add some common sense and balance to this debate. Instead, local governments have a free hand from the Supreme Court to do pretty much anything they want.

For example, the politics associated with the plight of the spotted owl may have induced the U.S. Department of the Interior to reduce timber harvests in the Pacific Northwest by about 80 percent,[7] thereby making the spotted owl the symbol of environmental regulations gone nuts, but hundreds of other endangered species from the Fresno kangaroo rat to the Alabama beach mouse have also been used by environmentalists to take away property rights. This has created a disincentive for property owners to have species "found" on their properties; after all, having the endangered Key Largo cotton mouse found on your southern Florida beach property can destroy your retirement plans, so any sane homeowner either wouldn't mention the presence of the mice, or would spread out some rat poison.

In this debate over the constitutionality of Endangered Species Act restrictions, property-rights advocates have not been arguing that the endangered species should be left in peril. They are simply saying that the public should pay for what it is taking, and that a smarter way to help species is to use free-market incentives so that it is in the property owners' interest to help a species by preserving critical habitat. This could easily be accomplished with tax breaks and other incentives.

Pushback against the deterioration of the Fifth Amendment gained some traction during President Ronald Reagan's administration. Richard Epstein's book, *Takings: Private Property and the Power of Eminent Domain* (1985), argued that if a citizen can show a violation of rights by a corporate polluter or by anyone else, then he or she should be able to file a lawsuit. In this way private property owners would have a means and an incentive to safeguard species, clean water, and so on. In March 1988, President Ronald Reagan signed Executive Order 12630, which codified Epstein's doctrine by requiring that "[e]xecutive departments and agencies should review their actions carefully to prevent unnecessary takings...."

During the successful 1994 Republican campaign for control of Congress, takings was incorporated into the Republican "Contract with America" as part of the proposed Job Creation and Wage Enhancement Act. Unlike Reagan's takings order, the version of takings promoted by congressional Republicans required financial compensation for "regulatory takings" of a property if the property's value is reduced more than 20 percent. Though H.R. 925, a bill that required such federal compensation for regulatory takings, passed the U.S. House of Representatives by 277–148 in 1995, the legislation was ultimately defeated after intense lobbying from labor groups, environmental organizations, and other Democratic-leaning groups.

Property-rights advocates, however, have won a few battles. For instance, in November 2004, 60 percent of Oregon's voters passed "Measure 37," a referendum to require government compensation for regulatory takings.

The impasse here is that within this constitutional battle between the Left and the Right, the Supreme Court has never articulated a workable test to determine when a regulation becomes a takings. In *Penn Central Co. v. New York City* the Court did establish that three factors must be considered to determine whether a regulation amounts to a taking: (1) the economic impact on the property owner; (2) the extent to which the regulation interferes with investment backed expectations in the land; and (3) the character or extent of the government action.

But all of those are vague, undefined benchmarks.

Subsequently, the case of *Agins* v. *City of Tiburon* (1980) added to the *Penn Central* analysis that to determine if there has been a takings, the courts must also weigh private and public interests, as if judges should be chewing over interests and thereby writing policies instead of simply blindly administering the law and sending uncertainties to elected legislatures for clarification. This ruling is clearly judicial activism.

However, one thing courts have consistently acknowledged is that a total loss of a property's value is a takings. For example, in *Lucas* v. *South Carolina* (1992), the Supreme Court held that when a legislature imposes regulations on private land use that result in a total economic loss, it is a takings and so just compensation must be paid. In *Lucas,* South Carolina law prevented a beachfront landowner from building on his land because the state wanted to stop beach erosion. The Court, however, did give the government a loophole: if the state can accomplish the same land use limitation under its nuisance or related property laws, then there wouldn't be a regulatory takings. So, to obtain compensation from the government under *Lucas,* a landowner must prove that the regulation has essentially rendered a piece of property valueless. Also, there mustn't be a nuisance law or other common law property rule that might justify the regulation.

A number of recent Supreme Court decisions show some return to the protection of private property rights. In *Dolan* v. *City of Tigard* (1994), for example, the Supreme Court held a lengthy discussion on the loss in real value from "green-space" preservation laws, while never mentioning the possible benefits of the land-use restrictions. As environmental value is not measureable in dollars, it makes perfect sense that courts would ignore it; this small neutering of environmentalists' line of reasoning is a victory for common sense.

There are other signs of hope for property rights. The U.S. Court of Federal Claims' decision in *Tulare Lake Basin Water Storage District* v. *United States* (2001) held that efforts to protect species under the Endangered Species Act constitute a taking of property in violation of the Fifth Amendment. Indeed, the court's opinion in this case was blunt and beautiful: "The federal government is certainly free to preserve the fish; it must simply pay for the water it takes to do so."

The debate over whether government can simply take private property is still ongoing, but if the trend continues to weaken landowner's rights, property ownership will become nothing more than a liability.

How the IRS Tax Code
Undermines the Fifth

Perhaps most importantly, the Fifth Amendment protects us from being forced to incriminate ourselves. It says, "No person shall ... be compelled in any criminal case to be a witness against himself, nor be deprived of life, liberty, or property, without due process of law." As anyone who has seen a police drama knows, to "plead the Fifth" is to refuse to answer a question because the response might provide self-incriminating evidence. What many people don't know, however, is that the federal income tax code can legally require individuals to file information that may be used against them in criminal cases.

If you're wondering why our Founding Fathers didn't see this coming, it's because they deemed the Federal income tax to be unconstitutional. The first U.S. income tax was imposed in July 1861, at 3 percent of all incomes over $800 in order to pay for the American Civil War. This income tax was discontinued in 1872.

In 1894, Democrats in Congress passed the Wilson-Gorman Tariff Act, which imposed the first peacetime income tax. Its rate was 2 percent on income over $4,000 annually. The alleged purpose of the income tax was to make up for revenue that would be lost by tariff reductions. In 1894 the *New York Times* reported that many Democrats in the East "prefer to take the income tax, odious as it is, and unpopular as it is bound to be with their constituents," than to defeat the Wilson-Gorman Tariff Act.[8]

Soon after, the Supreme Court, in *Pollock* v. *Farmers' Loan & Trust Co.* (1895), found the income tax to be unconstitutional. The progressive Woodrow Wilson argued for a constitutional fix. When Wilson was president of the United States, the Democratically controlled congress proposed the Sixteenth Amendment to make the income tax constitutional. The Sixteenth Amendment passed and was ratified by the requisite number of states in 1913 as: "The Congress shall have power to lay and collect taxes on incomes, from whatever source derived, without apportionment among the several States, and without regard to any census or enumeration."

Read the Sixteenth Amendment again, this time aloud. Can you hear Thomas Jefferson uttering such a broad-based federal power? It would have made even Alexander Hamilton blush—and he was the Founding Father who gave us the first sin tax (on whiskey), which started the Whiskey Rebellion.

Broad powers usurped by the federal government always work to subjugate individual rights, and the Sixteenth Amendment has not been an exception. The income tax has since grown so cumbersome and onerous even tax attorneys can't agree on its meaning. This growth has even affected the Fifth Amendment's right not to incriminate ourselves. For example, after the income tax was passed, the Supreme Court, in *United States* v. *Sullivan* (1927), ruled that a taxpayer could not invoke the Fifth Amendment's protections as a basis for refusing to file a required federal income tax return.

The Court stated: "If the form of return provided called for answers that the defendant was privileged from making[,] he could have raised the objection in the return, but could not on that account refuse to make any return at all. We are not called on to decide what, if anything, he might have withheld."

Talk about a dense, mind-numbing piece of writing. This means the person filing the required paperwork could raise the objection in the IRS form. But of course if he or she fills out the compulsory fields in the IRS form, then they've potentially incriminated themselves. But they can't know that because they can't judge "what, if anything, he might have withheld." Ultimately, this is the Court's way of saying you're damned if you do and damned if you don't, but either way, the IRS is empowered to do the damning.

Basically, the Court tried to justify the Sixteenth Amendment with the Fourth and Fifth Amendments, which wasn't possible, so they squirmed between the obvious contradictions and let it ride.

Many courts have since had to limbo under this legal barrier. For example, in *Garner* v. *United States* (1976), a defendant was convicted of crimes involving a conspiracy to "fix" sporting contests and to transmit illegal bets. During the trial, the prosecutor introduced as evidence the taxpayer's federal income tax returns for various years. In one return the taxpayer had showed his occupation to be a "professional gambler." In various returns the taxpayer had reported income from "gambling" or "wagering." The prosecution used this to help contradict Mr. Garner's argument that his involvement was innocent.

Garner tried unsuccessfully to keep the prosecutor from introducing the tax returns as evidence, arguing that since he was legally required to report the illegal income on the returns, he was being compelled to be a witness against himself. The Supreme Court agreed that he was legally required to report the illegal income on the returns, but ruled that the right not to incriminate oneself did not apply. The Court stated that "if a witness under compulsion to testify makes disclosures instead of claiming the privilege, the Government has not 'compelled' him to incriminate himself."

The *Sullivan* and *Garner* decisions are viewed by some legal scholars to say that on a required federal income tax return, a taxpayer would probably have to report the amount of the illegal income, but might validly claim the privilege by labeling the item "Fifth Amendment" (instead of "illegal gambling income" or "illegal drug sales"). So the Fifth Amendment, according to this line of reasoning, mandates we incriminate ourselves, but it at least allows us not to use words like "illegal."

Since President Woodrow Wilson and the Democrats in the progressive era made the income tax constitutional, the government has written invasive banking laws, income reporting requirements, and enough exemptions, tax brackets, and clauses to confuse even tax attorneys while leaving taxpayers with little of the privacy that was originally protected by the Constitution. The IRS is now unaccountable to the people, and big-government statists like it that way. Massive tax reform is necessary if Americans are to save their Bill of Rights and thereby retake their lost Fourth and Fifth Amendment freedoms.

AMENDMENT VI

In all criminal prosecutions, the accused shall enjoy the right to a speedy and public trial, by an impartial jury of the State and district wherein the crime shall have been committed, which district shall have been previously ascertained by law, and to be informed of the nature and cause of the accusation; to be confronted with the witnesses against him; to have compulsory process for obtaining witnesses in his favor, and to have the Assistance of Counsel for his defence.

"If a juror accepts as the law that which the judge states then that juror has accepted the exercise of absolute authority of a government employee and has surrendered a power and a right that once was the citizen's safeguard of liberty."[1]
—George Bancroft

L aura Kriho didn't mean to become a constitutional activist. She was selected to be a juror in Gilpin County Colorado in May of 1996, just one of a dozen chosen to hear some small-town methamphetamine possession case. She got the jury notice and reported hoping not to be selected. But she was chosen, so she sat quietly in the juror box and took instructions from Gilpin County Judge Fred Rodgers. She then listened as the attorneys tried the case. But, even after the closing arguments, she still wasn't certain the defendant was guilty.

Kriho went with the other jurors into the privacy of the jury room and soon found that the other eleven jurors were fairly certain the defendant was guilty. Kriho was, in fact, the lone holdout. Kriho later explained, "I had reasonable doubts based on the lack of evidence."[2] She never thought she'd make the type of dramatic stand Henry Fonda's character, Robert Cummings, took in the classic movie *Twelve Angry Men*. But she found herself debating the other jurors and questioning the evidence.

The jury hung that evening.

A year later, in February 1997, Kriho was back in court. This time she was on trial for speaking her mind in the sanctity of the jury room. The jurors she'd deliberated with actually testified against her. The prosecutor reached inside the sanctity of the jury room and used what she had said against her. By trying a juror for speaking their mind in the privacy of the jury room, the court was setting a precedent that would make other juries afraid to speak freely. This didn't happen in *Twelve Angry Men*. Kriho didn't know this was even possible in the land of the free.

Kriho had the Sixth Amendment right to a trial by jury in state court because in 1948 the Supreme Court had applied the protections of the Sixth Amendment to the states through the "due process" clause of the Fourteenth Amendment.[3] But she never imagined she'd be convicted of contempt of court, in part, for failing to volunteer knowledge about the doctrine of "jury nullification" during jury selection. According to the common-law doctrine of jury nullification, a juror can nullify a law—refuse to convict a defendant despite instructions from a judge—if they believe the law is unjust or that the application of the law in a specific instance is unjust.

Her lawyer pointed out she wasn't asked about jury nullification during jury selection. Nevertheless, Gilpin District Judge Henry Nieto fined Kriho $1,200.

Kriho says, "I was not trying to 'nullify' the drug laws....I only mentioned my (then) vague understanding of jury nullification as a last resort."

As Kriho appealed the $1,200 fine for saying "improper" things in the privacy of the jury room, she fought back in the court of public opinion by writing editorials for local newspapers:

> I have discovered that there is a nation-wide movement among judges to actively mislead jurors about their power to use their discretion. To my surprise, I discovered that one of the leaders of this movement [was] Gilpin County Judge Fred Rodgers, who wrote an article in a national legal journal about the issue. The article outlined strategies for judges to use to keep jurors ignorant of their power to "nullify" unjust law and for prosecuting "obstructionist" jurors.[4]

Judge Rodgers seemed to see prosecuting Kriho as a good test case to expand the power of the judiciary by making "we the people" into sheep the state could handle as it likes. Some judges and attorneys have certainly been working to purge juries of citizens who know they have the power to nullify a law; in fact, Kriho explained in various newspapers: "After reading this article, you too will possess forbidden knowledge that will exclude you from serving on a jury in many courts, if you choose to reveal your thought crime to the court."

After a lot of public attention, in April 1999, the Colorado Court of Appeals reversed Kriho's contempt conviction. The Court of Appeals ruled that the trial court had improperly invaded the secrecy of the jury room by allowing testimony from other jurors about jury room deliberations. Then, on August 4, 2000, First Judicial District Chief Judge Thomas Woodford signed a motion filed by the district attorney to dismiss the contempt-of-court case against Kriho.

Paul Grant, Kriho's attorney, said, "The very purpose of a jury trial is to resist oppression by the government, without interference or intimidation from any quarter, including the court."[5] Kriho won this battle for jury rights, but the war is being lost.

Historically the jury's power to sit in judgment of not only their peers, but also of the law, is what led to many of the freedoms we cherish today. Jury rights prevailed in England after the trial of William Penn (1644–1718) in 1670. Penn was an English real estate entrepreneur who converted to Quakerism, and, due to persecution, helped purchase land for a Quaker settlement that became the future Commonwealth of Pennsylvania. In fact, under Penn's direction, the city of Philadelphia was planned and developed.

Before Penn led a group of Quakers to America, he wrote pamphlets to protest the persecution of Quakers in England. At the time the King and the Church of England were confiscating the Quakers' property and putting thousands of Quakers in jail. In 1688, Penn's attacks on the Church of England landed him in the Tower of London. The Bishop of London ordered that Penn be held until he publicly recanted. The official charge was publication without a license, but the real crime was blasphemy. Penn responded, "My prison shall be my grave before I will budge a jot: for I owe my conscience to no mortal man."[6]

Penn, however, was released after eight months of imprisonment and went back to opposing the Church of England. Penn was arrested again in 1670 for violating the Conventicles Act of 1670, which made it illegal for any religious group, except the Church of England, to have a religious assembly. Penn deliberately broke this law.

When before a judge, Penn asked to see a copy of the charges against him. The law allowed Penn to view the charges. The judge, however, refused. Furthermore, the judge directed the jury to come to a verdict of guilty without hearing the defense.

The jury deliberated but returned a verdict of not guilty. When the judge instructed them to reconsider their verdict and to select a new foreman, they refused. The judge then fined and jailed the jury. Over the proceeding months the members of the jury stayed stubborn. Their cause became known as "Bushel's Case," after Edward Bushel, a member of the jury, and fomented public support.

Penn was freed when his father, who was then on his deathbed, paid his fine. Meanwhile, Penn's jury, which held firm even though four of the jurors spent nine weeks in prison, sparked a popular uprising that was instrumental in establishing not only the rights of juries, but also the freedom of religion, the freedom of speech, and *habeas corpus,* a right that requires the government to produce charges and to release someone being held illegally. These rights were won, to some extent, because this jury exercised its right to judge not only the facts in a case but also whether a law is just.

In 1735, an American jury asserted the same rights. John Peter Zenger, editor of the *New York Weekly Journal,* was clearly guilty of printing seditious criticisms of the governor of New York. Nevertheless, a jury refused to convict Zenger. Andrew Hamilton, Zenger's attorney, convinced the jury that something isn't libelous if it's true. Hamilton informed the jury that they had the common law authority to ignore the law and to instead rule according to their consciences. The jury subsequently acquitted Zenger, setting a precedent that led to increased debate about the importance of press freedom and, eventually, to the First Amendment.

Jury nullification has these glorious roots in people's struggles for freedom from tyranny, yet an American court reached into the jury room and fined Laura Kriho for speaking her conscience. Kriho found justice in a higher court, but people need to once again understand that juries weigh, as they must, the facts and laws that cement the American republic together, but they also have the common law right to draw on their consciences. Juries draw on the inalienable rights Thomas Jefferson referred to in the preamble to the Declaration of Independence when he wrote, "We hold these truths to be self-evident, that all men are created equal, that they are endowed by their Creator with certain unalienable rights, that among these are Life, Liberty, and the pursuit of Happiness. That to secure these rights, Governments are instituted among Men, deriving their just powers from the consent of the governed."

The understanding that man has inalienable rights—rights that are not transferable to another or capable of being taken away by a king or parliament and that therefore stand above, even in judgment of, government—led the English people to create a jury system of peers that acted as a moral check on the state. This is also why America adopted the jury system, separate from the power of the government, as a moral cross-section of peers who stand apart from the government's bureaucracy and determine the guilt or innocence of an individual. Jurors may acquit if they think a law unjust, or that a just law has been applied unfairly. This makes the case against Kriho all the more frightening; if higher courts had let her conviction for contempt stand, they would have set a precedent that would have devolved the rights of free Americans back to before the Penn trial in 1670, back to a time when government could do as it wanted with justice and the people.

To undermine these historical precedents and to kick jury rights back to an age when government did as it pleased, liberal-progressives today argue we don't have natural rights, merely legal rights granted to us by the government. They say we don't have absolute rights granted to us by God or nature that we have until someone else, such as a government, takes them away. This is why liberals don't think jurors have the right to overrule the government on moral grounds. They find government authority to be sacrosanct, not the rights of a free people.

In defense of the freedom of juries to stand apart from the government, three decades after the Zenger trial, in 1765, William Blackstone (1723–1780), an English judge and author, wrote that a jury's power to nullify a law is "the most transcendent privilege which any subject can enjoy, or wish for, that he cannot be affected either in his property, his liberty, or his person, but by the unanimous consent of twelve of his neighbours and equals."[7] This well-established safeguard of freedom was why the first U.S. Congress put the right to trial by jury into the Bill of Rights, thereby restoring what Supreme Court Justice James Iredell would describe in 1836 as that "noble palladium of liberty."[8]

Subsequently, during the American Revolution, colonialists demanded the right to a jury; in fact, the complaint of not having the right to a jury of peers was listed in the Declaration of Independence. It became one of the rights Americans won in the war for independence.

Historically though, jury nullification hasn't been important merely because it's a check on the state. When a jury acquits a defendant who clearly appears to be guilty, the acquittal conveys important information about community standards and provides a guideline for future prosecutorial discretion. For instance, some juries refused to return freed slaves to the South before the American Civil War, even though the Fugitive Slave Act required them to do so. In 1851, for example, a court indicted twenty-four people for helping a slave escape from a jail in Syracuse, New York. The first four trials of the group resulted in three acquittals and one conviction, which finally led the government, in exasperation, to drop the remaining charges. In another case, after a crowd broke into a Boston courtroom and rescued a slave, a grand jury indicted three of those involved, but after an acquittal and several hung juries, the government dropped those charges.[9]

America actually has a long history of jurors refraining from applying unjust laws. Other juries practiced jury nullification during Prohibition (which banned the consumption of alcohol in America from 1920 to 1933) by refusing to convict people who'd simply had a drink. Juries actually nullified alcohol control laws as much as 60 percent of the time.[10] This resistance is considered to have contributed to the adoption of the Twenty-First Amendment, which repealed the Eighteenth Amendment's establishment of Prohibition.

Also, left-leaning judges would be wise to remember that even during the Vietnam War era, jury nullification was used to stop the government from jailing protestors. For example, the pediatrician and author Benjamin M. Spock was convicted of conspiracy to counsel, aid, and abet registrants to avoid the draft. During Spock's trial, the presiding judge instructed the jury that they had to apply the law as he explained it, not according to their consciences. But later, the U.S. Court of Appeals in the First Circuit overturned the conviction because the judge had committed a "prejudicial error" by putting to the jury ten special yes-or-no questions designed to prevent them from voting their consciences.[11] The right of jurors to use their moral compasses freed Benjamin M. Spock.

Jury nullification, of course, can and has resulted in unfortunate judgments. During the twentieth century's civil-rights era, for example, some all-white juries acquitted white defendants who were accused of murdering blacks. In more recent cases, juries who believe the police didn't act ethically acquitted some "popular" drug dealers, such as Larry Davis.[12] Such judgments expose community beliefs that need to be addressed. However, despite the jury's history of winning freedoms for the people, liberal-progressives now argue that juries can't decide complex criminal and civil cases because the medical facts or the financial regulations are too complex for laymen to comprehend. Of course, this complexity is all the more reason why juries should decide difficult cases, as a jury will look for the moral right and wrong within the stultifying laws and regulations. A jury of peers also forces the government to find, through its attorneys, simple, understandable ways to explain why a given law is necessary and right. This keeps the bureaucracy responsive to the public.

Over 2,000 years ago, Cicero, a Roman statesman, pinpointed why the government loves complexity when he said, "More law equals less justice."[13] Cicero was pointing out that a republic only stays free as long as its government is accountable to its people. Arguing that the complexity of the law created by the government and its bureaucracy is a justification for destroying the individuals' right to a jury would allow the government to create a problem and then solve the problem by taking away the individual right to a jury of peers.

Nonetheless, some judges, such as the one who went after Kriho, are actively trying to take from juries the power to use their consciences; for example, the Criminal Pattern Jury Instructions developed by the U.S. Court of Appeals for the Tenth Circuit for use by U.S. district courts now instructs juries that they don't have the right to use their moral compasses:

> You, as jurors, are the judges of the facts. But in determining what actually happened–that is, in reaching your decision as to the facts–it is your sworn duty to follow all of the rules of law as I explain them to you. You have no right to disregard or give special attention to any one instruction, or to question the wisdom or correctness of any rule I may state to you. You must not substitute or follow your own notion or opinion as to what the law is or ought to be. It is your duty to apply the law as I explain it to you, regardless of the consequences. However, you should not read into these instructions, or anything else I may have said or done, any suggestion as to what your verdict should be. That is entirely up to you.
>
> It is also your duty to base your verdict solely upon the evidence, without prejudice or sympathy. That was the promise you made and the oath you took.[14]

The move to require jurors to ignore their consciences is actually troubling from a legal angle. Requiring jurors to ignore their sense of morality by only judging cases according to laws actually prevents jurors from legally distinguishing right from wrong; after all, what is moral and what is legal aren't necessarily the same thing. Ironically, this modern, statist mandate means jurors are instructed to be legally "insane," as not knowing right from wrong is one legal definition of insanity.

Few courts, however, have attempted direct assaults on jury nullification. They haven't had to, because in 1895 the Supreme Court, in *Sparf* v. *U.S.*, ruled 5–4 that a judge doesn't have to inform a jury of its right to nullify laws. In fact, a 1969 U.S. Court of Appeals for the Fourth Circuit decision (*United States* v. *Moylan*), affirmed the right of jury nullification, but also upheld the power of the court to refuse to allow jurors to learn they have such a power.

In *Moylan* the Court held:

> [B]y clearly stating to the jury that they may disregard the law, telling them that they may decide according to their prejudices or consciences (for there is no check to insure that the judgment is based upon conscience rather than prejudice), we would indeed be negating the rule of law in favor of the rule of lawlessness. This should not be allowed.

Worse still, in *United States* v. *Thomas* (1997), the U.S. Court of Appeals for the Second Circuit ruled that jurors could be removed if there is evidence they intend to nullify the law. This court cited the Federal Rules of Criminal Procedure 23(b), which says "a jury of fewer than 12 persons may return a verdict if the court finds it necessary to excuse a juror for good cause after the trial begins."

In *Thomas* the Second Circuit ruled:

> We categorically reject the idea that, in a society committed to the rule of law, jury nullification is desirable or that courts may permit it to occur when it is within their authority to prevent. Accordingly, we conclude that a juror who intends to nullify the applicable law is no less subject to dismissal than is a juror who disregards the court's instructions due to an event or relationship that renders him biased or otherwise unable to render a fair and impartial verdict.

This attack on jury rights is not just coming from some liberal, power-hungry judges. Statist attorneys also grind their teeth when someone mentions the longstanding precedent that juries have the power to rule according to their consciences; for example, Erick J. Haynie, an attorney who practices in Portland, Oregon, wrote recently,

> [I]t is highly questionable whether jurors should be instructed to "make" the law when a legislative body has already done the job for them. Congress and the state legislatures have superior expertise, resources, and perspective to make macro-social decisions, and much more time to reach a well-reasoned decision than does "a group of twelve citizens of no particular distinction snatched away from their primary vocations" to spend a couple of days in court.[15]

Haynie's elitist views would have made American colonialists cringe. Battling back the injustices that inevitably come from centralized bureaucracies is the very reason the jury system evolved in England and was fortified in the United States with the Sixth Amendment.

Today, according to the Fully Informed Jury Association, the constitutions of only two states—Maryland and Indiana—clearly declare the nullification right, although two others—Georgia and Oregon—refer to it indirectly. But despite the attacks from the Left, the concept is still rooted in common law. As Thomas Jefferson put it in a letter to Thomas Paine in 1789, "I consider trial by jury as the only anchor ever yet imagined by man, by which a government can be held to the principles of its constitution."

Does a Jury Need Twelve People?

In 1930 the Supreme Court held that the Sixth Amendment protected a right to "a trial by jury as understood and applied at common law ... recognized in this country and England when the Constitution was adopted."[16] Therefore, juries had to be composed of twelve people, and criminal verdicts had to be unanimous, as was customary in England.

However, after the Supreme Court extended the Sixth Amendment right of a trial by jury to defendants in state courts in 1948, the Court began to re-examine some of these standards.

The Supreme Court, in *Williams* v. *Florida* (1970), held that twelve came to be the number of jurors by "historical accident." Therefore, the Supreme Court decided that a jury of six would be sufficient, but anything less would deprive the defendant of a right to trial by jury. This new, yet no less arbitrary, historical accident broke precedent with English and American history.

Two 1972 cases heard together—*Apodaca* v. *Oregon* and *Johnson* v. *Louisiana*—were more damaging to the original protections afforded by the Sixth Amendment. In these cases the Court considered state laws that allowed criminal defendants to be convicted by less-than-unanimous votes by juries. Oregon allowed convictions on 10–2 votes, while Louisiana went further by allowing convictions on 9–3 votes—meaning it would take four "angry men" to hold up a jury verdict in Louisiana.

The Court, voting 5–4, upheld both state laws. The Court did this even though five justices actually stated the opinion that, to convict, the Sixth Amendment required unanimous jury decisions. This counterintuitive result occurred because Justice Lewis F. Powell Jr. concluded that the Sixth Amendment imposes greater requirements on the federal government than it does on the states. Justice Powell, who was nominated by President Richard Nixon, had a reputation of being able to straddle fences better than most politicians, but even so this parsing is a bit much.

The Supreme Court found that though the right to a unanimous jury verdict might have been expected at the time the Bill of Rights was adopted, because the first U.S. Congress rejected language that would have added a unanimity requirement to the Sixth Amendment, the Supreme Court decided it could make up its own definition. In fact, a concurring opinion by Justice Harry Blackmun—who is perhaps most infamous for authoring *Roe* v. *Wade* (1973), as discussed earlier—suggested that he would have had a constitutional problem with 8–4 and perhaps with 7–5 verdicts, but 9–3 was all right. The four dissenting justices, however, argued that laws that allow non-unanimous jury verdicts in criminal cases unconstitutionally weakened the "requirement of proof beyond a reasonable doubt" mandate. But they were out-voted.

Thankfully, six years later, in *Ballew* v. *Georgia* (1978), the Court decided it had gone far enough. Justice Blackmun wrote the opinion for the Court, which decided that Georgia's law allowing criminal juries of just five people violated the Sixth Amendment.

The Supreme Court visited the issue of jury size and unanimity just one more time in 1979. In *Burch* v. *Louisiana*, the Court found a Louisiana law allowing criminal convictions on 5–1 votes violated the Sixth Amendment to a jury trial. If a jury is to be as small as six, the Court said, the verdict has to be unanimous. So though defendants can now count on a jury trial in criminal cases in the states as well as from the federal government, in the states a jury, for some very flippant reasons, can be smaller and less sure of itself.

Defendants in criminal cases also still have the right to the Sixth Amendment's requirement that a trial be "speedy." But there is a big caveat: the Supreme Court has never explicitly ruled that some particular time limit must apply to this Sixth Amendment right. The prosecution may not excessively delay the trial for its own advantage, but a trial may be delayed to secure the presence of an absent witness or for investigators to gather all the facts.

In *Barker* v. *Wingo* (1972) the Supreme Court developed a four-part ad hoc balancing test for determining whether the person's right to a speedy trial has been violated:

1. A delay of a year or more from the date on which the speedy trial right "attaches" (the date of arrest or indictment, whichever occurs first) was termed "presumptively prejudicial," but the Court has never explicitly ruled that any absolute time limit applies.

2. The prosecution may not excessively delay the trial for its own advantage, but a trial may be delayed to secure

the presence of an absent witness or other practical considerations.

3. The time and manner in which the defendant has asserted their right: if a defendant agrees to the delay when it works to their own benefit, they cannot later claim that their trial has been unduly delayed.

4. The degree of prejudice to the defendant that the delay has caused.

Then, in *Strunk* v. *United States* (1973), the Supreme Court ruled that if the reviewing court finds that a defendant's right to a speedy trial was violated, the indictment must be dismissed and/or the conviction overturned. Therefore, a reversal or dismissal of a criminal case on speedy trial grounds means that no further prosecution for the alleged offense can take place. This works as an effective check on government power, as it reprimands the state for not adhering to the Constitution.

But this ruling too was subject to a glaring exception: in *Sheppard* v. *Maxwell* (1966), the Supreme Court had found that the right to a public trial is not absolute. In cases where excess publicity would serve to undermine the defendant's right to due process, limitations can be put on public access to the proceedings. According to *Press-Enterprise Co.* v. *Superior Court* (1986), trials can be closed at the behest of the government if there is "an overriding interest based on findings that closure is essential to preserve higher values and is narrowly tailored to serve that interest."

Actually, the right to a jury has always depended on the nature of the offense charged. Petty offenses—those punishable by imprisonment for not more than six months—are not typically covered by the jury requirement. Even where multiple petty offenses are concerned, the right to a jury trial does not necessarily exist. Also, except for serious offenses (such as murder), minors are typically tried in a juvenile court, which can lessen the sentences allowed, but forfeits the right to a jury.

How Solid Is the Right to a Lawyer?

Supreme Court Justice William J. Brennan once quipped, "I cannot accept the notion that lawyers are one of the punishments a person receives merely for being accused of a crime."[17] However, the Supreme Court hasn't completely agreed with a person's right to have a lawyer or to waive this right, if they so choose.

The Sixth Amendment protects the right "to have the Assistance of Counsel for his defence." In *Faretta* v. *California* (1975), the power to choose or waive counsel lies with the accused, but the Court later held in *Godinez* v. *Moran* (1993), that a state can deny this right if it believes the accused can't adequately proceed without counsel. Also, in *Bounds* v. *Smith* (1977), the Supreme Court held that the constitutional right of "meaningful access to the courts" can be satisfied by counsel or access to legal materials. *Bounds* has been interpreted, by several federal courts of appeals, to mean a defendant does not have a constitutional right to access a prison law library to research his or her defense if access to the courts has been provided through appointed counsel. So even if the state-appointed attorney is a moron, a defendant in prison can't necessarily see if something more can be done in his or her defense.

So the power of a jury to rest on its conscience has long been both a protection and a catalyst for freedom. Removing the jury's power to nullify laws would rip the sword from Lady Justice's left hand, leaving Lady Justice as an unarmed slave to the state. Intelligent, informed juries that retain the power to sit not only in judgment of their peers, but also of the government, are an important buttress to protect the individual rights originally secured in the Constitution. The only way to save these rights is to first know they exist.

AMENDMENT VII

*In Suits at common law, where the value in controversy
shall exceed twenty dollars, the right of trial by jury shall be
preserved, and no fact tried by a jury, shall be otherwise
re-examined in any Court of the United States, than according
to the rules of the common law.*

"Lawsuit: A machine which you go into as a pig
and come out of as a sausage."[1]
–Ambrose Bierce

W hatever your economic situation or politics, you probably find just enough truth in the Shakespeare quote, "The first thing we do, let's kill all the lawyers,"[2] to chuckle a moment. This viewpoint is so commonsensical Dante Alighieri, an Italian poet who lived from about 1265 to 1321, even expressed it in his *Inferno* by placing attorneys who thwart justice with slippery rhetoric, loopholes, and technicalities in the Eighth Circle of Hell. He gave these "evil counselors" clothes made of flames because, one supposes, being burned endlessly would prevent the attorneys from articulating a legal technicality that might, given their talents with sophistry, convince even the Devil to spare them from damnation.

Actually, once you see what attorneys have done to the Seventh Amendment, you'll hope Dante is getting his way.

The Seventh Amendment's requirement that the federal government seat a jury in civil trials where more than $20 is at stake has been undermined to benefit trial attorneys. The ramifications of this amendment's corrosion affects everything we do. This is why every time we help an accident victim, coach a little league team, start a small business, or decide whether to allow neighborhood children to play on our property, we have to weigh the odds of being sued. With an estimated 16 million lawsuits filed annually in the United States,[3] individuals as well as corporations and government entities have to practice extreme lawsuit avoidance. As the rules governing lawsuits favor trial attorneys, individual Americans have lost the right to swim beyond a lawyer-determined area at public lakes, to let a dog off a leash so they can throw a ball in a quiet portion of a public park, to obtain access to most private properties, to tell someone to go fly a kite, in some states to pump their own gas, and in others to smoke, even outdoors....

To name just a few specific examples of the affects lawsuits have on liberty, in 2010, a lawsuit prompted schools in Cabell County, West Virginia, to take down their swing sets.[4] Another lawsuit forced Basketball Town, a special events facility for basketball, volleyball, and other sports, in Rancho Cordova, California, to close even though they'd broken no laws.[5] And a lawsuit drained the Mt. Laurel Pool in Hazleton, Pennsylvania, after a person, who cut their heel when diving from a location where diving was forbidden, sued for $100,000.[6]

Of course, a lot of idiotic individuals add weight to this civil-litigation landslide every year. For example, in November 2010 a man sued a restaurant over "exploding" escargot.[7] Also in 2010, another restaurant was sued for failing to offer instructions on how to eat an artichoke.[8] And incredibly, a legendary drug dealer named "Freeway" Rick Ross sued rapper Rick Ross, claiming his ill-famed name is trademarked.[9]

How does this nonsense even get into court? People who file frivolous lawsuits, think: *Why not play the lawsuit lottery?* After all, though many countries require the loser to pay the legal costs of the person or entity they sued, the United States doesn't make the loser pay. And attorneys often waive fees by telling potential plaintiffs they'll only take a percentage of any win or settlement. So people can roll the dice in civil courts without even putting money on the table.

Another underlying reason why such lawsuits are being filed is that as the government has grown in power, its liability has increased. While this could be easily checked with simple tort reforms—for example, deciding that a legal adult who swims beyond the ropes is taking his life in his own hands and so therefore he, or his loved ones, have no right to suit if someone gets hurt—the trial bar doesn't want us to have our individual accountability back. They don't want their hands pried from the public's deep pockets or from corporate profits, so they lobby to keep the rules loose and the loopholes coming. They want to keep the state, as well as homeowners and corporations, liable for even someone else's negligence.

The people who lose in this storm of litigation are individual Americans. Because someone could suit for just about anything, because these people can win with only "a preponderance of evidence," because just going to court is costly, and because civil litigation can lead to huge sums of money being awarded, we've all lost our right to behave as responsible adults.

To regain our freedom to live as we see fit, we first have to clearly understand what some lawyers, judges, and politicians have done to the Seventh Amendment. The Founding Generation knew real justice must be erected on solid individual rights. These rights must include a jury system that can overrule the government's wishes. English judges won this independence from their king after the Glorious Revolution with the passage of the Act of Settlement of 1701; however, American colonial judges weren't extended this freedom. King George III even abolished trial by jury in the American colonies. The injustices that ensued from this omnipotent foreign control of even very local affairs became one of the central grievances that ignited the American Revolution; in fact, the ninth complaint listed in the Declaration of Independence is: "He [the King of Great Britain] has made judges dependent on his will alone for the tenure of their offices and the amount and payment of their salaries." The colonists wanted their judges to be accountable to the people in their communities, not to some distant puppeteer. They wanted the same rights Englishmen enjoyed.

This prompted the first U.S. Congress to solidify the right to a jury in federal cases—in criminal trials with the Sixth Amendment and in civil trials with the Seventh Amendment. The Framers thought that though a runaway jury can be a problem (such as giving $2.86 million to Stella Liebeck because she burned herself with a McDonald's coffee[10]), a runaway judge can pose an even greater threat to justice. As Thomas Jefferson explained:

We all know that permanent judges acquire an esprit de corps; that, being known, they are liable to be tempted by bribery; that they are misled by favor, by relationship, by a spirit of party, by a devotion to the executive or legislative; that it is better to leave a cause to the decision of cross and pile [heads or tails] than to that of a judge biased to one side; and that the opinion of twelve honest jurymen gives still a better hope of right than cross and pile does. It is left therefore, to the juries, if they think the permanent judges are under any bias whatever in any cause, to take on themselves to judge the law as well as the fact. They never exercise this power but when they suspect partiality in the judges; and by the exercise of this power they have been the firmest bulwarks of English liberty.[11]

The Framers certainly understood that as the federal bureaucracy grew in America it would one day seek to weaken the jury system, as juries were originally designed to be a check on the state. This was the primary reason the federal government was limited to the powers outlined in the Constitution. And it's why the Anti-Federalists insisted on a bill of rights.

However, the modern liberal-progressive view that the federal government should reign supreme over the people was also expressed early in American history. This statist viewpoint, for example, was articulated in 1800 by Supreme Court Justice Samuel Chase (1741–1811). Until the late nineteenth century, Supreme Court justices had the added duty of serving as individuals on circuit courts. While serving in such a capacity during the trial of James T. Callender (1758–1803)–a case that found Callender guilty of printing seditious libel about President John Adams, according to the Alien and Sedition Acts of 1798–Justice Chase said:

If inferior courts commit error, it may be rectified; but if juries make mistakes, there can be no revision or control over their verdicts, and therefore, there can be no mode to obtain uniformity in their decisions. Besides, petit juries are under no obligation by the terms of their oath, to decide the constitutionality of any law; their determination, therefore, will be extra judicial. I should also imagine, that no jury would wish to have a right to determine such great, important, and difficult questions; and I hope no jury can be found, who will exercise the power desired over the statutes of congress, against the opinion of the federal courts.[12]

Though Justice Chase never explained why he thought federal judges could be trusted to honor their oaths whereas jurors could not, Chase was subsequently impeached—partly for his conduct during the Callender trial. In a letter to Congressman Joseph Hopper Nicholson of Maryland, Thomas Jefferson asked, "Ought the seditious and official attack [by Justice Chase] on the principles of our Constitution … go unpunished?"[13] Subsequently, the U.S. House of Representatives Articles of Impeachment Against Samuel Chase alleged that he was "marked, during the whole course of the [Callender] trial, by manifest injustice, partiality, and intemperance."[14]

Nevertheless, the U.S. Senate voted to acquit Justice Chase of all charges on March 1, 1805. Justice Chase then returned to his duties on the Court. As Chief Justice William Rehnquist noted in his book *Grand Inquests*, some senators declined to convict Justice Chase, despite their partisan dislike of him, likely because they thought Justice Chase's political ideology wasn't grounds for removal. No Supreme Court justice has been impeached since. Many historians say Justice Chase's acquittal helped ensure the independence of the judiciary, and in fact, in the two centuries since Justice Chase's impeachment, all subsequent impeachments of federal judges have been based on allegations of legal or ethical misconduct, not on judicial performance.

So though one result of Justice Chase's impeachment and acquittal has been enhanced judicial freedom, the legislative branch's refusal to even threaten impeachment for more than two centuries has also meant that Supreme Court justices aren't afraid to make politically partisan and even unconstitutional rulings. The checks and balances of our branches of government that all school kids learn about have not applied to the judicial branch. The Supreme Court acts as a check on the legislative branch, but the legislative branch has long since lost its will to check the judicial branch.

Judicial restraint wasn't the only loser in the impeachment trial of Justice Chase. After Jefferson became president of the United States, Callender asked Jefferson to appoint him Postmaster of Richmond, Virginia. Jefferson, however, refused to make the controversial appointment. Callender then attained the position of editor of the *Richmond Recorder* and decided to strike back at Jefferson's rebuke by revealing that Jefferson had funded his pamphleteering against Adams. After Jefferson denied doing any such thing, Callender published letters he'd gotten from Jefferson. Then, after some of Jefferson's supporters fought back by spreading rumors that Callender had abandoned his wife, leaving her to die of a venereal disease,[15] Callender penned a series of articles about how Jefferson had fathered children with his slave Sally Hemings.[16] (And people say today's politics are ghastly.)

Despite this political sideshow and Justice Chase's acquittal, for generations after this battle between the legislative and judicial branches, judges mostly understood that jurors were supposed to deliberate both the facts and the laws. For example, the first Chief Justice of the U.S. Supreme Court, John Jay, informed a civil jury in 1794 that while the Court usually determined the law and the jury found the facts, the jury nevertheless had "a right to take upon yourselves to judge of both, and to determine the law as well as the fact in controversy."[17]

During the twentieth century, however, the judiciary began to abandon the idea that juries are empowered to act as a check on the judicial branch in civil trials. Judges have since asserted control over the evidence, the law, and even the facts. Judges can now even overturn civil jury decisions outright; for example, the Eighth Circuit's 2008 "Civil Juror Instructions" commands: "You are the sole judges of the facts; but you must follow the law as stated in my instructions, whether you agree with it or not."[18]

As a result, juries are no longer paramount in civil trials; for example, a judgment notwithstanding the verdict–what lawyers sometimes call "judgment non obstante veredicto" or "JNOV"–currently allows a presiding judge in a civil trial to overrule the decision of a jury and reverse or amend the verdict. This intervention, which is often requested though rarely granted, permits a judge to alter "extreme" jury decisions.[19] However, because of the right against double jeopardy (a right protected by the Fifth Amendment), a judge is not allowed to enter a JNOV of "guilty" following a jury acquittal; though, if the judge grants a motion to set aside judgment after the jury convicts, the ruling may later be reversed on appeal.

Reversal of a jury's verdict by a judge can occur when a judge believes a jury made a decision counter to the facts, or if a judge thinks a jury's verdict did not correctly apply the law. As a result, in civil cases–which often require only a majority vote by jurors–the jury can no longer use its common law power of nullification to override an immoral law, or an immoral use of a law. The government has effectively quashed that power.

Also, in civil litigation a judgment is often decided on whether there is a "preponderance of the evidence" benefitting one side. This gives the judge enormous power to sway a jury; after all, if a jury believes there is more than a 50 percent probability that the defendant was negligent in causing the plaintiff's injury, the plaintiff pressing the lawsuit wins. This is a very low standard, especially when you consider that the defendant might be ordered to pay millions of dollars. Criminal law, on the other hand, requires that the jury declare a guilty verdict only when they think the defendant is guilty "beyond a reasonable doubt." A few tort claims (such as fraud) typically require that the plaintiff prove his/her case at a level of "clear and convincing evidence," which is a standard higher than preponderance, but it is still far short of guilty "beyond a reasonable doubt."

In civil cases in these litigious times, a judge may also order a jury to arrive at a particular verdict (called a "directed verdict"). A directed verdict is occasionally made when a jury refuses to follow a judge's instructions to arrive at a certain verdict.[20] In a criminal case, a judge may only order a directed verdict for acquittal; however, in a civil case, a judge may decide to direct a verdict of not guilty if there is a scarcity of evidence. The phrase "directed verdict" first arose when judges actually directed a jury to leave the courtroom, deliberate, and return with a verdict that was predetermined by the judge. This term has largely been replaced with the more politically correct phrase "judgment as a matter of law." However you parse it, this rule enables a judge to apply the law as he or she sees fit, which thereby prevents the jury from nullifying a law and voting on their consciences.

As a result of this judicial usurpation of the jury's constitutional rights, Judge Robert Bork said the United States is now a regime governed by a "judicial oligarchy,"[21] which has been brought about by what he described as a "judicial coup d'état" of individual rights. In less hyperbolic words, the government has seen fit to create rules to overrule the people.

Though common law has long allowed a judge to set aside a jury verdict when the judge thinks the verdict is contrary to the evidence or the law, common law precluded the judge from entering a verdict; a new trial, with a new jury, was the only course permissible. In *Slocum* v. *New York Insurance Co.* (1913) the Supreme Court upheld this common law rule that simply allowed a judge to let another jury adjudicate the case. Later cases, however, have undermined *Slocum*, which has allowed the Court to develop exceptions to Seventh Amendment rights. Generally, such newfound judicial power has only been exercised in extreme cases. Bork and other conservatives are alarmed, however, because cases build precedents that result in new precedents that slowly, case by case, separate the judiciary from the Constitution.

This is all occurring on a state-by-state basis because the Supreme Court doesn't think the Seventh Amendment requirement of a jury in civil trials is a fundamental right. In his majority opinion in *Palko* v. *Connecticut* (1937), Justice Benjamin Cardozo ruled that not all rights are equal; he found that some rights are "superior," while "justice …

would not perish" without others. The Supreme Court has not incorporated the Seventh Amendment, as it hasn't found that justice would perish without this amendment. So state and local governments do not have to obey the Seventh Amendment; however, the Supreme Court has found that state and local governments must adhere to most of the Bill of Rights. For example, the First Amendment and the Second Amendment have been incorporated by the Supreme Court, so they also restrict state and local governments. The Third Amendment hasn't been incorporated by the Supreme Court, but a Second Circuit found it to be incorporated. The Fourth Amendment has been fully incorporated. The Fifth Amendment has been fully incorporated except for the clause guaranteeing criminal prosecution only on a grand jury indictment. The Sixth Amendment has been fully incorporated, whereas the Seventh Amendment has not. The Eighth Amendment has been incorporated with respect to its protection against "cruel and unusual punishments," but no specific Supreme Court ruling on the incorporation of the "excessive fines" and "excessive bail" protections has been found to restrict state and local governments.[22]

The notion that some rights are inferior to others and so needn't be found to restrict state and local governments didn't occur to the Founding Fathers. They wrote and ratified the Bill of Rights as restrictions only on the federal government. They left states free to write and pass their own bills of rights. Since 1937, selective incorporation has, however, been largely accepted as standing precedent. Today even conservative justices are reluctant to debate the constitutionality of selective incorporation, as decades of case law have now been built upon this theory. Nevertheless, states today do make jury trials available for most civil cases above the level of small claims court.

Despite the problems resulting from an unbridled judiciary, it's what the flood of civil litigation has done to individual rights that would most disturb the Founding generation. This is why tort reform isn't as dry as it sounds.

Why Freedom Requires Tort Reform

Most Americans are with Dante. According to the American Bar Association, the United States has over one million lawyers—more per capita than any other country. And the abundance of attorneys hasn't made them more popular. According to a 2009 Rasmussen poll: "57 percent of voters nationwide favor limiting the amount of money a jury can award a plaintiff in a medical malpractice lawsuit." Despite this plurality, tort reform has proven to be too technically stupefying to become a viable campaign issue.

Regardless, the fundamental reason the Seventh Amendment was included in the Bill of Rights isn't so mind-numbing: the Seventh Amendment was ratified to protect individual freedom through a jury of our peers in civil trials. As such, these juries were designed to act as a check on federal power. The Founders knew that if judges were only accountable to the ruling political party, then the government would wield an absolute power over private industry. As corporations don't only defend themselves against civil-liability claims, but also have to aggressively defend their patents, products, and services in court, the courts need to be impartial, not weapons for politicians to utilize to raise campaign donations or support. The jury saved America from such authoritarianism via a politically controlled judiciary, but by subsequently making the rules of civil litigation overly friendly to trial attorneys, the government has sold many of our individual freedoms to what has been nicknamed "Trial Lawyers, Inc."

According to Bernie Marcus, a private investor and a co-founder of The Home Depot: "Class-action lawsuit filings rose more than 1,000 percent in state courts and 300 percent in federal courts during the 1990s. The costs, too, have been staggering and are reflected in higher prices for products and services—about $233 billion a year, or $3,200 for every family of four."[23]

Additionally, a study conducted by NERA Economic Consulting for the U.S. Chamber of Commerce found that small businesses paid $105.4 billion in liability costs in 2008. Small businesses have created 64 percent of all new jobs in the United States over the past fifteen years. As the U.S. Chamber of Commerce's Lisa Rickard said, "As America struggles out of this current economic downturn, this study shows that lawsuits continue to be a drag on job-creating small businesses." The study "Tort Liability Claims for Small Businesses" examined the enormous costs of the medical liability system for doctors in small groups and medical labs and found the liability price tag for these businesses totaled $28 billion in 2008. When medical malpractice costs were added to all other tort liability costs, the total for small businesses was $133.4 billion. What percentage of this money went legitimately to people who were harmed is difficult to estimate; also, how many billions went to the lawyers on both sides is tough to calculate–though we can presume at least one third did. The costs to everyday honest Americans, however, can be found in everything we buy, from car insurance to dog food.

Despite the costs and the public's view of tort reform, personal-injury lawyers have mostly been able to kill civil tort reform by obscuring the crux of the argument. They've shifted the tort-reform debate to what "preventative medicine" really adds to health-care costs, to whether punitive damages should be capped when corporations are making profits, and to other statistical smokescreens that obscure the liberty the Seventh Amendment was originally ratified to safeguard.

If civil libertarians are to attain real tort reform–which would then lower the costs of everything from shampoo to health insurance while at the same time winning back lost freedoms–they have to point out the liberties Americans are no longer permitted because everyone from our grandmothers to the federal government have to make decisions based on lawsuit avoidance. Despite the liberty the Seventh Amendment was originally ratified to protect, Americans now live in fear of lawsuits because the trial bar doesn't want them to be able to act as rational adults with responsibility for their own actions.

For much of this we can blame Democrats. According to OpenSecrets.org, in the past twenty years the American Association for Justice (AAJ)–formerly the Association of Trial Lawyers of America–ranks sixth overall in the amount of campaign contributions given. The AAJ is the trial lawyers' Washington lobbying group, and 90 percent of its $30.7 million in contributions since 1989 has gone into the pockets of Democrats.

Democrats are particularly indebted to the attorneys who use these loose rules to win verdicts and settlements. In the 2009–2010 election cycle, Senator Harry Reid (D-NV) reaped the biggest payday from the trial bar with $2,660,931, while the two Democratic senators from New York, Charles E. Schumer and Kirsten Gillibrand, followed close behind. In fact, in the 2009–2010 election cycle, Democrats raked in $78.1 million from attorneys, while Republicans took in $22.9 million.[24]

These political action committee (PAC) contributions are only the beginning, as contribution limits favor the people who can "bundle" donations. The plaintiffs' bar is well suited to raise money this way, as they have thousands of wealthy members willing to write $2,000 checks. Corporations are not so well distributed, nor are their interests so focused. The trial lawyers, on the other hand, have a narrow mandate: They simply lobby to maintain the lawsuit industry and to expand legal-liability rules that then result in yet more lawsuits.

In fact, cumulatively since 1990, the amount donated to federal political candidates by lawyers–excluding lobbyists–surpassed $1 billion, according to the Center for Responsive Politics (CRP). Given the amount of money the trial bar is pumping into the Democratic Party, perhaps it is not so remarkable that the first piece of legislation signed by President Obama–the Lilly Ledbetter Fair Pay Act of 2009–weakened statutes of limitation in employment lawsuits to give attorneys more time to suit. Such tweaks to the law to benefit trial attorneys is why, in 2002, the late Fred Baron, a Texas trial lawyer and Democratic fundraiser, reacted to a *Wall Street Journal* editorial that asserted the trial bar was "all but running the Senate" by quipping, "I really, strongly disagree with that. Particularly the 'all but.'"[25]

Baron wasn't kidding. The Lilly Ledbetter Fair Pay Act of 2009 amended the Civil Rights Act of 1964 by stating that the 180-day statute of limitations for filing an equal-pay lawsuit regarding pay discrimination wouldn't be tied to the time the pay was agreed on, but would rather reset with each new "discriminatory paycheck." This change extended the period in which people could suit, in some cases by years. Laws such as these destroy merit pay increases, as an employer is afraid to give a raise to one particularly hardworking or enterprising employee without giving the same bump in pay to all the others, as one of the others could scream discrimination and suit. The law was another gift to the trial bar. The Supreme Court decision *Ledbetter* v. *Goodyear Tire & Rubber Co.* (2007) held that the statute of limitations for presenting an equal-pay lawsuit begins at the date the pay was agreed upon, not at the date of the most recent paycheck. The trial bar lobbied and changed that.

This was too technical a change for the public to become passionate about, but it was another small tweak in the law that allows Trial Lawyers, Inc. to continue sopping America's corporations and governments with lawsuits that act to erode the fundamental freedoms the Seventh Amendment was written to protect.

For example, Americans might find it astounding that lawyers have so rigged the system that by flooding the federal government with lawsuits they virtually guarantee that the government will be responsible for their fees—to the tune of $250 per hour. Two sources of federal money provide reimbursement for legal fees for any individual or organization that files a lawsuit against the federal government and wins. One, called the Judgment Fund, is a congressional line-item appropriation used solely for cases related to the Endangered Species Act, the Clean Water Act, and other environmental laws. The second method is through the Equal Access to Justice Act (EAJA), which was supposedly enacted to help individuals and small businesses take on the federal government. The EAJA prohibits reimbursement to for-profit corporations worth more than $7 million; however, non-profit groups are exempt from this restriction.

Groups such as the Center for Biological Diversity, an extreme leftwing environmental nonprofit group, play this fixed game. In fact, according to Karen Budd-Fallen, a senior partner at Budd-Fallen Law Offices L.L.C., the Center for Biological Diversity filed more than

400 lawsuits and 150 appeals in federal courts in the last ten years. Why? "It's a numbers game," says Bud-Fallen. Many of these environmental lawsuits are based on technicalities, such as the federal government's failure to meet a strict filing deadline or to follow a specific environmental procedure. When the federal government fails according to these technical criteria, they have to pay the lawyer's fees of the person or group suiting.

Most of the lawsuits have little to do with actually preserving wildlife or the environment. In one such case, in April 2010, the Center for Biological Diversity filed a bulk petition requesting the U.S. Fish and Wildlife Service (USFWS) to review 404 species from the southeastern United States. According to the law, the USFWS has ninety days to consider each animal listed in the petition and a year to make a final determination whether to list the species as endangered or threatened. It's all but impossible to make those deadlines when the system is overwhelmed, but that's exactly why these groups file bulk petitions. When the agencies fail to meet any benchmark, the environmental attorneys get $250 per hour.

To shed light on this environmental slush fund, Representative Cynthia Lummis (R-WY) sponsored the Open EAJA Act of 2010, which would list exactly who is receiving these legal fees. Yes, that's right, the government hasn't even been required to keep track of which group and/or person is being paid by these funds. This bill would at least let the American people know who is getting their tax money from the government. Then some savvy watchdog can start a website as a sort of public rogue-attorney gallery of the biggest bilkers for each year. This oversight from an outraged public is just what attorneys want to avoid.

Overall, the civil-litigation rules are so friendly to the trial bar that America is one of the few countries in the world that allows punitive damages. Generally, punitive damages are not awarded in order to compensate the plaintiff, but in order to punish and make an example of the defendant. Punitive damages are awarded only in special cases where conduct is thought to be egregiously invidious. These awards are subject to the limitations imposed by the due process of law clauses of the Fifth and the

Fourteenth Amendments. Despite these conditions, punitive damages actually run counter to the criminal-justice system; after all, the civil-justice system in the United States does not have the same procedural protections as the criminal-justice system. Allowing punitive damages punishes people for wrongful conduct without allowing them the ordinary procedural protections that are present in a criminal trial.

Punitive damages can be shocking; for example, in 1999, a Los Angeles County jury awarded $4.8 billion in punitive damages against General Motors to a group of six people whose 1979 Chevrolet Malibu was rear-ended by a drunk driver, causing it to catch fire. A judge reduced the amount to $1.2 billion.[26] Some argue that such eye-popping damage awards are a result of the jury system, but in this case a judge still went for $1.2 billion! Whether a judge or a jury decides these cases, sound laws—including caps on awards—need to create a more just system. Without such a sensible tort reform, all of us will keep being nickel-and-dimed so a few can strike it rich in the lawsuit lottery.

Though trial lawyers and some politicians claim that restorative justice, which these punitive judgments are based on, actually dates back to antiquity—in ancient Israel the Pentateuch specified restitution for property crimes; in the kingdom of Sumer, some 2,000 years before Christ, the Code of Ur-Nammu required restitution for offenses of violence; and in England the Laws of Ethelbert of Kent, at about 600 AD, included detailed restitution guidelines—even these ancient laws stipulated amounts or caps on restitution by qualifying the money owed to some real value.

Critics of caps on damages contend that legislatures violate the principle of separation of powers when they attempt to impose damage caps on juries. In *Best* v. *Taylor Machine Works* (1997), the Illinois Supreme Court ruled that a $500,000 cap on non-economic damages functioned as a "legislative remittitur" and invaded the power of the judiciary, in violation of the separation of powers clause. The court decided that only judges are empowered to reduce excessive verdicts and so ruled the legislature couldn't intervene—forget runaway juries, this ruling is an example of a runaway judiciary. Legislatures in every state and at the federal level set sentencing guidelines, fines, and more, yet they can't enact caps on civil damages? Legislatures need to remember there is a constitutional process for dealing with such tyrants in robes.

Other tort reforms are necessary in the United States. According to The American Tort Reform Association (ATRA), these include: limitations on liability for medical malpractice; the abolition of the rule of joint and several liability; the abolition of the collateral source doctrine; limiting the period in which someone can suit; limitations on noneconomic damages; and other reforms so that individuals, insurance companies, and corporations can at least keep their risk within calculable reason.

That such changes are necessary is even obvious to European socialists, so much so that they mock the United States for being a "compensation culture." For example, in some international civil cases, lawyers actually prefer that the case be heard in America, as U.S. laws regarding civil trials make it much easier for them to win huge sums of money from corporations in U.S. courts.

To be fair, tort compensation does get complex when looking at specific personal injuries. Though compensation can easily be applied to property damage where the replacement value can be based on a market price, it is difficult to quantify the injuries to a person's body and/or mind, as there is no legal market for severed legs and sanity is priceless. To address this, some countries have developed creepy scales of damage awards. For instance, in the United Kingdom, the loss of a thumb is compensated at £18,000, an arm is worth £72,000, and two arms is £150,000.[27] These heartless, statist attempts at justice would be horrifying if they weren't so perversely funny; however, it's not possible to calculate damages for pain and suffering by any such morbid scale; for example, you could double or triple or even divide all the awards by the "golden ratio" (1.618) and they would still make just as much sense as the amounts the English decided on.

For tort reform to be just, it must give the jury a cap on damages (caps set by elected representatives). A jury could then use their consciences to decide on an exact amount. Meanwhile, punitive damages should be decided in a criminal court. A civil court shouldn't punish a company that has done something criminally wrong–arbitrary punitive damages are not a fair way to adjudicate criminal justice, as they are not consistent.

Some say they could fix all this by simply repealing the Sixth and Seventh Amendments and allowing juries of experts to decide these cases. In fact, the tort reform advocacy group Common Good proposed creating specialized medical courts where medically trained judges render decisions. This "solution," however, would do exactly what the Framers wanted to avoid: it would mean that civil trials would be completely ruled by the government via agents of the state. This wouldn't advance individual rights, it would empower the state.

To address some of these tort-reform issues, Republicans backed the U.S. Class Action Fairness Act of 2005. This Act was the first major legislation passed after President George W. Bush won in 2004. Business groups and tort reform supporters lobbied for the legislation, arguing that it was needed to curb class-action lawsuit abuse. The Act gave federal courts jurisdiction to certain class-action lawsuits when the amount being sought exceeds $5 million. The Act was designed to reduce "forum shopping" by plaintiffs in friendly state courts by expanding federal jurisdiction to class actions where there is not "complete diversity" giving federal jurisdiction over class actions against out-of-state defendants. Proponents argued that civil law attorneys were venue-shopping cases to "judicial hellholes," such as Madison County, Illinois, where they knew they had a higher chance of getting a jury to grant huge sums to the plaintiffs.

The Act also requires greater federal scrutiny of procedures for the review of class-action settlements and can reduce attorney's fees that are deemed excessive. For example, in an Alabama class-action lawsuit involving Bank of Boston, the attorneys' fees actually exceeded the settlement. In this case the plaintiffs actually lost money to their attorneys for the "victory."[28]

Only one Republican member of Congress voted against the U.S. Class Action Fairness Act of 2005, and a Republican president signed it into law. However, the debate over tort reform is not always a partisan affair. As a senator, Barack Obama voted for the Class Action Fairness Act of 2005. Nevertheless, the trial bar, which mostly supports Democrats because Democrats mostly support them, argued that the legislation would deprive Americans of legal recourse, as the bill pushed some class-action suits into federal court, where the Seventh Amendment applies. Critics also argued that the expansion of federal jurisdiction came at the expense of states' rights, something Republicans have historically protested; however, proponents responded that the bill is consistent with the Framers' original intent for the role of federal courts and diversity jurisdiction as was expressed by Alexander Hamilton in Federalist No. 80.

The American Tort Reform Association (ATRA) argues that the "cost of the U.S. tort system for 2003 was $246 billion, or $845 per citizen or $3,380 for a family of four." But Trial Lawyers, Inc. consistently denies there has been a "liability crisis" running up costs. It's important to realize that this whole statistical war is deceptive. As Mark Twain quipped, "There are three kinds of lies: Lies, damned lies, and statistics." What is at stake is our individual liberty. While the jury system has largely kept the political party in power from using the judiciary to simply punish its opponents, the civil system has been rigged to benefit trial attorneys at the expense of individual liberty.

To regain the right to swim beyond the ropes and to allow neighbors on our property without fear of being liable when some kid trips, we have to regain control of civil litigation with tort reform. When conservative politicians realize and articulate this, we will begin to win back our American freedoms.

AMENDMENT VIII

Excessive bail shall not be required, nor excessive fines imposed,
nor cruel and unusual punishments inflicted.

"The Court must be living in another world. Day by day,
case by case, it is busy designing a Constitution for a country
I do not recognize."[1]
–Justice Antonin Scalia

I n the middle of a sultry night on August 11, 1967, William Micke, a father of five children, woke to noises in his Savannah, Georgia, home. He investigated and found a burglar, William Henry Furman, in his kitchen. What Micke said or did next we'll never know because Furman pulled a revolver and killed Micke. Furman then fled into the night. Moments later Micke's wife and children found him dying of a chest wound on their kitchen floor. His wife phoned for help.

Police soon captured Furman. He still had the murder weapon in his possession. This made it easy for a jury, a year later, to give Furman a sentence of death.

The state, however, never did kill Furman. His case was appealed all the way to the U.S. Supreme Court on the grounds that the death penalty should be unconstitutional. William Henry Furman became famous. The Left said he was a poster child of overzealous law-enforcement and cruel laws. Attorneys looking for a way to end the death penalty made him the central figure in what became *Furman* v. *Georgia* (1972), a class-action case in which the Supreme Court halted the use of the death penalty in all fifty states until the Court changed its mind in 1976. In this 5–4 decision, the Court ruled that "arbitrary" procedures used to administer the death penalty in the states violated the "cruel and unusual punishments" clause of the Eighth Amendment. This spared Furman and other prisoners on death row, and left families like the Mickes without the justice they expected in such clear murder cases.

The Supreme Court was able to stop the states from utilizing the death penalty because, in a previous case, *Louisiana ex rel. Francis* v. *Resweber* (1947), the Supreme Court assumed that the Eighth Amendment's "cruel and unusual punishments" clause also applies to state and local governments through the Fourteenth Amendment. This gave the Supreme Court the ability to squelch what had always been a state power. (The Court, however, hasn't ruled on whether the "excessive bail" or "excessive fines" clauses apply to the states; as a result, there are major differences in bails set in various states, as well as fines levied for similar offenses.)

In *Furman* v. *Georgia,* Justice Thurgood Marshall argued he had to morally determine what the voting public *really* wanted; after all, if the people could only stand at his intellectual height, then they would certainly concur with his enlightened opinion of the death penalty:

> It has often been noted that American citizens know almost nothing about capital punishment….I believe that the great mass of citizens would conclude on the basis of the material already considered that the death penalty is immoral and therefore unconstitutional….Assuming knowledge of all the facts presently available regarding capital punishment the average citizen would, in my opinion, find it shocking to his conscience and sense of justice. For this reason alone capital punishment cannot stand.[2]

Between other paternal pats on the people's heads by the liberal block of judges, Justice William Brennan outlined what the majority of the Court required of the states: "There are, then, four principles by which we may determine whether a particular punishment is 'cruel and unusual.'" A "punishment must not by its severity be degrading to human dignity"; it cannot be "inflicted in wholly arbitrary fashion"; a punishment can't be inflicted "that is clearly and totally rejected throughout society"; and the state can't enact a "severe punishment that is patently unnecessary."

Historically, punishments considered to be cruel and unusual were things like being burned at the stake, being disemboweled, and being put on a rack and stretched until your ligaments tore free. But this new test didn't mean just those horrible things—it also meant whatever five or nine justices might find objectionable. In fact, to make certain they had the power to do as they liked with the Constitution, Justice Brennan wrote that he didn't expect any state to pass a law that obviously violated any one of these principles, so Court decisions regarding the Eighth Amendment would need to involve a "cumulative" analysis of the implication of each of the four principles, so the justices could add them up and see if they violated the Eighth Amendment. This vague test puts all the power in the hands of the Court and allows the justices to rule without any specific reason whatsoever.

Indeed, by instituting this vague and subjective "cumulative" test, Justice Brennan positioned the Court so that a majority of justices can do as they please with the Eighth Amendment. He rigged the system so the little people—the common folk who just don't know what's best for them in this constitutional republic—can be morally guided by the philosophers on the Supreme Court. Before this ruling, the Eighth Amendment only stopped the government from doing "cruel and unusual" things that the people found objectionable to American citizens; after this ruling, the Court could overrule the people's will and do as they pleased.

Micke's five children, however, didn't have justice served up by the Court's intelligentsia. After the *Furman* decision put an administrative hold on capital punishment in 1972, states amended their death penalty statutes to meet the Court's new guidelines. Subsequently, many of the named defendants that led to the case collectively referred to as *Furman* were again given death sentences in their respective states. State supreme courts then upheld their death sentences according to the new rules outlined in *Furman.* The defendants appealed to the Supreme Court to review their death sentences, asking the Supreme Court this time to go beyond *Furman* and declare once and for all the death penalty to be a "cruel and unusual punishment" forever barred by the Eighth Amendment.

Of course, despite any claim to moral superiority by the liberals on the Court, the justices couldn't go quite so far. After all, even an unenlightened everyday American can clearly see the death penalty is constitutional because the U.S. Constitution mentions capital crimes four times. For example, the Fifth Amendment says: "No person shall be held to answer for any capital, or otherwise infamous crime, unless on a presentment or indictment of a Grand Jury...." The Constitution actually only requires three things before a sentence of death may be imposed: a grand jury indictment, no double jeopardy, and a jury trial. And yet the Supreme Court banned the death penalty for being unconstitutional.

This obvious break with the Constitution forced the Supreme Court to back down–though only after legislating from the bench. In *Greg* v. *Georgia* (1976), the Supreme Court developed two broad guidelines that legislatures must follow in order to craft sentencing procedures for capital crimes. First, the state and federal laws must provide objective criteria to direct and limit the sentencing discretion of a jury. For example, a rule must be instituted that a jury that finds guilt can't also decide if the guilty person should live or die. A sentence of death must then pass appellate review. Also, the law must allow the judge or jury to take into account the character and record of an individual defendant.

So the question the Court resolved in these cases wasn't whether the death sentence imposed on each of the individual defendants was cruel, but rather whether the process by which those sentences were imposed was rational, objectively reviewable, and done according to the Court's multi-faceted regulations and the justices' subjective view of society.

Now though the Court was certainly attempting to establish clearer moral guidelines, the conservatives on the bench pointed out that such regulations should be passed by elected representatives, not adjudicated by a majority of nine people with lifetime appointments. As former judge Robert H. Bork wrote, "If the people have enacted an immoral law, it is the judge's duty to enforce it or resign."[3] A judge can rule whether a law is constitutional, and they can rule on what the law says, but they aren't supposed to decide if a law is moral, no matter what Justice Marshall claims.

By playing philosophers, the justices stole justice from the Micke family. William Henry Furman, who was jailed in 1967 after murdering William Micke, avoided the death penalty and was paroled in 1984. However, as this book was being written, Furman was back in jail for another attempted robbery. Furman got twenty years for a 2004 robbery conviction in Bibb County, Georgia. Furman had broken into a home occupied by a mother and her 10-year-old daughter. The mother called 911 while Furman was in the house. She spoke to a dispatcher while fooling the not-so-bright Furman by speaking as if she were talking to a friend. The police raced over and arrested Furman. The mother and daughter were unharmed. But later, when the police searched Furman, they found a pair of the 10-year-old girl's panties in his pocket.[4]

This hero of the Left who should have paid with his life nearly destroyed more innocent American lives. Nevertheless, the so-called "mainstream media" ignored the re-arrest of this murderer.

What Is a "Cruel and Unusual" Punishment?

The phrase "cruel and unusual punishment" first appeared in the English Bill of Rights in 1689. To put this right into context, realize that in England in 1689, the set punishment for treason was to hang the convicted person, not until they were dead, but just until they were pretty well terrorized. The person was then cut down and tied so he could watch someone disembowel him and burn his innards right before his still-living eyes. Finally, an executioner would behead and quarter the then-writhing enemy of the state just like a butcher would dismember a cow in a slaughterhouse. The British in the seventeenth century only did this to men convicted of treason. Any woman convicted of treason was supposed to be burned at the stake.

Whether being burned alive is more merciful than being gutted is hard to say. The point is that the Eighth Amendment's "cruel and unusual" clause refers to what a society can—or cannot—stomach.

In 1791—the year the states ratified the Bill of Rights—federal law found that larceny could be punished with a whip. Other physical punishments, such as branding, ear cropping, and pillorying, were also common in late-eighteenth century America. Most executions were done with a rope, though a firing squad might be a traitor's fate. These days, however, such punishments are considered to be cruel and certainly unusual; however, the Eighth Amendment didn't play a role in these changes. The Supreme Court didn't spend the nineteenth century ruling thumbscrews and lashings to be unconstitutional. The Eighth Amendment was actually rarely mentioned in the nineteenth century. People, through their elected representatives, evolved laws to mirror the public's conception of what was too cruel and unusual to be permitted.

Whereas in 1776 common punishments included public hangings and public pillories (a device that confined a convicted person's neck and wrists and forced them to stand in a compromising position in the public square), the pillory was formally abolished as a form of punishment in England and Wales in 1837, but remained legal, though infrequently used, in parts of the United States until 1872. In 1834, Pennsylvania became the first state to move executions away from the public eye. In 1846, Michigan became the first state to abolish the death penalty for all crimes except treason. Most states continue to use capital punishment today; in fact, as of 2010, only fifteen states and the District of Columbia did not allow its practice. Capital punishment is still viewed as a state right.

Obviously, the standard of what is cruel and unusual has been evolving throughout U.S. history. Though the Supreme Court rarely adjudicated the Eighth Amendment until well into the twentieth century, in one of the few nineteenth century cases, *Wilkerson* v. *Utah* (1878), the Supreme Court commented that drawing and quartering, public dissecting, burning alive, and disemboweling would all constitute cruel and unusual punishment. However, it wasn't until 1910, in *Weems* v. *United States*, that the Supreme Court for the first time overturned a criminal sentence as cruel and unusual. In this case the punishment, called "cadena temporal," mandated "hard and painful labor" and shackling for the duration of the sentence. The Court found this to be cruel, if not unusual.

So given this slow change in what constitutes "cruel and unusual," did the Framers intend only to ban punishments, such as drawing and quartering or having prisoners boiled in oil, which were recognized as cruel at the time of the amendment's adoption in America? Or did they expect that what constitutes a cruel and unusual punishment would change over time as society's "sense of decency" evolved?

One clue to the expectations of the Framers comes from the debates of the First Congress, which proposed the Eighth Amendment in 1789. On the floor of the House, Representative Livermore complained about the vagueness of the amendment's language: "It is sometimes necessary to hang a man, villains often deserve a whipping, and perhaps having their ears cut off, but are we in the future to be prevented from inflicting those punishments because they are 'cruel'?" Despite Livermore's thoughtful ramblings, the vague "cruel and unusual punishments" clause, which is subject to new interpretation over time, was left unchanged, and the amendment was ratified. This is why most scholars say that what is cruel and unusual was meant to evolve (or devolve) according to the standards of society.

Indeed, according to William Blackstone's *Commentaries on the Laws of England*, a treatise published in volumes from 1765 to 1769: "[H]owever unlimited the power of the court may seem, it is far from being wholly arbitrary; but its discretion is regulated by law. For the bill of rights has particularly declared, that excessive fines ought not to be imposed, nor cruel and unusual punishments inflicted...."[5]

After the American Revolution, George Mason, Patrick Henry, and others wanted to ensure this restriction would also be applied as a limitation on the new federal government. Mason warned that, otherwise, Congress may "inflict unusual and severe punishments."[6] Henry emphasized that, without this restriction, the federal government might depart from precedent. Henry said, "What has distinguished our ancestors?–That they would not admit of tortures, or cruel and barbarous punishment."[7] Ultimately, Henry and Mason prevailed, and the Eighth Amendment was adopted. James Madison strengthened the wording by changing "ought" to "shall" ("Excessive bail *shall* not be required, nor excessive fines imposed, nor cruel and unusual punishments inflicted") and proposed the amendment to Congress in 1789.[8]

So though other amendments–despite what "living Constitution" liberals claim–are not subject to the changing viewpoints of society (they can only be altered by further amendments to the Constitution or by runaway judiciaries), the Eighth Amendment has basically followed what a majority of Americans define to be "cruel and unusual." This understanding prompted Justice Joseph Story, in 1833, to write that the Eighth Amendment "would seem to be wholly unnecessary in a free government, since it is scarcely possible that any departure of such a government should authorize or justify such atrocious conduct."[9] If what is "cruel and unusual" changes as society does, then the protection is unnecessary.

Story's point, however, relies on the premise that a free, democratically elected government wouldn't be able to use cruel and unusual punishments because the public would vote them out if they did. This firm ground disappears, however, when a rogue Supreme Court with lifetime appointments decides to enforce its will, regardless of the Constitution and the opinion of the people, upon every state and the federal government. This is why it's alarming that the Supreme Court was able to rule the death penalty unconstitutional from 1972 to 1976, as a majority of the American people and the states have always been in favor of capital punishment for the most extreme crimes.

The "Evolving Standards of Decency Test"

To shape the Eighth Amendment according to their worldview, not necessarily the peoples' will via elected representatives, Supreme Court justices devised the "Evolving Standards of Decency Test." This judicial test was invented by the Supreme Court in *Trop* v. *Dulles* (1958) when Chief Justice Earl Warren deemed that "the [Eighth] Amendment must draw its meaning from the evolving standards of decency that mark the progress of a maturing society."[10] *Trop* v. *Dulles* was a federal case in which the Supreme Court ruled 5–4 that it was unconstitutional for the government to revoke a person's citizenship as a punishment for a crime. He thought the decency of Americans wouldn't then allow such a punishment.

Justice Warren was correct that society has long viewed the Eighth Amendment according to its changing standards of decency; it's just that before *Trop* v. *Dulles,* the Supreme Court had mostly allowed legislatures to define what "cruel and unusual" meant and only acted to apply the law as written. Subsequent to *Trop* v. *Dulles,* however, the Court began looking to "societal developments" to determine what the American people's "evolving standards of decency" should be. This enabled the Court to do as it pleased. Before the Court took this tack the government, according to the Eighth Amendment, was simply restricted from administering punishments that the people found objectionable—meaning the government was at the mercy of the people. When justices decided they knew best, the people and their representative government were at the mercy of the will of five out of nine people with lifetime appointments.

As Professor John Stinneford pointed out, the evolving-standards test misinterprets intent of the Framers of the Bill of Rights who understood the word "unusual" to mean "contrary to long usage." The Eighth Amendment's original meaning requires the Supreme Court to compare punishments with the longstanding principles and precedents of common law and elected legislatures, not with their own nebulous notions of "societal consensus" and contemporary "standards of decency."[11]

With this "Evolving Standards of Decency Test" in its arsenal, in the second half of the twentieth century the Supreme Court got busy defining the Eighth Amendment. In *Trop* v. *Dulles,* the case the Court used to create this new test, the Supreme Court held that punishing a natural-born citizen for a crime by taking away his citizenship is unconstitutional, as it was "more primitive than torture." The Court ruled that because taking away citizenship involved the "total destruction of the individual's status in organized society," it was "cruel and unusual." When a legislature decides a peculiar thing like this, it becomes a campaign issue; when the Supreme Court does, the people's will becomes irrelevant.

Within a few years of *Trop* v. *Dulles*, the Supreme Court started to really stick its nose into American lives. In *Robinson* v. *California* (1962), the Supreme Court decided that a California law authorizing a 90-day jail sentence for "be[ing] addicted to the use of narcotics" violated the Eighth Amendment, as narcotics addiction "is apparently an illness," and California was attempting to punish people based on the state of this illness. The Court wrote: "To be sure, imprisonment for ninety days is not, in the abstract, a punishment which is either cruel or unusual. But the question cannot be considered in the abstract. Even one day in prison would be a cruel and unusual punishment for the 'crime' of having a common cold."

However, in *Powell* v. *Texas* (1968) the Court upheld a statute barring public intoxication by distinguishing from *Robinson* on the basis that *Powell* dealt with a person who was drunk in public, not someone addicted to alcohol. Traditionally, the length of a prison sentence was not subject to scrutiny under the Eighth Amendment, regardless of the crime for which the sentence was imposed.

The next big Eighth Amendment case was *Furman* v. *Georgia* (1972) (mentioned earlier), which banned the death penalty until the Court created its legislation for how the death penalty must be administered in *Greg* v. *Georgia* (1976). The Supreme Court has since placed further limitations on the death penalty in *Atkins* v. *Virginia* (2002), which found the death penalty to be unconstitutional for persons with an IQ below 70 (the baseline for mental retardation). And in *Roper* v. *Simmons* (2005) the Court found that the death penalty is unconstitutional if the defendant is under the age of eighteen at the time the crime was committed.

In the middle of all this tweaking and evolving, it was not until *Solem* v. *Helm* (1983) that the Supreme Court held that incarceration could constitute cruel and unusual punishment if it were "disproportionate" in duration to the offense. The Court outlined three factors to determine if the sentence is excessive: "(i) the gravity of the offense and the harshness of the penalty; (ii) the sentences imposed on other criminals in the same jurisdiction; and (iii) the sentences imposed for commission of the same crime in other jurisdictions." The Court held that in the circumstances of the case before it and the factors to be considered, a sentence of life imprisonment without parole for cashing a $100 check on a closed account was cruel and unusual. Of course, such a hypothetical has never occurred and would result in public outrage if it did, but the Court was going to extremes—even if the extremes didn't exist—to get its way.

So then, would it be unconstitutional to give a life sentence for possession of cocaine? This question was the issue presented in *Harmelin* v. *Michigan* (1991), in which the Supreme Court (5–4) upheld the sentence of life imprisonment for a first-time offense of possession of cocaine. However, in *Harmelin* a fractured Court found the excessive sentence test outlined in *Solem* v. *Helm* to be inadequate and held that for non-capital sentences, the Eighth Amendment only constrains the length of prison terms by a "gross disproportionality principle." Under this principle, the Court sustained a mandatory sentence of life without parole imposed for possession of 672 grams or more of cocaine.

In *Harmelin*, Justice Scalia, joined by Chief Justice Rehnquist, said, "The Eighth Amendment contains no proportionality guarantee." Justice Scalia added, "If 'cruel and unusual punishments' included disproportionate punishments, the separate prohibition of disproportionate fines (which are certainly punishments) would have been entirely superfluous." Justice Scalia is right. Why would the Framers of the Bill of Rights separate a proportional punishment unless they meant it to be separate?

The proportionality of crimes has actually often come up with regards to cruel and unusual punishment. In England, sheriffs originally determined whether to grant bail to criminal suspects. Since some abused their power, Parliament passed a statute in 1275 that defined bailable and non-bailable offenses. The king's judges, however, often subverted the provisions of the law. It was held that an individual could be held without bail upon the Sovereign's command. Eventually, the Petition Right of 1628 argued that the king did not have such authority. Later, technicalities in the law were exploited to keep the accused imprisoned without bail even where the offenses were bailable; such loopholes were for the most part closed by the Habeas Corpus Act of 1679. Thereafter, judges were compelled to set bail, though they sometimes required amounts that couldn't be raised. Finally, the English Bill of Rights (1689) held that "excessive bail ought not to be required." Nevertheless, the bill did not determine the distinction between bailable and non-bailable offenses. Thus, the Eighth Amendment has been interpreted to mean that bail may be denied if the charges are sufficiently serious.

The Supreme Court has also permitted "preventive" detention without bail. In *United States* v. *Salerno* (1987), the Supreme Court held that the only limitation imposed by the bail clause is that "the government's proposed conditions of release or detention not be 'excessive' in light of the perceived evil."

The Supreme Court isn't elected by the people, it's comprised of nine people with lifetime appointments, and it changes too slowly to be a true reflection of the people's will. So without even looking to the powers it was vested by the Constitution, it's clear the Court can't effectively write sentencing guidelines and other specific regulations. Nor is it supposed to write legislation. These are just some of the reasons why the Court's attempts to adjudicate its view of what is "cruel and unusual" quickly becomes problematic, as it actually thwarts the will of the voting public. This is especially true in the states—a majority of voters in California don't always agree with a majority of voters in Wyoming, and both populaces like it that way. The Supreme Court too often ignores this state rights principal and sets a national policy that curbs individual and state freedoms. Often they do this in areas that were not even supposed to be federal areas of the law.

This fact was clearly exhibited in *Hudson* v. *McMillan* (1992). Keith Hudson, an inmate at the state penitentiary in Angola, Louisiana, sued three corrections security officers for punching him in the face and stomach. One of the officers held Hudson in place while another beat him.

The Supreme Court voted 7–2 that the beating was a violation of the "cruel and unusual punishment" clause. Justice Clarence Thomas wrote the dissenting opinion, joined by Justice Scalia. Thomas argued that the judgment had not only ignored the "significant injury" requirement, but had loosened the Eighth Amendment "from its historical moorings." What, after all, did the Framers mean by "barbarous" punishment? They clearly meant disemboweling, the thumbscrew, and maybe drawing and quartering. How could mere fisticuffs, something that occurs on playgrounds every day, be found to be a "cruel and unusual" punishment? Thus Thomas concluded, "A use of force that causes only insignificant harm to a prisoner may be immoral, it may be tortuous, it may be criminal, and it may even be remediable under other provisions of the Federal Constitution, but it is not 'cruel and unusual punishment.'"

Ruling this assault to be "cruel and unusual" opens the door to just about any physical or physiological assault by the police or other public officials being ruled unconstitutional under the Eighth Amendment. Such an expansive view of the Eighth Amendment might even give some enterprising attorneys the notion they can use the "cruel and unusual punishments" clause as another means to suit for every insult or mishap that results from government actions. To expose the absurdity of this liberal logic, a conservative might even point out that the IRS tax code, according to such an expansive definition, is a "cruel and unusual" punishment; after all, there's no doubt an astute legal team could form a class-action suit from victims of IRS audits who'd done everything in their power to comprehend the five-million-word tax code and all its exemptions, clauses, and mealy-mouthed legal language, yet just couldn't. Such victims of the bureaucracy certainly suffer mental anguish, and the physical search and seizures of the records can be tortuous.

In 1972, Chief Justice Warren Burger cut through all this liberal obfuscation of the Eighth Amendment's original intent and articulated what the role of the Supreme Court should be when he wrote in his dissent to *Furman* v. *Georgia*:

> [O]f all our fundamental guarantees, the ban on "cruel and unusual punishments" is one of the most difficult to translate into judicially manageable terms....[Therefore] it is essential to our role as a court that we not seize upon the enigmatic character of the guarantee as an invitation to enact our personal predilections into law.[12]

The idea that judges should simply apply the law is a straightforward, just, and historically accurate job description of what a judge is paid to do. Liberals justices abhor this elegantly simple definition because it restricts their power. The Left wants an empowered liberal judiciary that can even extend constitutional rights to terrorists who are not U.S. citizens.

Do Terrorists Get Eighth Amendment Rights?

The Eighth Amendment's biggest test is coming from how we fight the "War on Terror." Liberals claim the high moral ground with regards to the Eighth Amendment's ban on torture, but do they really stand on such lofty heights? The Left champions two basic arguments that are currently defining the Eighth Amendment: first, they say waterboarding and other "enhanced interrogation techniques" are torture barred by both the Eighth Amendment and international law; and second, they say the foreign terrorists being held in the Guantánamo Bay detainment facility in Cuba deserve U.S. constitutional rights, including Eighth Amendment protections.

Are they right?

The Eighth Amendment prohibits "cruel and unusual punishments." This at first seems to bar torture in all instances. Yet, as Harvard University Professor Alan Dershowitz pointed out in his book *Why Terrorism Works,* the Eighth Amendment has long been limited to punishments proscribed to convicted felons in the U.S. penal system. In fact, the Supreme Court explained as much in *Ingraham* v. *Wright* (1977): "An examination of the history of the [Eighth] Amendment and the decisions of this Court construing the proscription against cruel and unusual punishment confirms that it was designed to protect those convicted of crimes. We adhere to this long-standing limitation." This constraint alone determines that the Guantanamo detainees don't have Eighth Amendment rights.

After all, the words "torture" and "punishment" are not synonyms. Torture is something that is administered—whether legally or not—to obtain a confession or information. Torture is not, by definition, wielded by a jury or a judge, whereas judges and juries do exercise punishments for crimes. So before this debate is begun, it must be pointed out that the dictionary clearly indicates that the Eighth Amendment isn't referring to torture. Other laws certainly outlaw torture; the Eighth Amendment refers only to punishments.

There are also numerous precedents dealing with "lawful combatants" during World War II and other conflicts that have found non-U.S. citizens being held outside U.S. territory don't have U.S. constitutional protections. This is why the Geneva Conventions outline specific procedures for dealing with enemies captured on the battlefield. These agreements were written and signed so that governments couldn't and wouldn't use their own standards.

Of course, though 194 countries have ratified the Geneva Conventions, al-Qaeda and the Taliban haven't put pen to paper and promised not to cut off any more heads or to target civilians. And, as unlawful combatants not fighting for a country's flag, they don't seem to have legal rights under the Geneva Conventions.

Still, the United States has signed the Geneva Conventions, and torture and other forms of cruel, inhuman, and degrading treatment are prohibited under American criminal statutes and by international law, including several human rights treaties that were ratified by the United States in the 1990s. Because the Constitution's "supremacy" clause says treaties are "the supreme Law of the Land," these treaties certainly apply.

As a result, the International Convention on Civil and Political Rights (ICCPR) and the United Nations Convention Against Torture and Cruel, Inhuman and Degrading Treatments (UNCAT)—both of which were ratified by the United States—prohibit the United States from using cruel, inhuman, and degrading treatment.

However, when Congress ratified these treaties, they tweaked them so that the treaties legally define what is cruel and inhuman treatment according to the Eighth Amendment's definition—they didn't leave the definition open to international law and to the opinions of foreign activists and European law professors. So what we're still talking about here is the Eighth Amendment, as the United States uses its definition for these treaties. So then are the "enhanced interrogation techniques" torture according to the Eighth Amendment?

Before we begin to answer that question, it's necessary to point out that another wrench was thrown into the debate. In 2008 the U.S. Supreme Court further knotted this issue by ruling 5–4—with Justice Anthony Kennedy voting with the liberal bloc as the swing vote—in *Boumediene* v. *Bush* that the prisoners at Guantánamo Bay have habeas corpus rights found in the U.S. Constitution. The Court ruled: "The detainees in these cases are entitled to a prompt habeas corpus hearing...." A writ of habeas corpus is a summons with the force of a court order demanding that a prisoner be taken before the court, and that the officials present proof of authority, allowing the Court to determine if the government has the lawful power to detain the person. If the government does not have such authority, it must release the prisoner.

Basically this ruling has been forcing the government to act on each detainee's case. However, Attorney General Eric Holder, with the backing of President Barack Obama, has still been able to attempt to have Khalid Sheikh Mohammed, whom the *9/11 Commission Report* called "the principal architect of the 9/11 attacks," tried in New York City. Why? Because the Supreme Court also said its ruling "does not address the content of the law that governs" the Guantánamo detainees. The Court said whether U.S. criminal law or military law should be used "is a matter yet to be determined." So though *Boumediene* v. *Bush* overruled lower court decisions and gave the prisoners of the War on Terror habeas corpus rights under the U.S. Constitution, it didn't extend the entirety of the Constitution to Guantánamo Bay detainees. This 5–4 decision, however, does open the Constitution to further expansions of government power, because for the first time the Court gave limited rights to foreigners captured overseas.

In addition to this unprecedented 5–4 Supreme Court decision, there are other recent Supreme Court decisions, a lot more international law, U.S. Military regulations, and memos on torture written by the U.S. Justice Department for President George W. Bush, which together make it easy to get bogged down in this debate over "enhanced interrogation techniques" and the Eighth Amendment.

So to focus this debate on the Eight Amendment's role, it's helpful to realize that the only "enhanced interrogation technique" that has come under real legal challenge is "waterboarding." Waterboarding is typically accomplished by tying someone down, placing a cloth over their face, and pouring water into their nose and mouth to cause a gag reflex–the same desperate gulp for air a person has when he is drowning. When administered by a trained professional, there is presumably no actual threat of drowning.

So then, given that even international treaties mostly rely on the Eighth Amendment's definition of torture in the United States, is waterboarding torture? Waterboarding is not considered to be very painful, and it causes no lasting physical injuries. A 2005 U.S. Justice Department memo even indicated that Khalid Sheikh Mohammed was waterboarded 183 times in March 2003 alone as the government tried to force him to give critical information about people who are actively trying to murder Americans. Yet Khalid Sheikh Mohammed wasn't physically injured by all those gasps for air.[13] That doesn't sound very cruel.

In *Furman* v. *Georgia,* the Supreme Court did say a punishment is cruel and unusual if it's "degrading to human dignity." Of course, full-body airport scanners now used on U.S. citizens are also degrading to human dignity. But the *Furman* test doesn't really work either, as it utilizes a "cumulative" test to judge if something is torture. Whether the technique is "degrading" was only one segment of a four-part test to see if something is torture. The test also said a punishment cannot be "inflicted in wholly arbitrary fashion." Waterboarding Khalid Sheikh Mohammed is hardly arbitrary. The test found that a punishment can't be inflicted if it's "rejected throughout society." After Umar Farouk Abdulmutallab, the "underwear bomber," was captured, Rasmussen Reports found that 58 percent of U.S. voters said waterboarding should be used on him,[14] so it's not rejected by society. And the Court found a punishment can't be "patently unnecessary." Stopping the next terrorist attack isn't unnecessary.

With "degrading" being the only box checked in the cumulative test, waterboarding captured terrorists who are not U.S. citizens is not torture according to the *Furman* test. (Americans, however, would likely "reject throughout society" the waterboarding of U.S. citizens, which would prohibit it according to two parts of *Furman's* cumulative test.)

Perhaps because waterboarding is obviously *not* torture, the late Senator Edward Kennedy (D-MA) decided to obscure the possibility of an honest debate by citing a World War II-era war crimes prosecution in which the United States convicted a Japanese soldier for using a "water torture" on an American. Senator Kennedy neglected to note that the Japanese soldier was also charged with "beating" the American with his "hands, fists, [a] club," as well as, "burning" him with "cigarettes." Waterboarding was hardly the central issue in this case and was not dealt with individually.

Though the hyperbolic debate over waterboarding has been dishonest and deceptive, Congress did clearly decide that "unlawful combatants" deserve justice served up by the military. When clarifying what American intelligence services could do with captured terrorists, Congress passed the Military Commissions Act of 2006, which made it clear that issues of detention and interrogation would be controlled, not by Common Article 3 of the Geneva Conventions, but by American military law. The Act stated, "No alien unlawful enemy combatant subject to trial by military commission under this chapter may invoke the Geneva Conventions as a source of rights."

This is in the alleged terrorists' best interests, as the United Nations has hardly proven to be an effective bulwark for human rights. As of this writing, the current members of the UN Human Rights Council include China, Saudi Arabia, Russia, Cuba, and Libya, none of which gives unlawful combatants, let alone their own citizens, the human rights that many in the Western World now take for granted.

Also, Sharia law–the very rules the captured militants were fighting for–allows for capital punishment and even mutilation. So, given such options, any sensible terrorist would prefer justice from a jury of American officers. But, as of this writing, Attorney General Eric Holder, with the backing of President Barack Obama, had not yet ruled out trying captured terrorists, including 9/11 mastermind Khalid Sheikh Mohammed, in American criminal courts. As a result, which body of law is to be used is still flitting about in the political winds.

Attorney General Holder has said he can decide whether to use military tribunals or civilian courts on a case-by-case basis. This, of course, tosses "equal justice under law" out the window, as justice requires two things to be truly just: a punishment that is proportionate to the crime and justice that is so blind that the exact same crime is punished in precisely the same way every time. With Attorney General Holder flippantly deciding whether to use civilian or military courts depending on what he had for breakfast, justice is far from equal. But that's how liberals–who believe in "social justice," not equal justice–like it.

Meanwhile, amidst all of this political and legal parsing, President Obama banned waterboarding. So does this mean that America is keeping its hands clean by allowing other nations to do their dirty work? Or does this close the alleged torture issue before a real debate can take place? Not necessarily. A majority of the American people still maintain that rather than banning waterboarding forever, this tactic should be reserved for rare use when a terrorist is captured who is thought to have information about an active plot to murder civilians. President Obama's ban is, after all, threatening national security by keeping actionable information off the table.

Indeed, if there is a legal time when the federal government should use waterboarding on a captured terrorist suspect, then this tool must be reserved for states of emergency. Neither conservatives nor liberals, nor anyone in between, want the federal government to have the ability to call a "state of emergency" and then start torturing people. This is a country with a bill of rights, individual liberties we're trying to save, not hand over to statists. However, preventing such tyrannical actions from the government wouldn't be all that difficult. Federal legislation could be passed that would ban just about all waterboarding, but that would leave the president with this last-resort tool in his or her arsenal to save American lives.

Such legislation could mandate that the use of this interrogation technique be made public after a certain amount of time has elapsed; this would enable public opinion to influence its future use and would ensure there is a political price to pay for using, or not using, this technique. Legislation could also require that a presidential decision to use waterboarding must be first approved by a congressional committee or by a panel of federal judges. Indeed, only two terrorists are known to have ever undergone waterboarding, so President George W. Bush certainly saw it as a desperate, last-resort tactic. In fact, this is why President Bush had the U.S. Justice Department investigate the legality of waterboarding before he approved its limited use on two terrorists. In this way, reasonable restrictions on its use could easily be made compatible with America's constitutional government.

To determine if this is ethical, ask yourself which shocks your conscience more: waterboarding an alleged terrorist who is thought to know about an imminent attack on civilians, or giving such an al-Qaeda operative Miranda rights and, before they can even be questioned, granting the terrorist a lawyer? This is a plausible scenario; after all, Attorney General Eric Holder quickly gave Umar Farouk Abdulmutallab (a.k.a. the "underwear bomber") Miranda rights just hours after Abdulmutallab tried to blow up a plane bound for Detroit on December 25, 2009; as a result, the

United States lost the opportunity to attain actionable, and timely, information from Abdulmutallab about just who made the bomb.

The Left has not been realistic or even honest. Instead, they've put American lives in jeopardy for very weak reasons. In fact, because what constitutes a "cruel and unusual punishment" according to the Eighth Amendment has long been defined by the "evolving standards of decency" of a majority of Americans, and because most Americans think waterboarding is an ethical option for extreme use on a terrorist thought to have actionable information, such a use is clearly constitutional.

Hence this debate over waterboarding could be resolved in an open and transparent way that could keep Americans as safe as possible and that would keep American values intact, as well as the Eighth Amendment, if the Left would only be intellectually honest.

The Eighth Amendment was written and ratified to restrain the federal government to what the consciences of the people think appropriate. Liberal and/or progressive Supreme Court justices have instead placed the judgment of how far the government can go in their own unelected hands. The Left has gone along with this statist power grab. Therefore, to save this portion of the Bill of Rights, Americans need to remember that whether the topic is administering the death penalty, using waterboarding on Khalid Sheikh Mohammed, or attaching a ball and chain to a convict, the measure of what is cruel and unusual needs to be placed back into the hands of the citizenry, not in the government's judicial branch.

AMENDMENT IX

The enumeration in the Constitution, of certain rights, shall not be construed to deny or disparage others retained by the people.

"Can the liberties of a nation be thought secure when we have
removed their only firm basis, a conviction in the minds of the
people that these liberties are of the gift of God?"[1]
–Thomas Jefferson

The Bill of Rights is erected upon the fundamental belief that we inherently have a body of other rights, natural rights, until someone else takes them away. In the Declaration of Independence, Thomas Jefferson said natural rights (he called them "unalienable rights") were granted to us by "the Creator." Others believe they are philosophical rights that developed in nature. Regardless of where someone believes this foundation of moral justice comes from, the secular Left denies natural rights even exist. They don't want to acknowledge that the Ninth Amendment protects a deeper philosophical, or perhaps theological, foundation for our rights, because such rights have long acted as a moral check on government.

The Framers of the Constitution and Bill of Rights believed natural rights were the bedrock of individual rights. They knew good and evil are real, even if hard to define. They didn't believe right and wrong are purely relativistic as liberals claim they are today. Indeed, the underlying principal that we all have natural rights to life, liberty, and property is protected by the "Golden Rule." The Bible words the Golden Rule thus: "Do unto others as you would have them do unto you."[2] When a person obeys the Golden Rule, they're respecting natural rights. This fundamental rule stretches across time and cultures; for example, in the first century B.C., Rabbi Hillel, a Jewish religious leader, acknowledged that the Golden Rule is the basis for the Bible when he said, "That which is hateful to you, do not do to your fellow; that is the whole Torah; the rest is the explanation;

go and learn."[3] The Golden Rule is even found in the *Analects of Confucius*: "Zigong asked: 'Is there any single word that could guide one's entire life?' The master said, 'Should it not be reciprocity? What you do not wish for yourself, do not do to others.'"

This concept is found across cultures and time because it is natural.

During the U.S. Constitutional period, in *The Federalist Papers* (no. 84), Alexander Hamilton asked, "Why declare that things shall not be done which there is no power to do?" Hamilton thought a bill of rights would be superfluous because the federal government was already restricted to the powers it is granted in the Constitution. Other politicians, however, mainly the Anti-Federalists such as Patrick Henry and George Mason, saw the need for a bill of rights to spell out an additional list of limitations on the federal government to prevent a centralized bureaucracy from exceeding its constitutional limitations. The Anti-Federalists wanted to protect individuals not just with the restrictions on government that they could spell out in a bill of rights, but also by making it clear there are many other rights not listed that the people retain—hence the Ninth and Tenth Amendments. As a result, Madison included the Ninth Amendment's open-ended declaration of natural rights in the Bill of Rights.

Natural rights are the liberties that exist even without government, even in anarchy. John Locke (1632–1704) defined them as "life, liberty, and estate." Thomas Hobbes (1588–1679), in *Leviathan* (1651), said natural rights extend from the "state of nature," thus Hobbes argued that man has the essential human right "to use his own power, as he will himself, for the preservation of his own Nature; that is to say, of his own Life; and consequently, of doing any thing, which in his own judgment, and Reason, he shall conceive to be the aptest means thereunto." The idea that we have the natural right to preserve "our own nature" underlies our rights to self-defense, to protect our own property, to speak the truth as we see it, and so on. This is why natural rights are the foundation of the Bill of Rights.

The Framers of the U.S. Constitution basically thought that a constitution is a social contract between individuals but does not invalidate natural rights; as a result, society's laws in a republic like the United States are only just when they treat every member of society equally and when they don't infringe upon natural rights. Anyone who has ever stood before a jury has benefited from a group of peers standing apart from, or even above government, from people drawing on their consciences as they apply the law or decide to overrule an unjust, improperly applied, or even unconstitutional law. This is one profound reason why many conservatives and libertarians today dispute the claim that the federal government can justly, or even legally, regulate every facet of our daily lives, as the government does not have the right to morally infringe upon our right to life, liberty, and property.

This fundamental belief is in keeping with American constitutionalism. As Thomas Jefferson said in a letter to Francis Gilmer in 1816: "No man has a natural right to commit aggression on the equal rights of another, and this is all from which the laws ought to restrain him." Natural rights are philosophical or theological values, which is why Jefferson said they were "endowed by their Creator" in the Declaration of Independence. They are difficult-to-define moral values that the youngest child acknowledges as soon as he or she says, "But that's not fair." Natural rights are the foundation for the motto chosen for the face of the U.S. Supreme Court building: "Equal Justice Under Law," as everyone, no matter what their genetics or gender, equally enjoys these same basic human rights.

However, to subjugate the moral will of the people to the power of the state, many liberal and progressive Americans now argue that natural rights don't exist. They say that the power to grant or restrict rights lies solely in the hands of the state. They maintain we only have legal rights granted by the government, not absolute rights granted by God or nature. They ignore the fact that the Constitution was written as restrictions on the federal government—that it is a list of what the federal government can and can't do—not as a check on the people.

Nevertheless, liberal-progressives can't admit there are real moral restrictions on government, as moral rules that cover everyone equally prevent any king or government from infringing on the people's inherent rights. Indeed, conceding there are moral absolutes based in natural rights would drain the swamp of the liberal-progressives' moral relativism, and then, if they were intellectually honest, would force them to become conservatives; thus the existence of natural rights has long been denied by oligarchs, kings, and liberals. And this is why Communists and liberals often attack religion, as theology presents, with profound lists of moral values such as the Ten Commandments, tangible moral guidelines that can't be superseded by the state. Such moral rules are a check on government power.

The ambiguity of natural rights, however, causes conservatives to avoid citing the Ninth Amendment. They fear that if the Ninth Amendment is legislated from the bench it will be used to constitutionalize activist justices' personal views into the gray areas of the law. After all, natural rights escape firm definitions that everyone can agree upon, so much so they've been the fodder of philosophers from Plato to Locke. Consequently, natural rights are best left to the morality of jurors and voters.

One problem with the inclusion of the Ninth Amendment in the Bill of Rights is that it gives such justices a means to read anything they want into the Constitution. For example, some Supreme Court justices have asserted that the Ninth Amendment can be used to interpret the Fourteenth Amendment. Justice Arthur Goldberg (joined by Chief Justice Earl Warren and Justice William Brennan) expressed this view in a concurring opinion in the case of *Griswold* v. *Connecticut* (1965): "The Framers did not intend that the first eight amendments be construed to exhaust the basic and fundamental rights...."

Subsequent to *Griswold*, progressive justices used the Ninth Amendment to justify rights that are not listed in the Constitution. For example, the district court that heard the case *Roe* v. *Wade* (1973) ruled in favor of a "Ninth Amendment right to choose to have an abortion," although it stressed that the right was "not unqualified or unfettered."

Supreme Court Justice William O. Douglas disagreed; in a concurring opinion, he wrote, "The Ninth Amendment obviously does not create federally enforceable rights." Justice Douglas, however, joined the majority opinion of the Supreme Court in *Roe* v. *Wade*, which stated that a federally enforceable right to privacy "whether it be founded in the Fourteenth Amendment's concept of personal liberty and restrictions upon state action, as we feel it is, or, as the District Court determined, in the Ninth Amendment's reservation of rights to the people, is broad enough to encompass a woman's decision whether or not to terminate her pregnancy."

The progressive tendency to read their worldview into the Constitution is why the Ninth Amendment is dangerous in the hands of an activist Supreme Court looking for a means to have its way. Such justices disregard the Constitution and create new rights they think society should embrace.

Justice Antonin Scalia threw speed bumps into this debate by arguing, in *Troxel* v. *Granville* (2000), that the "Declaration of Independence ... is not a legal prescription conferring powers upon the courts; and the Constitution's refusal to 'deny or disparage' other rights is far removed from affirming any one of them, and even farther removed from authorizing judges to identify what they might be, and to enforce the judges' list against laws duly enacted by the people." Justice Scalia believes in judicial restraint because he doesn't think courts should be able to usurp the rights of the people by treating the Constitution like a "living" document that can be semantically reinterpreted as desire dictates.

Robert Bork, an originalist whose Supreme Court nomination was rejected by a Democratic controlled U.S. Senate in a 58–42 vote, agrees with Justice Scalia. Bork argued in *The Tempting of America* (1990) that if a provision of the Constitution were covered by an actual inkblot, judges should not be permitted to make up what might be under the inkblot. Doing so would allow a majority of justices to twist the meaning of the Constitution to their own ends. Because the Ninth Amendment's allusion to natural rights points to a broad and hard-to-define area dealing with justice and morality, Bork doesn't think judges should be permitted to adjudicate what they think natural rights might cover.

However, despite the philosophical ambiguity of natural rights, understanding the Ninth Amendment's underlying protection of this other body of rights is fundamental to a nation of people who wish to remain free;

after all, we use natural rights every day. In perhaps their most dramatic application, every time a jury looks into the eyes of a person charged with murder they take the Ninth Amendment on their shoulders. They weigh, as they must, the facts and laws that cement the American republic together, but they also call on the natural rights found between the lines of the laws. Though today juries are often instructed only to weigh the facts as presented to them, judges used to order juries to draw on "the facts and their consciences." Today judges more often tell juries they can only make legal, not moral, decisions. Such statists don't want juries to draw on their consciences, on natural rights.

Though many in our legalistic society deny it today, a jury of peers is separate from the power of the government. A jury may even use natural rights to nullify a law it finds immoral. When weighing a self-defense case or a temporary-insanity plea, a jury has to utilize these other moral values, rights often referred to as natural rights, and may decide not to convict despite overwhelming evidence. For example, early in American history, juries often refused to convict journalists that the John Adams administration was attempting to convict under the Alien and Sedition Acts of 1798. As discussed earlier, jury nullification was also used in the pre-Civil War era when juries sometimes declined to convict people for violations of the Fugitive Slave Act. Even during the Prohibition period (1920–1933), many juries acquitted people who'd been caught drinking because the jurors didn't think the law was just.

The debate as to whether certain rights are natural or inalienable actually dates back to the Stoics in late Antiquity. The Stoics held that no one was a slave by nature, but that rather slavery is an external condition. Seneca the Younger wrote, "It is a mistake to imagine that slavery pervades a man's whole being; the better part of him is exempt from it: the body indeed is subjected and in the power of a master, but the mind is independent, and indeed is so free and wild, that it cannot be restrained even by this prison of the body, wherein it is confined."[4]

Of fundamental importance to the development of the idea of natural rights was the emergence of the idea of natural human equality. In 1932,

Charles H. McIlwain observed that "the idea of the equality of men is the profoundest contribution of the Stoics to political thought" and that "its greatest influence is in the changed conception of law that in part resulted from it."[5] Indeed, the Roman statesman Cicero argued in *De Legibus* that "we are born for Justice, and that right is based, not upon opinions, but upon Nature."[6] Cicero lived in a time and place where slavery was common, yet he looked to nature and human morality and found everyone inherently has the same rights.

In the thirteenth century, St. Thomas Aquinas (1225–1274), in his *Summa Theologica,* picked up where Cicero left the debate by asserting that natural law is a rational creature's participation in the eternal law; however, since human reason can't fully comprehend God's law, it needs to be alluded to and protected with documents such as the Bill of Rights. In keeping with this logic, Aquinas taught that an unjust law is not a law; he argued that an unjust law retains merely the appearance of law insofar as it is duly constituted and enforced in the same way a just law is, but is actually a "perversion of law."[7]

At this point, natural law not only could pass judgment on the moral worth of various laws, but also could determine what the law said in the first place. This idea led to the creation of jury nullification—a power an English jury fought for and won during the trial of William Penn in 1670—and later became a philosophical and moral justification for opposing slavery in America.

The philosophy of Locke and others then provided the basis for the anti-slavery movement to argue not simply against involuntary slavery, but also against any explicit or implied contractual forms of slavery. Any contract that tried to legally alienate natural rights was inherently invalid according to Locke's natural law theory.

These themes had also converged in the debate about American Independence. While Jefferson was writing the Declaration of Independence, Richard Price in England sided with the Americans' claim "that Great Britain is attempting to rob them of that liberty to which every member of society and all civil communities have a natural and unalienable title."[8] Price went on to say that any social contract or compact trying alienate these rights would be necessarily void:

> Neither can any state acquire such an authority over other states in virtue of any compacts or cessions. This is a case in which compacts are not binding. Civil liberty is, in this respect, on the same footing with religious liberty. As no people can lawfully surrender their religious liberty by giving up their right of judging for themselves in religion, or by allowing any human beings to prescribe to them what faith they shall embrace, or what mode of worship they shall practise, so neither can any civil societies lawfully surrender their civil liberty by giving up to any extraneous jurisdiction their power of legislating for themselves and disposing their property.

Thus the preservation of the natural rights to life, liberty, and property was claimed as a central justification for the rebellion of the American colonies. As George Mason stated in his draft for the Virginia Declaration of Rights: "… all men are born equally free," and hold "certain inherent natural rights, of which they cannot, by any compact, deprive or divest their posterity."[9]

Thomas Paine (1731–1809), who so well articulated why America must free itself from English rule in *Common Sense* (1776), further elaborated on what natural rights are in his book *Rights of Man* (1791). Paine said, "It is a perversion of terms to say that a charter gives rights. It operates by a contrary effect–that of taking rights away. Rights are inherently in all the inhabitants; but charters, by annulling those rights, in the majority, leave the right, by exclusion, in the hands of a few….They … consequently are instruments of injustice."[10]

Paine would be alarmed at the way our charter, the U.S. Constitution, has been upended. The Constitution was designed to restrict the U.S. government to the enumerated powers it was granted by a free people. By definition, argued Paine, these enumerated powers take away some

rights from the people. This was why Paine called government a "necessary evil" in his 1776 treatise *Common Sense.* Paine would have been all the
more alarmed with how this necessary evil has been able to turn the
Constitution into an all-expansive document that allows the government's
bureaucracy to do just about anything it wants.

To prevent the growth of an ever-expanding government from imped-
ing the rights of the people, the Bill of Rights was written as a list of restrictions on the federal government, not as positive rights the government
must grant to the people. Conversely, this is why President Barack Obama
referred to the Constitution as a list of "negative liberties." President
Obama would like the government to have the power to enforce positive
liberties, such as universal health care and a right to employment. Of
course, by its own definition, "positive liberty" is a contradiction in terms,
because to create positive liberties the government has to take away individual liberties in order to mandate that collective rights be given to all.
For example, if the government created a "positive right" that granted
every person the right to a job (this was in President Franklin D. Roosevelt's proposed "second bill of rights"), then people who own and run
businesses would lose the right to fire incompetent employees.

In keeping with the idea that natural rights could invalidate immoral
laws, such as those created with so-called positive rights, future Chief
Justice Salmon P. Chase (1808–1873) argued before the Supreme Court
in the case of John Van Zandt: "The law of the Creator, which invests
every human being with an inalienable title to freedom, cannot be
repealed by any interior law which asserts that man is property." Van
Zandt had been charged with violating the Fugitive Slave Act. Though he
lost the case, and with it his land, property, and children, he continued to
help runaway slaves; in fact, Van Zandt is believed to have been the basis
for John Van Trompe, a character in Harriet Beecher Stowe's *Uncle Tom's
Cabin.*

Modern progressives ignore the fact that because every person has
natural rights, all are inherently free and can thus only be enslaved by
immoral laws. This same right to natural freedoms was expressed during

the Enlightenment when natural law (which is closely associated with natural rights) was used to challenge the so-called divine right of kings and thereby to win people freedom from tyranny. The "divine right of kings" asserts that a monarch derives his right to rule directly from the will of God. A divine king is thus not subject to the will of his people or even to the church. According to this doctrine, since only God can judge an unjust king, the people can only follow a king. The doctrine implies that any attempt to depose a king or to restrict his powers runs contrary to the will of God and thus would constitute heresy. In 1215, the English people tossed out this concept and said they had natural, unalienable rights by shoving the Magna Carta down King John's not-so-divine throat. Americans did the same thing to King George III in 1776.

Natural rights can be used today to wrestle back basic human freedoms that have been seized by an overbearing federal government. To prevent such curbs on state power, liberal-progressives argue that the only rights that exist are legal ones. They believe the government has given rights to the people by collectively seizing them from the selfish clutches of anarchy or from individualists (capitalists). Ayn Rand showed the injustice in this belief when she wrote, "Remember also that the smallest minority on earth is the individual. Those who deny individual rights, cannot claim to be defenders of minorities."[11]

Yet liberal-progressives claim to be the true defenders of minorities, even as they judge people by their skin tone and gender, categorizing them in their quest for employment (with affirmative action) or justice (with hate-crimes legislation). Conservatives and libertarians, on the other hand, insist that the natural rights of every person require them to be judged by the decisions they make as individuals, not according to their looks or gender. Conservatives insist on equal justice under law.

Clearly the debate over natural rights is still alive, and is being carried on in the courts and legislatures. It even popped up in 2010 in what became known as the "Texas Textbook Wars," when the Texas Board of Education debated whether to include natural rights as part of the foundation of the Declaration of Independence. Every ten years Texas reviews its school textbooks. As Texas is a big state (it is the largest school textbook buyer in the country), the changes it wants often affect the textbooks that other states receive. In 2010 they found themselves dealing with things that would outrage the average American; for example, during the review process, liberals wanted to replace the word "Christmas" with "Diwali." They also wanted to remove Daniel Boone and Independence Day from the texts.[12] The battle to stop this Orwellian rewriting of American history was largely won after a very public fight in the spring of 2010. David Barton, an author and constitutional scholar who worked as a consultant for the Texas Board of Education, said, "We mostly won this battle and kept natural rights—an idea so basic it's found throughout history and in our Declaration of Independence—in our school textbooks."[13]

This attempt to expunge historical figures and the morality that natural rights protect is telling. In this pivotal time in America, denying that natural rights exist is to deny that kings and legislatures have limitations on their power. A government that is not moored to the natural rights of man isn't subject to equal justice under law. It is, rather, a government unhinged from morality. To deny, as liberals do, that natural rights exist is to deny the very individual freedoms that made America possible. Taking away the Ninth Amendment concept that we have natural rights would free the government from basic human morality and allow the state to do whatever it desires, regardless of individual rights. This is why keeping the Ninth Amendment intact is fundamental to our freedom.

AMENDMENT X

The powers not delegated to the United States by the Constitution, nor prohibited by it to the States, are reserved to the States respectively, or to the people.

"There are more instances of the abridgement of the freedom of the people by the gradual and silent encroachment of those in power, than by violent and sudden usurpation."[1]
–*James Madison*

T he Tenth Amendment is not a modern, mealy-mouthed law written by lobbyists and loaded with loopholes by lawyers. People who'd just taken up arms to win their freedoms from an unjust empire wrote the Tenth Amendment's unambiguous twenty-eight words. As these revolutionaries didn't want to relinquish the individual freedoms they'd just won to a new federal government, they wrote the Tenth Amendment to plainly restrict the U.S. government to the powers granted by the people in the Constitution.

Nevertheless, since America's founding, the U.S. government has nearly worked itself free from the Tenth Amendment's bonds. The federal government has grown so large that some politicians and judges see individual rights as obstacles to their power—restrictions they have been increasingly successful at loosening. As a result, to find our way back to the constitutional republic with restricted powers granted by the people, it's worth remembering that it took a popular uprising just to get the Bill of Rights included in the U.S. Constitution. During America's founding period, some Federalist politicians thought a bill of rights would be superfluous, as the scope of the federal government was by definition restricted by the Constitution. James Madison said as much: "The powers delegated by the ... Constitution to the federal government are few and defined," while "[t]hose which are to remain in the State governments are numerous and indefinite."[2]

Some of the Founding Fathers thought differently. They wanted individual and state rights etched in constitutional stone. They feared the federal government might break free from its constitutional bonds and run amok over the peoples' liberties and the states' rights. Anti-Federalists, such as George Mason, Patrick Henry, and Samuel Adams, were so bothered by the Constitution's lack of a bill of rights that they opposed ratification of the Constitution unless one was added. Their argument was so compelling to the American public and to state politicians that it nearly prevented the ratification of the Constitution.

In Massachusetts, for example, the Constitution was in serious jeopardy of not being ratified by the state legislature. During debate in Massachusetts, Anti-Federalists demanded to be allowed to amend the Constitution, but Federalists said it had to be accepted or rejected without changes. Federalists knew it would be impossible ever to get the Constitution ratified by the necessary number of states if every state legislature amended it at will. Some Anti-Federalists agreed—they thought this was a clever way to prevent ratification of the Constitution, a document some thought gave too much power to the proposed central government.

This standoff was only resolved when two leading Anti-Federalists, Samuel Adams and John Hancock, negotiated a compromise that permitted state politicians to recommend amendments to the Constitution that would be sent with the ratification papers to Congress. The Massachusetts convention subsequently voted to ratify the Constitution; however, even with the compromise, it barely passed by a vote of 187–168. After Massachusetts voted to ratify, four of the next five states voted to ratify and included proposed amendments that they sent to the U.S. Congress. Since many of these recommendations protected individual rights, this further pressured Congress into adding a bill of rights.

Meanwhile, during the ratification process, James Madison acquiesced by promising that America's first U.S. Congress would pass a bill of rights that the states could then ratify or vote down. He said these rights would restrict the federal government's authority from infringing on individual liberties and state rights. The Constitution was then ratified and Madison kept his promise. The first U.S. Congress wrote and passed twelve amendments and sent them to the states for ratification. The states ratified ten of the twelve amendments. These ten amendments became known as the U.S. Bill of Rights.

A congressional committee, however, didn't write the Bill of Rights from just the proposed amendments. Many of the amendments in the Bill of Rights actually came from other bills of rights and were simply tweaked and debated by the first Congress; for example, the Tenth Amendment, which says that "powers not granted to the federal government nor prohibited to the states by the constitution of the United States are reserved to the states or the people," is actually similar to an earlier provision of the Articles of Confederation: "Each state retains its sovereignty, freedom, and independence, and every power, jurisdiction, and right, which is not by this Confederation expressly delegated to the United States, in Congress assembled."[3]

So the Bill of Rights was popularly fought for and passed to restrain the federal government. Also, the Tenth Amendment was simply included in the Bill of Rights to put an exclamation point on the fact that the federal government is restricted to the powers it is granted by the Constitution. This basic premise is important to remember in this age of out-of-control government, as the federal government has increasingly been able to find ways to ignore, obscure, or even to override its constitutional limitations.

One fundamental way the federal government has been able to expand its power has been with the Constitution's Commerce Clause ("The Congress shall have Power ... To regulate Commerce with foreign Nations, and among the several States..."). This clause's biggest expansion came in *Wickard* v. *Filburn* (1942), when the Supreme Court ruled that the federal government could regulate the growing of wheat even when the wheat is only used for "home consumption."

Roscoe Filburn, an Ohio farmer, had been growing wheat to feed his chickens when he ran afoul of President Franklin D. Roosevelt's administration. The U.S. government had imposed limits on wheat production based on the acreage owned by each farmer. FDR wanted to drive up wheat prices during the Great Depression by using central planning to control the amount of wheat raised. To accomplish this, Congress passed the Agricultural Adjustment Act of 1938, and FDR signed it into law.

As he wasn't planning to sell the wheat, Filburn ignored the Act's government quotas and grew as much as he needed. Federal bureaucrats subsequently checked Filburn's private land, saw his "excess" wheat, and ordered him to destroy his crop and to pay a fine.

Filburn refused and took the government to court. He argued logically that because the "excess" wheat he was growing was for his private consumption it couldn't be treated as commerce between the states. Filburn was obviously right, as wheat fed to his chickens wasn't ever going to be interstate commerce. The federal government, however, argued that because the wheat was withheld from commerce, it was affecting the price of wheat; after all, if his wheat was sold across state lines it would increase the overall amount and would theoretically reduce the overall price of wheat. Therefore, it was interstate commerce.

A federal district court ruled in favor of Filburn, saying that the Commerce Clause couldn't be used regulate wheat that didn't even go to the market. The U.S. government appealed to the Supreme Court.

By 1942, all but one of the Supreme Court justices had been appointed by President Roosevelt, so the Court had been ideologically molded into a progressive rubber stamp for FDR's policies. As a result, few were surprised when the justices ruled unanimously that the federal government could regulate wheat production that was never intended to enter commerce between the states. This progressive ruling massively expanded the federal government's power via the Commerce Clause and thereby anulled the Tenth Amendment.

To put this federal overreach into perspective, consider that as Joseph Stalin was starving the Russian people with his "command economy" and collective farming, President Roosevelt was taking America down a path toward centralized control by penalizing a farmer who was using his own wheat during the Great Depression to feed his chickens.

After the *Filburn* decision, a half-century passed before the door of the progressive tomb holding the Tenth Amendment was cracked back open.

In the 1990s the Supreme Court, led by Chief Justice William Rehnquist, who had been nominated by President Ronald Reagan in 1986, began to return some balance to the Commerce Clause and through it to the Tenth Amendment.

First, in *New York* v. *United States* (1992), the Supreme Court invalidated a portion of a federal law because it violated the Tenth Amendment. This particular case challenged a portion of the Low-Level Radioactive Waste Policy Amendments Act of 1985. The Act included three segments designed to compel states to comply with federal rules covering the disposal of low-level radioactive waste. The first two incentives were federal monies. The third required states to be liable for radioactive waste not disposed of before January 1, 1996. It was this last provision that New York fought because it forced state officials to enforce federal statutes, which is a clear Tenth Amendment infringement on state rights.

Incredibly, the Supreme Court, in a 6–3 decision, actually read the Constitution and ruled that this federal obligation violated the Tenth Amendment because it mandated that states have their workers do federal bidding. If such an idea were allowed to stand, state rights and their constitutions would be meaningless, as the federal government could micromanage every decision made in the fifty states and force state officials to be de facto federal employees.

Justice Sandra Day O'Connor wrote for the majority in *New York* v. *United States* that the federal government could encourage the states to adopt certain regulations by dangling economic incentives, such as by attaching specific conditions to federal funds. But Congress can't directly compel states to enforce federal regulations.

As a result of *New York* v. *United States*, Congress today typically exercises its will over the states by economically incentivizing the states to implement national minimum standards, a system known as "cooperative federalism." For example, federal educational funds often now come with the caveat that any state that accepts the funds must then comply with federal rules, such as by using the funds to teach specific subjects or to institute equal-protection guidelines. This federal meddling in education is actually a new phenomenon, as President Jimmy Carter created the

U.S. Department of Education in 1979. Currently, in this new age of federal control, the U.S. government is attaching conditions to payouts that would impress Don Corleone. For example, federal funds were used to compel the states to adhere to the .08 legal blood alcohol limit and, via this power of the congressional purse, the federal government also coerced the states into raising the drinking age to twenty-one.

Next, the Supreme Court actually issued a bold ruling for states rights. In *United States* v. *Lopez* (1995), the Supreme Court ruled 5–4 to strike down a portion of the Gun-Free School Zones Act, a federal law that created "gun-free zones" on and around public school campuses. The Court's reasoning was that because there was no clause in the Constitution authorizing this restriction on Second Amendment rights, the federal government couldn't enforce "gun-free zones" on and around public school campuses. Liberals couldn't believe that the Supreme Court actually ruled the federal government couldn't do something unless the Constitution said so.

After decades of suffocation, the Supreme Court was actually breathing life into the Tenth Amendment!

This case began when Alfonso Lopez Jr. brought a gun to school. Lopez was a twelfth grade student attending Edison High School in San Antonio, Texas. On March 10, 1992, school authorities were tipped that he had a handgun. When confronted, Lopez handed over the firearm. The police then arrested him. None of that was particularly remarkable. What was remarkable was that the next day Lopez was charged with violating the federal Gun-Free School Zones Act of 1990. Though Lopez had clearly broken state laws and could have been dealt with appropriately in Texas, the feds decided they were in charge.

Lopez's attorney moved to dismiss the indictment on the grounds that the Gun-Free School Zones Act was unconstitutional, as it is beyond the power of Congress to legislate control over state public schools. The federal government countered that the presence of firearms within a school was dangerous; as a result of this danger, students would be too frightened to go to school; as the students would be too scared to attend class this would, in turn, inhibit learning; the students' lack of learning would then lead to a weaker national economy, since education is fundamental to U.S. corporations' ability to compete in the world market; finally, this weakened domestic economy resulting from students who are too scared of guns to study would then dampen interstate commerce. And they weren't kidding!

If the government's contrived position seems laughably nonsensical to you, and if bringing a gun to school, though clearly illegal under state statutes, doesn't sound like commerce to you, then you're starting to see how the growth of federal power over the states has been justified. Given enough "what ifs," any child and, it seems, the federal government, can concoct an excuse. In this case, the excuse would allow the federal government to supersede state laws by expanding the federal government's constitutional powers. Such an expansion of federal power is precisely what the Tenth Amendment was written and ratified to prevent.

Nevertheless, a trial court denied the motion to dismiss and convicted Lopez; however, on appeal the Fifth Circuit Court of Appeals ruled that the Act did exceed the limitations of the Commerce Clause. The Fifth Circuit found that the U.S. government invented a complex way to justify new and expansive powers under the Constitution's Commerce Clause, a power grab that was unconstitutional. No kidding.

The U.S. attorneys pushing the case weren't worried. They expected yet another expansive decision from the Supreme Court, as their law schools clearly taught them the Commerce Clause allows the federal government to do most anything. Indeed, progressive Supreme Court justices had spent much of the twentieth century going along with federal government ruses that the Commerce Clause was boundless. So the federal government confidently appealed the *Lopez* case to the Supreme Court.

But this time the Supreme Court ruled in a 5–4 decision that while Congress has broad lawmaking authority under the Commerce Clause, the power doesn't extend so far from "commerce" that it authorized a ban on guns in and around schools. Chief Justice William Rehnquist wrote:

To uphold the Government's contentions here, we have to pile inference upon inference in a manner that would bid fair to convert congressional authority under the Commerce Clause to a general police power of the sort retained by the States. Admittedly, some of our prior cases have taken long steps down that road, giving great deference to congressional action. The broad language in these opinions has suggested the possibility of additional expansion, but we decline here to proceed any further. To do so would require us to conclude that the Constitution's enumeration of powers does not presuppose something not enumerated, and that there never will be a distinction between what is truly national and what is truly local. This we are unwilling to do.

This case is heralded as the first modern Supreme Court opinion that didn't go along with the federal government's big, fat lie that the Commerce Clause allows the federal government to do just about anything it wants. The Court actually read the law and used it to limit the government's power under the Commerce Clause. Liberals were shocked.

In his dissenting opinion, Justice Stephen Breyer, who found himself on the losing side of this 5–4 decision, outlined three principles the liberals on the Court wanted to use to define the Commerce Clause: 1) the Commerce Clause included the power to regulate local activities so long as the activities "significantly affect" interstate commerce; 2) a court must consider not only the individual act being regulated, but also the cumulative effect of all similar acts; and 3) a court must specifically determine not whether the regulated activity significantly affected interstate commerce, but whether Congress could have had a rational basis for its decision.

According to Justice Breyer's nebulous principles, the federal government should be able to outlaw firearms on or near school campuses under the Commerce Clause because, as long as a majority of nine justices decide a law is "rational," it is therefore constitutional no matter what the

Constitution actually says. This statist view of how the high court should interpret the Constitution is precisely what allowed the federal government to expand its authority into every facet of Americans' lives, as it allows the federal government and the high court to supplant the Constitution with vague, subjective tests that have enough wiggle room to allow almost anything.

A few years later, the Supreme Court ruled in *Printz* v. *United States* (1997) that the Brady Handgun Violence Prevention Act was unconstitutional according to the Tenth Amendment. The Left considered this Act one of President Bill Clinton's shining achievements. The Act required state and local law enforcement officials to conduct background checks on anyone who wanted to buy a handgun. Justice Scalia, writing for the majority, referred to *New York* v. *United States* to show that the law violated the Tenth Amendment since the Act "forced participation of the State's executive in the actual administration of a federal program." This portion of the Act was ruled unconstitutional, as it would have allowed the federal government to micromanage the states by demanding they spend their revenues to do federal bidding—if found constitutional, the states would simply have become slaves to the federal government's will.

As a result of these rulings, the Tenth Amendment, though still just an apparition, was at least up to haunting state houses and the U.S. Capitol.

However, after the Tenth Amendment was at last found to still have some vitality, the Supreme Court ruled that the 1942 *Filburn* decision (which had found that even wheat grown for personal consumption could be regulated by the Commerce Clause) was still good law. In *Gonzales* v. *Raich* (2005) a California woman sued the Drug Enforcement Administration (DEA) after federal agents had destroyed her "medical marijuana crop." Proposition 215 had legalized medical marijuana under California state law; however, marijuana is prohibited at the federal level by the Controlled Substances Act. This set up a power struggle between California and the U.S. government. Even though the woman grew the marijuana strictly for her own consumption and never sold a single joint to anyone, the Supreme Court ruled 6–3 that growing one's own marijuana affects the illegal interstate market of marijuana; as a result, the Court decided in favor of the federal government's Commerce Clause.

Justice Rehnquist voted with the liberals in *Gonzales* v. *Raich* because he believed the Constitution's Necessary and Proper Clause ("The Congress shall have Power to make all Laws which shall be necessary and proper for carrying into Execution the forgoing Powers, and all other Powers vested by this Constitution in the Government of the United States, or in any Department or Officer thereof") gave the federal government the power to deal with the illegal trade of narcotics.

As a result, the Supreme Court allowed the government not only to regulate wheat grown for personal use, but also substances the federal government deems to be illegal. However, as a state right to grow marijuana isn't something that resonates with most Americans, the ruling didn't raise many eyebrows.

In his dissent in *Gonzales* v. *Raich*, Justice Clarence Thomas summed up the Constitution's limitations well: "Respondent's local cultivation and consumption of marijuana is not 'Commerce … among the several States.'" Such clear thinking isn't something liberal justices prefer, as the Constitution and the Bill of Rights were written and ratified by men who were mostly of a libertarian or conservative point of view. As a result, the only way liberals can win these constitutional debates is to obfuscate, spin, and outright lie. This is why clear constitutional analysis scares liberals.

The Rise of Tenth Amendment Activism

However, perhaps the Tenth Amendment has some chance of rising from the dead after all.

Former Speaker of the House Representative Nancy Pelosi (D-CA) saw the ghost of the Tenth Amendment during a press conference in October 2009 when a reporter asked her, "Madam Speaker, where specifically does the Constitution grant Congress the authority to enact an individual health-insurance mandate?"

Representative Pelosi blurted the first words that leapt into her rattled mind: "Are you serious? Are you serious?"

"Yes," said the reporter, "yes I am."[4]

Perhaps with some help from Botox, Representative Pelosi regained her composure and cast the Tenth Amendment's restriction on federal power back out of the House by refusing to answer.

Other Democrats, however, are so blinded by arrogance they can't even see the specter of the Tenth Amendment. At a town hall meeting on July 24, 2009, for instance, a woman reminded Representative Pete Stark (D-CA), a congressman who has been in office since the Nixon administration, that the Constitution "specifically enumerates certain powers to the federal government and leaves all other authority to the states."

Representative Stark didn't even flinch when the spirit of the Tenth Amendment appeared. He just smugly created a YouTube hit by replying, "I think that there are very few constitutional limits that would prevent the federal government from rules that could affect your private life. The basis for that would be how would it affect other people."

The woman pressed further, asking, "Is your answer that [the federal government] can do anything?"

Representative Stark coolly replied, "The federal government yes, can do most anything in this country.[5]

The town hall shook with boos and the woman accused, "You sir, and people like you, are destroying this nation."

Regardless, Representative Stark simply retained the expression of a monarch amused by his subjects' childlike naïveté.

Meanwhile, the Tenth Amendment has had some success retaking the solid form originally afforded by its twenty-eight words as legislators in state houses from Alaska to Tennessee once again grow bold enough to seek its return from the grave. According to the Tenth Amendment Center—an organization trying to resurrect the Tenth Amendment's mandate that the "powers not delegated to the United States by the Constitution ... are reserved to the States respectively, or to the people"—at least thirty-seven state legislatures have proposed "Tenth Amendment resolutions" since 2008. As of January 2011, seven states had passed these resolutions (Alaska, Idaho, North Dakota, South Dakota, Oklahoma, Louisiana, and Tennessee). These are unbinding declarations, following an old-fashioned custom whereby, before a duel, one gentleman had to declare his outrage by slapping another with an empty glove. In the same way, these declarations at least show with gentlemanly forbearance that the gauntlet has been thrown down.

More confrontationally, the rise of the Tea Party—a movement extolling the original constitutional restrictions placed on government—is also keeping this fundamental fight lively. This movement has made it politically possible for Louisiana Governor Bobby Jindal to throw his weight behind a lawsuit to defeat the federal moratorium on offshore oil drilling, and for Arizona Governor Jan Brewer to challenge federal immigration policies. The Tea Party's state-rights stance made it easier for eighteen governors to sign a letter demanding that the U.S. Senate protect their states against Environmental Protection Agency (EPA) climate rules. This pro-Constitution wave prompted Idaho's Governor C. L. "Butch" Otter to begin publicly toying with the theory that the states can nullify a federal power grab. And, as of January 2011, this opposition to growing statism in America resulted in a total of twenty-seven states gathering together to sue to overthrow the Patient Protection and Affordable Care Act ("ObamaCare").

In another effort to pick a constitutional brouhaha, since 2008 some states have passed "Firearms Freedom Act Legislation." These bills typically declare "that any firearms made and retained in-state are beyond the authority of Congress under its constitutional power to regulate commerce among the states." As of January 2011, such legislation had passed in eight states and had been introduced in twenty others.[6] To force the federal government to respect Montana's legislation, a lawsuit was brought by the Montana Shooting Sports Association and Second Amendment Foundation against the federal government.

U.S. Attorney General Eric Holder's first response to the lawsuit was to file a "Motion to Dismiss" by claiming that the plaintiffs lack standing to sue because federal firearms laws trump state laws, even when firearms are made and sold in the same state. Holder believes the Commerce Clause ("The Congress shall have Power ... To regulate Commerce with foreign Nations, and among the several States...") gives the federal government the power to regulate all transactions, whether or not the products physically enter interstate commerce "among the several states." The trouble is, according to a standing Supreme Court precedent (*Wickard* v. *Filburn*), he's right ... at least until the Supreme Court weighs in on the constitutionality of ObamaCare.

Which gets us to the coming battle for your rights: Democrats in 2010 next tried to steamroll the last remaining limitations to the Commerce Clause by including the individual mandate in the Patient Protection and Affordable Care Act.

The Biggest Constitutional Question of Our Age

In March 2010, a Democratic Congress and president pushed through ObamaCare, a 2,700-page bill that includes a "Minimum Essential Coverage Provision," a mandate that everyone buy federally approved health insurance. If found constitutional by the U.S. Supreme Court, this provision would topple the Commerce Clause's last limitations. This attempt to vastly expand the federal government's power poses the fundamental question: does the Commerce Clause give the federal government the clout to mandate that citizens buy a federally approved product from a private company?

How the Supreme Court—and perhaps once again the U.S. Congress—answers this question in the coming years will decide if America will continue to veer left toward centrally planned authoritarianism, or if it can right itself back toward individual rights and a limited constitutional government.

If the Commerce Clause is expanded further by allowing the federal government to mandate that Americans purchase a product, then the government could dictate purchases related to dietary decisions (Sorry, you've reached your fast-food quota for this month), housing (Why do some fat-cats need 8,000-square-foot homes?), transportation (Uncle Sam says you must buy a Chevy Volt!), and everything in between.

The Tenth Amendment originally prevented such infringements on individual rights by restricting the federal government to its enumerated powers as listed in the Constitution. This restriction on government supremacy left the people free to pursue their American dreams, or as the Declaration of Independence puts it, to engage in their personal "pursuit of happiness."

Benjamin Franklin saw this fundamental fight coming. This is why, as he walked out of the Constitutional Convention in Philadelphia in 1787 and was asked, "What have we got—a Republic or a Monarchy?" he replied, "A Republic... if you can keep it."[7]

The clear tug-of-war between individual rights and state power is something the Obama administration didn't want to confront. The Left prefers to spin the moral argument around by pointing to alleged victims of American capitalism, to those suffering from "preexisting conditions" who can't attain affordable health care outside an emergency room. The Left runs from the obvious fact that ObamaCare's mandates and penalties lessen American freedom faster than Dracula flees from a cross because when Americans realize their individual rights are at stake, they vote conservative. This is why even as the Left used straw men to pass ObamaCare, they refused to acknowledge that the states with the least amount of freedom (the most stringent regulatory schemes) are the same states that have the fewest insurance providers and the most expensive insurance plans. Indeed, the states with the most costly health insurance plans are those that require insurance providers to cover everything from psychotherapy and chiropractic treatment to more traditional procedures. The Left wouldn't acknowledge that Cadillac plans are expensive because they're Cadillac plans;

even worse, they wouldn't acknowledge that forcing people to buy only Cadillac plans reduces freedom and raises costs.

In fact, the price tags and regulations associated with ObamaCare are so onerous they triggered the National Federation of Independent Business (NFIB) to determine that ObamaCare's "federal mandate requiring that nearly all U.S. residents carry health insurance by 2014 seriously threatens our basic constitutional rights and individual freedoms." ObamaCare's costs to small business and its infringements on individual liberty also prompted the NFIB to join a lawsuit with twenty-seven states mounting a constitutional challenge to ObamaCare. After entering this fight, the NFIB began arguing that the real victims aren't the uninsured, but are the small business owners and those they employ. Government mandates, rules, regulations, and the lack of tort reform are driving up costs and curtailing the ability of entrepreneurs and low-wage workers to obtain affordable health care.

During the debate over ObamaCare, Democrats refused to even acknowledge that just passing a spending plan that would buy insurance for the needy would be vastly less expensive than ObamaCare. But this entire debate is really best left up to the enumerated powers outlined in the Constitution. Thankfully, that is where U.S. District Court Judge Henry E. Hudson kept it when he ruled on the constitutionality of ObamaCare in December 2010.

This case was set in motion on the day President Obama signed ObamaCare into law—March 23, 2010. Just after Democrats rammed through ObamaCare, Virginia's Attorney General Kenneth T. Cuccinelli II filed a lawsuit stipulating that ObamaCare is an infringement on state and individual rights, as the bill mandates that, as of 2014, every American must buy a product approved by the U.S. Congress or be fined for not doing so. Failure to buy government-approved health insurance results in a penalty included on the taxpayer's annual federal return. Of course, as 47 percent of Americans didn't have to pay income taxes in 2009,[8] many of the uninsured still won't pay the penalty. They can just continue to wait until they get sick and then utilize ObamaCare's provision that prevents insurance companies from refusing to grant insurance to those with "preexisting conditions."

After filing suit, Virginia Attorney General Cuccinelli said, "Just being alive is not interstate commerce. If it were, there would be no limit to the Constitution's Commerce Clause and to Congress's authority to regulate everything we do. There has never been a point in our history where the federal government has been given the authority to require citizens to buy goods or services."

Cuccinelli was taking a stand George Mason (1725–1792), the "Father of the Bill of Rights," might have taken. During the U.S. Constitutional Convention, Mason argued that individual rights need to be protected within the Constitution with a bill of rights in order to restrict federal power. When a bill of rights wasn't added to the Constitution at the convention, Mason refused to sign the document. Mason' efforts, along with pressure from several states during the ratification process, eventually succeeded in convincing the Federalists to pass a bill of rights during the first congressional session. These amendments, collectively known as the Bill of Rights, were based on the earlier Virginia Declaration of Rights, which Mason had drafted in 1776.

Regardless of this history, Kathleen Sebelius, the Secretary of the Department of Health and Human Services, attempted to justify Obama-Care's mandate that Americans buy a product by claiming it was the only way to keep the 2,700-page takeover of the private U.S. health-care system affordable. She argued the government has to force Americans to buy health insurance because the nanny state needs to make sure that each citizen can get coverage. So let me get this straight: because the government needs to find a way to pay for ObamaCare, the government should be able to mandate people buy health care? This is like a five-year-old saying, "But Mommy, I needed to steal the money because I just had to have the Gummy Bears."

Of course, neither the Bill of Rights nor the Constitution lists access to health care as a right. The Founders left such decisions up to individuals. This is why Sebelius and the Obama administration decided to use the catch-all Commerce Clause to enumerate this power. Why not, asked the Democrats, since according to the Supreme Court's *Filburn* decision the Commerce Clause can tell a farmer how much wheat he or she can grow even for purely private use? In fact, the Commerce Clause can even be construed to regulate the growth of tomatoes on a Manhattan apartment's balcony. So it certainly is expansive enough to force people to buy health insurance and to penalize them if they don't, at least according to liberal ideology.

However, on December 13, 2010, U.S. District Judge Henry E. Hudson cut right to the primary constitutional question: "This case does not turn on wisdom of Congress or the public policy implications of ACA [ObamaCare]. The Court's attention is focused solely on the constitutionality of the enactment."

This isn't the tack the Obama administration wants taken. Liberal justices pride themselves on how well they determine the common good. They style themselves as philosopher kings ready to decree what's best for the masses, not as judges who merely adjudicate the law. Judge Hudson, however, by coldly asking the basic constitutional question, was behaving as an American judge is required to act—he was first asking if the legislation is constitutional.

Because ObamaCare also runs counter to the Virginia Health Care Freedom Act, Judge Hudson said he'd additionally rule whether the mandate that everyone must buy federally approved health insurance runs afoul of the Tenth Amendment.

The Obama administration responded that because everyone will likely need health-care services at some time in their lives, even their passive inactivity affects the interstate commerce of health-care services; as a result they say the Commerce Clause can be used to justify this new federal power to force people to buy health insurance. By making this argument, the Obama administration is semantically trying to convert inactivity into activity so they can control even what people decide not to do. They think they can tax people for buying or not buying, driving or not driving, drinking or not drinking. They can use "sin taxes" to up the price of alcohol and cigarettes, but that's not enough, they also want "virtue taxes" so they can get the people who choose not to spend.

In fact, according to the Left's convoluted reasoning, a person's decision not to eat fast food, not to take a job, not to join the military, or not to buy a Toyota is an "activity that is commercial and economic in nature" that can be regulated and even required by Congress. Thus this expansion of the Commerce Clause would allow the federal government to mandate almost anything. This is also why it would finish off the Tenth Amendment's requirement that the federal government be held to its listed (enumerated) powers.

However, before Judge Hudson even got going, the government started changing the definitions of words. Though Democratic congressmen referred to the individual mandate as a "penalty" imposed on people who didn't buy health insurance, and even President Barack Obama adamantly said it wasn't a tax, Secretary Sebelius said in her brief to Hudson's court that it was actually a tax, regardless of what the president said and despite what the members of Congress who voted for it thought it was.

Of course, even ObamaCare calls the punishment for not buying federally approved health insurance a "penalty," so this was an uphill battle for the Obama administration–especially with a judge who doesn't call himself progressive. Nevertheless, Secretary Sebelius thought she could justify her attempt to redefine "penalty" to really mean "tax" by boasting in her brief that this mandate would raise $4 billion annually in revenue from Americans who wouldn't buy health insurance. Secretary Sebelius seems convinced that the amount of money taken from Americans might itself deem the provision a tax.

Judge Hudson parried these semantics by pointing out that the Supreme Court, in *U.S.* v. *La Franca* (1931), had ruled: "The two words [tax versus penalty] are not interchangeable … and if an exaction [is] clearly a penalty it cannot be converted into a tax by the simple expedient of calling it such." He also found that the Supreme Court has ruled that a "purported tax that is actually a penalty to force compliance with a regulatory scheme must be tied to an enumerated power other than the taxing power." And then Judge Hudson slammed the Obama administration's position by writing, "Congress specifically denominated this payment for failure to comply with the mandate as a 'penalty.'" Therefore, he ruled, it is a penalty, not a tax. In so doing, he ruled that the federal government can't use its taxing power to regulate something the Constitution doesn't allow them to regulate, such as economic inactivity.

Judge Hudson went on to rule: "Furthermore, the resulting regulatory tax, untethered to an enumerated power, is an unconstitutional encroachment on the state's power of regulation under the Tenth Amendment." In plain language, Judge Hudson said that the federal government can't do something the Constitution doesn't give it the authority to do—the Tenth Amendment gives all the powers not listed in the Constitution to the states or the people.

Judge Hudson even accused the Obama administration of deception: "The use of the term 'tax' appears to be a tactic to achieve enlarged regulatory license." That's judge parlance for "You're a big, fat liar."

Regardless of whether it's a tax or a penalty, says the Obama administration, the Commerce Clause still has to be paired with the "Necessary and Proper Clause" in Article One of the U.S. Constitution (section 8, clause 18) which states, "The Congress shall have Power to make all Laws which shall be necessary and proper for carrying into Execution the forgoing Powers, and all other Powers vested by this Constitution in the Government of the United States, or in any Department or Officer thereof." As a result, according to the Obama administration, the Necessary and Proper Clause gives the federal government broad, expansive powers that, when paired with the Commerce Clause, grant the federal government the authority even to force someone to purchase a product or service.

Constitutionalists like Cuccinelli deflate this broad claim by—*gasp!*—quoting the Constitution. They reject the idea that the Necessary and Proper Clause gives the Commerce Clause a regiment of steroids (and some Viagra besides). Conservatives point out that the Necessary and Proper Clause only gives the federal government the power to do things that are *granted* in the Constitution. How do we know this? It's simple. The Necessary and Proper Clause says it's restricted to what's listed in the Constitution: "The Congress shall have ... all other Powers vested by this Constitution."

However, the Obama administration thinks little things like the meaning of words and the breadth of constitutional powers are quaint and irrelevant when compared to their expansive view of the U.S. government's "living Constitution." This is the liberal idea that, like a human being, the Constitution can change its mind as it ages. Conservatives argue that, while the Constitution can change according to society's will—we change it every time we add an amendment—simply deciding that a word or phrase can suddenly mean something different only works in Wonderland.

Here in America, the concept of a "living Constitution" would take the Constitution out of the hands of the people and allow the government to do whatever it wants, regardless of what the Constitution says. Such things may happen in China and Zimbabwe, but America is attractive to immigrants and has created wealth because it has a stable, just democracy tethered to a Constitution that says what it means and means what it says.

So though Cuccinelli is obviously right in this debate, it's worth noting that the Necessary and Proper Clause was criticized during America's founding. Anti-Federalists expressed concern that the clause might be construed to grant the federal government boundless power (as liberals are now doing). Federalists, on the other hand, argued that the clause would only permit execution of power already granted by the Constitution. Just after the American Revolution, James Madison argued in *The Federalist Papers* (no. 44) that without this clause the Constitution would be a "dead letter." Meanwhile, at the Virginia Ratifying Convention, Patrick Henry took the opposing view, saying that he feared the clause would lead to limitless federal power that would inevitably menace civil liberties.[9]

This Anti-Federalist position at America's founding turned out to be visionary. Their trepidation that the Necessary and Proper Clause could result in a federal government with no bounds is part of the reason the Tenth Amendment was included in the Bill of Rights. The Tenth Amendment was included to boldly state that the federal government only has the power it's granted in the Constitution.

Judge Hudson showed he understood that even the federal government must obey its listed powers when he cut to the marrow of Obama-Care's individual mandate: "At its core, this dispute is not simply about regulating the business of insurance—or crafting a scheme of universal health-insurance coverage—it's about an individual's right to choose to participate." Judge Hudson then ruled in favor of the state of Virginia that the Commerce Clause does not give the U.S. government the ability to force someone to buy a product. If the Supreme Court is as constitutionally honest as Judge Hudson, then this provision, and possibly the entire 2,700-page Patient Protection and Affordable Care Act, will be held unconstitutional.

However, Judge Hudson's opinion was just one court battle in a larger war over the breadth of the constitutional powers of the federal government. Judges have come down on both sides of the issue. For example, a profound and judicially conservative ruling on the constitutionality of ObamaCare in January 2011 by Senior United States District Judge Roger Vinson found that:

> It is difficult to imagine that a nation which began, at least in part, as the result of opposition to a British mandate giving the East India Company a monopoly and imposing a nominal tax on all tea sold in America would have set out to create a government with the power to force people to buy tea in the first place. If Congress can penalize a passive individual for failing to engage in commerce, the enumeration of powers in the Constitution would have been in vain ... and we would have a Constitution in name only. Surely this is not what the Founding Fathers could have intended.[10]

Judge Vinson ruled that ObamaCare is unconstitutional and struck down the entire 2,700-page bill, as he found that the individual mandate that all citizens purchase health insurance wasn't severable from the rest of the act.

Judges who lean Left, however, see ObamaCare quite differently. Perhaps the most shocking liberal ruling came from Judge Gladys Kessler of the United States District Court for the District of Columbia. Judge Kessler thinks the federal government has broken its constitutional bonds so completely that bureaucrats can now even regulate our "mental activity."

Judge Kessler claimed this latest extension of government power in February 2011 when she found ObamaCare to be constitutional. In her decision she wrote: "It is pure semantics to argue that an individual who makes a choice to forgo health insurance is not 'acting,' especially given the serious economic and health-related consequences to every individual of that choice. Making a choice is an affirmative action, whether one decides to do something or not do something. They are two sides of the same coin. To pretend otherwise is to ignore reality."[11]

Judge Kessler's tortured liberal logic—a desperate effort to justify a government power that is clearly unconstitutional—again rests on the back of the Commerce Clause. How the federal government's power to regulate commerce "among the several states" allows the government to mandate that people purchase a product, such as health insurance, takes a lot of liberal Kool-Aid to comprehend.

After all, if regulating commerce among the states empowers the federal government to control even non-decisions by individual Americans, then there is no limit left to the federal government's power over private transactions. According to this view, any time a person chooses not to act they are still legally "acting." Therefore, says Judge Kessler, any decision not to act that could somehow be construed to affect commerce is an action the government can regulate and even require. For example, if the federal government decides it's in the best interest of the country for people to buy cars from GM or solar panels from GE, then it can make them do so—at least according to Judge Kessler and the Obama administration.

This struggle for freedom is headed for the Supreme Court and likely for more skirmishes in the U.S. Congress. Despite the legal and political wrangling, this is not a nebulous issue; in fact, in this rancorous debate over the future of America, the paths leading left and right are clear. A right turn leads back to the individual rights originally safeguarded by the Bill of Rights; a left turn leads to European-style socialism.

To shine a light down both forks in this road, it's worth comparing America's 7,200-word Constitution to the 76,000 words that comprise the European Union's (EU) constitution, now known as the Lisbon Treaty.

The U.S. Constitution and its twenty-seven amendments simply outline the structures of the federal government and the rights of individuals, whereas the EU constitution covers the structure of its central government, but is also filled with government powers so specific and overbearing that they dictate the rights of disabled people, they decide who can seek asylum, they outline the breadth of humanitarian missions, etc., etc.

The U.S. Constitution begins with "WE THE PEOPLE" in huge letters. The EU's inaugural charter, the Treaty of Rome, begins, "His Majesty the King of the Belgians."

The U.S. Constitution outlaws titles of nobility for federal officials and protects the freedom of speech, of religion, property rights, gun ownership, and many other individual rights. The Charter of Fundamental Rights of the European Union promises positive rights that impede individual rights, such as the right to affordable housing, protection against "unjustified dismissal," and free health care.

The EU's positive rights curtail individual rights because they empower the state to prevent an employer from sacking an incompetent employee, they take away the rights of property owners with rent-control-style bureaucracies, they force people to take part in national health-care systems, and so much more.

The U.S. Bill of Rights is basically a list of restrictions on government. The EU's Charter of Fundamental Rights is split into the categories

"Dignity," "Freedoms," "Equality," "Solidarity," "Citizens' rights," and "Justice," each of which empowers bureaucrats to weigh individual rights with the EU's powers as they decide how to define individual freedoms. The U.S. Bill of Rights, in contrast, is a simple, declarative list of restrictions on government power that was defined by the people; it was not designed to be subject to complex interpretations by unelected bureaucrats.

President Obama seems to prefer the EU constitution, which is why he called the U.S. Constitution a "charter of negative liberties."[12] He knows the Tenth Amendment was added to the U.S. Constitution to assure the people that the federal government wouldn't exceed its restricted powers (i.e.: "negative liberties"). This is why liberal-progressives abhor the Tenth Amendment and have worked to all but expunge it from the Constitution.

This is also why President Franklin D. Roosevelt proposed his "second bill of rights"[13] during his State of the Union address on January 11, 1944, a list of positive rights that is eerily similar to those found in the EU's constitution. And it's why President Barack Obama said, "While many believed that the new Constitution gave them liberty, it instead fitted them with the shackles of hypocrisy."[14] President Obama and the Left think that only the government can empower the people; America's Founding Fathers knew government can only take away liberty, which was why, in 1776, Thomas Paine called government a "necessary evil" in his tome for freedom, *Common Sense.*

President Obama's and FDR's push for positive rights would give Washington politicians and bureaucrats the ability to force all Americans to buy government-approved health insurance or to do anything else the government deems to be for the common good. It would lead to the end of individual freedom in America.

In fact, to complete the federal government's triumph over the individual, liberal-progressives now even deny the United States is a constitutional republic, as a constitutional republic protects individual rights from the majority; America does this with the U.S. Bill of Rights. Instead, liberal-progressives claim the United States is a pure democracy, which they construe to mean the majority rules over all things, including the Constitution. Thus an elected government can overrule individual rights if they think it is in the best interest of the majority to do so.

The Founders tried to avoid this government-centric authoritarianism. In *The Federalist Papers* (1787–1788) this concept was referred to as "the violence of majority faction."[15] In his book *Democracy in America* (1835–1840), Alexis de Tocqueville called a democracy that isn't restricted by individual rights a "tyranny of the majority." To prevent the majority from infringing on minority rights (remember, the smallest minority is the individual), the Framers restricted the federal government to its powers as listed in the Constitution. They then added a bill of rights during the first U.S. Congress that included the Tenth Amendment's straightforward declaration restricting the federal government to its constitutional powers. And they burdened the government with checks and balances designed to slow down government and thereby protect individuals from the politics of the moment.

Liberals can't abide these restrictions on government authority. Some even deny the Tenth Amendment still has meaning. For example, Representative James Clyburn (D-SC) articulated the Democratic Party's position a bit too honestly for some in his party when he said, "[T]here's nothing in the Constitution that says that the federal government has anything to do with most of the stuff we do."[16] Representative Clyburn's brash claim that the federal government has no constitutional boundaries prompted Republicans to open the 112th Congress by reading the Constitution. Some Democrats mocked this public show, but they knew deep down that a candid reading of the Constitution is dangerous to their power. Their entire movement requires that the Constitution be reduced to dead letters, that it be replaced by a "living Constitution" they can alter as their needs dictate.

Beyond the liberal smokescreen, the Constitution is really a very simple, easy-to-understand document. The First Amendment restricts the government from unreasonably infringing upon our free speech, on our freedom of religion, and from establishing a state religion; the Second

Amendment prevents the government from disarming the citizenry; the Fourth Amendment requires the government to leave us, and our houses, papers, and even digital records alone unless they first obtain a warrant. Each of the amendments protects a fundamental right and so clearly operates as a strong check on the power of the federal government. Saving the Bill of Rights requires us to honestly understand this plain truth and to actively demand our elected representatives do the same. After all, it is these individual rights that brought and still attract the tired, the poor, and the hungry to America with hope in their eyes and the eagerness to chase down and attain their dreams in their hearts.

That American Dream is precisely what's at stake in the battle to save the Bill of Rights.

THE BILL OF RIGHTS

The Preamble to the Bill of Rights

Congress of the United States begun and held at the City of New-York, on Wednesday the fourth of March, one thousand seven hundred and eighty nine.

THE Conventions of a number of the States, having at the time of their adopting the Constitution, expressed a desire, in order to prevent misconstruction or abuse of its powers, that further declaratory and restrictive clauses should be added: And as extending the ground of public confidence in the Government, will best ensure the beneficent ends of its institution.

RESOLVED by the Senate and House of Representatives of the United States of America, in Congress assembled, two thirds of both Houses concurring, that the following Articles be proposed to the Legislatures of the several States, as amendments to the Constitution of the United States, all, or any of which Articles, when ratified by three fourths of the said Legislatures, to be valid to all intents and purposes, as part of the said Constitution; viz.

ARTICLES in addition to, and Amendment of the Constitution of the United States of America, proposed by Congress, and ratified by the Legislatures of the several States, pursuant to the fifth Article of the original Constitution.

Amendment I

Congress shall make no law respecting an establishment of religion, or prohibiting the free exercise thereof; or abridging the freedom of speech, or of the press; or the right of the people peaceably to assemble, and to petition the Government for a redress of grievances.

Amendment II

A well regulated Militia, being necessary to the security of a free State, the right of the people to keep and bear Arms, shall not be infringed.

Amendment III

No Soldier shall, in time of peace be quartered in any house, without the consent of the Owner, nor in time of war, but in a manner to be prescribed by law.

Amendment IV

The right of the people to be secure in their persons, houses, papers, and effects, against unreasonable searches and seizures, shall not be violated, and no Warrants shall issue, but upon probable cause, supported by Oath or affirmation, and particularly describing the place to be searched, and the persons or things to be seized.

Amendment V

No person shall be held to answer for a capital, or otherwise infamous crime, unless on a presentment or indictment of a Grand Jury, except in cases arising in the land or naval forces, or in the Militia, when in actual service in time of War or public danger; nor shall any person be subject for the same offence to be twice put in jeopardy of life or limb; nor shall be compelled in any criminal case to be a witness against himself, nor be deprived of life, liberty, or property, without due process of law; nor shall private property be taken for public use, without just compensation.

Amendment VI

In all criminal prosecutions, the accused shall enjoy the right to a speedy and public trial, by an impartial jury of the State and district wherein the crime shall have been committed, which district shall have been previously ascertained by law, and to be informed of the nature and cause of the accusation; to be confronted with the witnesses against him; to have compulsory process for obtaining witnesses in his favor, and to have the Assistance of Counsel for his defence.

Amendment VII

In Suits at common law, where the value in controversy shall exceed twenty dollars, the right of trial by jury shall be preserved, and no fact tried by a jury, shall be otherwise re-examined in any Court of the United States, than according to the rules of the common law.

Amendment VIII

Excessive bail shall not be required, nor excessive fines imposed, nor cruel and unusual punishments inflicted.

Amendment IX

The enumeration in the Constitution, of certain rights, shall not be construed to deny or disparage others retained by the people.

Amendment X

The powers not delegated to the United States by the Constitution, nor prohibited by it to the States, are reserved to the States respectively, or to the people.

NOTES

The Preamble

1. H. L. Mencken, *On Politics: A Carnival of Buncombe*, 1920–1936, published posthumously in 1956.
2. Charles Darwin, *On the Origin of the Species*, 1860.
3. Pius XII, *Humani Generis*, Vatican, 1950.
4. Thomas Jefferson, Letter to Colonel Charles Yancey, January 6, 1816.
5. Bill Whittle, "Shame Cubed," National Review Online, October 27, 2008, http://article.nationalreview.com/376519/shame-cubed/bill-whittle (accessed March 10, 2011).
6. Franklin D. Roosevelt, "State of the Union Message to Congress," Franklin D. Roosevelt Presidential Library and Museum, http://www.fdrlibrary. marist.edu/archives/address_text.html (accessed March 10, 2011).
7. Barack Obama's "senior seminar" paper written at Columbia University. The subject of this paper, which totaled 44 pages, was American government, and the title was "Aristocracy Reborn."
8. John Stuart Mill, *On Liberty*, 1859.

Amendment I

1. Charlton Heston, Speech to the National Press Club, September 14, 1997.
2. Medea Benjamin, "Hugo Chavez could teach U.S. leaders a thing or two about winning votes," Press Release by CodePink, http://www.codepink-alert.org/article.php?id=117 (accessed March 17, 2011).
3. A. J. Liebling, "Do you belong in journalism?" *The New Yorker*, May 14, 1960, http://www.newyorker.com/archive/1960/05/14/1960_05_14_105_TNY_CARDS_000262077 (accessed March 17, 2011).
4. Evelyn Beatrice Hall, *The Friends of Voltaire* (London: Smith Elder, 1906).
5. Congressional Record S12585-6, October 14, 1999.

6. "President Signs Campain Finance Reform Act," the White House, http://georgewbush-whitehouse.archives.gov/news/releases/2002/03/20020327.html (accessed March 17, 2011).

7. *McConnell* v. *FEC*, U.S. Supreme Court, 2003 (Scalia dissenting).

8. Angelo M. Codevilla, "America's Ruling Class–And the Perils of Revolution," *The American Spectator*, July–August 2010.

9. Bradley A. Smith, Chairman Federal Election Commission, Letter to Michael Boos, Esq., Vice President & General Counsel Citizens United, September 10, 2004, http://www.democracy21.org/vertical/Sites/ %7B3D66FAFE-2697-446F-BB39-85FBBBA57812%7D/uploads/% 7BEB24246D-CC3F-4F27-A003-4B84CB0576CF%7D.PDF (accessed April 14, 2011).

10. The White House Press Room, "Remarks by the President in State of the Union Address," January 27, 2010, www.whitehouse.gov/the-press-office/remarks-president-state-union-address (accessed March 17, 2011).

11. Adam Liptak, "Justices, 5-4, Reject Corporate Spending Limit," *New York Times*, January 21, 2010, http://community.nytimes.com/comments/www.nytimes.com/2010/01/22/us/politics/22scotus.html (accessed March 17, 2011).

12. Nick Baumann, "Grayson: Court's Campaign Finance Decision 'Worst Since Dred Scott,'" *Mother Jones*, January 22, 2010, http://motherjones.com/mojo/2010/01/grayson-courts-campaign-finance-decision-worst-dredd-scott (accessed March 17, 2011).

13. "Group Calls For Constitutional Amendment to Overturn High Court's Campaign Finance Ruling," The Public Record, January 21, 2010, http://pubrecord.org/multimedia/6674/congresswoman-professor-movement/ (accessed March 17, 2011).

14. Jason Hancock, "Boswell pushed constitutional amendment to overturn SCOTUS ruling," *The Iowa Independent*, January 21, 2010, http://iowaindependent.com/26145/boswell-pushes-constitutional-amendment-to-overturn-scotus-ruling (accessed March 17, 2011).

15. Susan Crabtree, "Sen. Kerry backs changing Constitution to deal with Supreme Court decision," *The Hill*, February 2, 2010, http://thehill.com/homenews/senate/79289-kerry-backs-changing-constitution-to-deal-with-scotus-decision (accessed March 17, 2011).

16. Kasie Hunt, "John McCain, Russ Feingold diverge on court ruling," *Politico*, January 21, 2010, http://www.politico.com/news/stories/0110/31810.html (accessed March 17, 2011).

17. David Kirkpatrick, "Lobbyists Get Potent Weapon in Campaign Financing," *New York Times*, January 22, 2010, http://www.nytimes.com/2010/01/22/us/politics/22donate.html (accessed March 17, 2011).

18. Steve Padilla, "Obama's State of the Union Address, Criticism of the Supreme Court campaign finance ruling," *Los Angeles Times*, January 27, 2010, http://latimesblogs.latimes.com/washington/2010/01/obamas-state-of-the-union-address-criticism-of-the-supreme-court-campaign-finance-ruling.html (accessed March 17, 2011).

19. T. W. Farnam, "The Influence Industry: Disclose Act could deter involvement in elections," *The Washington Post*, May 13, 2010, http://www.washingtonpost.com/wp-dyn/content/article/2010/05/12/AR2010051205094.html (accessed March 17, 2011).

20. Author interview with R. Bruce Josten, executive vice president for government affairs at the U.S. Chamber of Commerce, August 18, 2010.

21. See www.discloseact.com.

22. Editorial, "A distasteful move by MoveOn.org," *Los Angeles Times*, August 19, 2010, http://articles.latimes.com/2010/aug/19/opinion/la-ed-moveon-20100819 (accessed March 17, 2011).

23. Eric Foner, *Give Me Liberty!* (New York: W.W. Norton and Company, 2008.)

24. James Morton Smith, *Freedom's Fetters: The Alien and Sedition Laws and American Civil Liberties* (Ithaca, NY: Cornell University Press, 1966).

25. Ralph Reiland, "Dr. Jack Cassell: A Hero," *Capitalism Magazine*, April 11, 2010.

26. Fred Lucas, "Obama Signs Bill Violating 'Equal Justice Under the Law,' Critics Say," CNSNews.com, October 29, 2009. http://www.cnsnews.com/node/56300 (accessed March 17, 2011).

27. Peter Brimacombe, *All the Queen's Men: The World of Elizabeth I* (New York: Palgrave Macmillan, 2000).

28. Warren Richey, "Supreme Court to decide case on animal cruelty and free speech," *Christian Science Monitor*, October 5, 2009, http://www.csmonitor.com/USA/Justice/2009/1005/p02s01-usju.html (accessed March 17, 2011).

29. "Just 21% Want FCC to Regulate Internet, Most Fear Regulation Would Promote Political Agenda," *Rasmussen Reports*, December 28, 2010, http://www.rasmussenreports.com/public_content/politics/general_politics/december_2010/just_21_want_fcc_to_regulate_internet_most_fear_regulation_would_promote_political_agenda (accessed March 17, 2011).

30. Rush Limbaugh, *The Rush Limbaugh Show*, March 16, 2010.

31. Ben Smith, "HHS buys 'Obamacare,'" *Politico*, December 17, 2010, http://www.politico.com/blogs/bensmith/1210/HHS_buys_ObamaCare.html (accessed March 17, 2011).

32.   Robert W. McChesney, "The U.S. Media Reform Movement," *Monthly Review*, September 15, 2008, http://monthlyreview.org/080915mcchesney. php (accessed March 17, 2011).

33.   "Media Capitalism, the State and 21st Century Media Democracy Struggles," An Interview with Robert McChesney, The Bullet Socialist Project, August 9, 2009, http://www.socialistproject.ca/bullet/246.php (accessed March 17, 2011).

34.   John Fund, "The Net Neutrality Coup," *The Wall Street Journal*, December 21, 2010, http://online.wsj.com/article/SB10001424052748703886904576 031512110086694.html (accessed March 17, 2011).

35.   Amy Schatz and Shayndi Raice, "Internet Gets New Rules of the Road," *The Wall Street Journal*, December 21, 2010, http://online.wsj.com/article/ SB10001424052748703581204576033513990668654.html (accessed March 17, 2011).

36.   Robert M. McDowell, "The FCC Threat to Internet Freedom," editorial in *The Wall Street Journal*, December 19, 2010, http://online.wsj.com/article/ SB10001424052748703395204576023452250748540.html (accessed March 17, 2011).

37.   Mark S. Fowler, *The Mark Levin Show*, February 16, 2009.

38.   Michael Calderon, "Sen. Harkin: 'We Need the Fairness Doctrine Back," *Politico*, February 11, 2009, http://www.politico.com/blogs/michaelcalde- rone/0209/Sen_Harkin_We_need_the_Fairness_Doctrine_back_.html (accessed March 17, 2011).

39.   John Gizzi, "Pelosi Supports 'Fairness' Doctrine," *Human Events*, October 25, 2008, http://www.humanevents.com/article.php?id=27185 (accessed March 17, 2011).

40.   John Eggerton, "Bill Clinton Talks of Re-Imposing Fairness Doctrine or At Least 'More Balance in Media,'" Broadcasting & Cable, February 13, 2009, http://www.broadcastingcable.com/article/174123-Bill_Clinton_Talks_of_ Re_Imposing_Fairness_Doctrine_or_At_Least_More_Balance_in_Media. php (accessed March 17, 2011).

41.   Sara Jerome, "FCC push to regulate news draws fire," *The Hill*, December 6, 2010, http://thehill.com/blogs/hillicon-valley/technology/132195-fcc- proposal-to-regulate-news-draws-fire (accessed March 17, 2011).

42.   "Uncovered Audio: Obam's Regulatory Czar Pushes Creepy Plan for Legally Controlling Internet Information," Breitbart.com, May 17, 2010, http://www.breitbart.tv/uncovered-audio-obamas-regulatory-czar-pushes-

creepy-plan-for-legally-controlling-internet-information/ (accessed March 17, 2011).

43. Senator Jim DeMint, "Public Broadcasting Should Go Private," *The Wall Street Journal*, March 4, 2011.

44. Ayn Rand interview with Alvin Toffler, *Playboy*, March 1964.

45. Matthew 5:14–16.

46. Interview with Reverend Donald D. Binder, Pohick Church, July 4, 2010.

47. Letter of October 7, 1801, from Danbury Baptist Association to Thomas Jefferson.

48. Thomas Jefferson, *Writings*, Vol. XVI, letter to the Danbury Baptist Association, January 1, 1802.

49. Thomas Jefferson, *Writings*, Vol. VIII, to Noah Webster, December 4, 1790.

50. Leviticus, 25:10.

51. U.S. Supreme Court, *Reynolds* v. *United States*, 1878.

52. Thomas Jefferson, *Notes on the State of Virginia*, Philadelphia: Mathew Carey, 1794.

53. "Obama Leaves 'By their Creator' Out of the Declaration of Independence at Hispanic Caucus Speech," posted by FreedomsLighthouse, September 18, 2010, http://www.youtube.com/watch?v=yR61uTGTFoM (accessed April 14, 2011).

54. Baron de Montesquieu, *The Spirit of the Laws*, 1748.

55. John Witherspoon, *The Works of John Witherspoon*, Edinburgh: J. Ogle, Parliament-Square, 1815.

56. Interview with David Barton, founder and president of Wallbuilders, November 17, 2010.

57. Representative Walter B. Jones, "Rep. Jones Vows to Continue the Fight to Restore Freedom of Speech to Houses of Worship," press release, October 2, 2002, http://jones.house.gov/News/DocumentSingle.aspx?Document ID=172024 (accessed March 17, 2011).

58. Andy Birkey, "IRS Loophole Gets Minnesota off Tax Violation Hook," *The Minnesota Independent*, August 24, 2009, http://minnesotaindependent. com/41720/irs-loophole-gets-minnesota-churches-off-tax-violation-hook (accessed March 17, 2011).

59. Dan Gilgoff, "Turning a blind eye, IRS enables church politicking," *USA Today*, January 29, 2007, http://www.usatoday.com/printedition/news/20070129/opledereligion62.art.htm (accessed March 17, 2011).

60. Andy Birkey, "IRS Loophole gets Minnesota churches off tax-violation hook," *The Minnesota Independent*.

Amendment II

1.   *McDonald* v. *Chicago*, U.S. Supreme Court, opinion of the court, 2010.

2.   Radley Balko, "Brian Aitken's Mistake," *Reason*, November 15, 2010, http://reason.com/archives/2010/11/15/brian-aitkens-mistake (accessed March 17, 2011).

3.   Peter May, "N.H. town fights for one of its own," *The Boston Globe*, December 25, 2010, http://www.boston.com/news/local/new_hampshire/articles/2010/12/25/prison_term_for_native_son_draws_ire_of_nh_town/ (accessed March 17, 2011).

4.   "Sacramento-area pilot punished for YouTube video," News10, December 22, 2010, http://www.news10.net/news/article.aspx?storyid=113529&provider=top&catid=188 (accessed March 17, 2011).

5.   George Mason, 3 Elliot, Debates at 380.

6.   George Mason, 3 Elliot, Debates at 425–426.

7.   Definition available at http://1828.mshaffer.com/d/search/word,militia (accessed March 17, 2011).

8.   ABC, *This Week*, interview with President Barack Obama, September 20, 2009, http://blogs.abcnews.com/george/2009/09/obama-mandate-is-not-a-tax.html (accessed March 17, 2011).

9.   Richard A. Posner, "In Defense of Looseness," *The New Republic*, August 27, 2008, http://www.tnr.com/article/books/defense-looseness (accessed March 17, 2011).

10. J. Harvie Wilkinson, "Of Guns, Abortions, and the Unraveling Rule of Law," *Virginia Law Review*, 2009, http://www.virginialawreview.org/articles.php?article=239 (accessed March 17, 2011).

11. Jeffrey M. Shaman, *The Wages of Originalist Sin: District of Columbia* v. *Heller*, July 17, 2008, http://ssrn.com/abstract=1162338 (accessed March 17, 2011).

12. Colleen Mastony, "The Public Face of Gun Rights," *Chicago Tribune*, January 30, 2010, http://articles.chicagotribune.com/2010-01-31/news/1001310077_1_handgun-ban-supreme-court-second-amendment (accessed March 17, 2011).

13. Ibid.

14. Ibid.

15. *McDonald* v. *Chicago*, U.S. Supreme Court, opinion of the court, 2010.

16. David B. Kopel, "The Klan's Favorite Law," *Reason*, February 15, 2005, http://reason.com/archives/2005/02/15/the-klans-favorite-law (accessed March 17, 2011).

17. Editorial, "An assault on citizen rights: In New Orleans, legally owned guns taken," *The Tribune-Democrat*, October 28, 2005, http://tribune-democrat. com/editorials/x519118924/An-assault-on-citizen-rights (accessed March 17, 2011).

Amendment III

1. *United States* v. *Valenzuala*, U.S. District Court for the Southern District of California, 95 F. Supp. 363, 366, 1951.
2. Author interviews with Jerrold Ziman.
3. *Engblom* v. *Carey*, U.S. Court of Appeals for the Second Circuit, 1982.
4. *Rakas* v. *Illinois*, U.S. Supreme Court, 1978.
5. "History of Rent Regulation in New York State 1943-1993," New York Division of Housing & Community Renewal.
6. William Tucker, "How Rent Control Drives Out Affordable Housing," Cato Institute, May 1997, http://www.cato.org/pubs/pas/pa-274.html (accessed March 17, 2011).
7. *Lorreto* v. *Teleprompter Manhattan CATV Corp.*, U.S. Supreme Court, 1982.

Amendment IV

1. Ayn Rand, *The Fountainhead*, Bobbs Merrill, 1943.
2. "Reps. Paul Ryan, Chris Van Hollen Talk Policy, Politics; Justice Stephen Breyer on New Book," *FOX News Sunday* with Chris Wallace, December 12, 2010, http://www.foxnews.com/on-air/fox-news-sunday/transcript/ reps-paul-ryan-chris-van-hollen-talk-policy-politics-justice-stephen-breyer-new-book?page=4 (accessed March 21, 2011).
3. *Annals of Congress*, 1st Congress, 1st Session, 452.
4. Osmand K. Fraenkel, "Concerning Searches and Seizures," *Harvard Law Review* (34) 1921.
5. *Griffin* v. *Wisconsin*, U.S. Supreme Court, 1987.
6. Robert B. Traynor, "*Mapp* v. *Ohio* at Large in the Fifty States," *Duke Law Journal*, 1962 (321–22).
7. Peter F. Nardulli, "The Societal Cost of the Exclusionary Rule: An Empirical Assessment," *American Bar Foundation Research Journal*, 1983 (585); and, "The Societal Costs of the Exclusionary Rule Revisited," *University of Illinois Law Review*, 1987.

8.   Daniel Webster, *The Writing and Speeches of Daniel Webster,* 10 volumes, Boston 1903.

9.   *Florida* v. *Riley,* U.S. Supreme Court, 1989.

10.   Declan McCullagh, "Feds push for tracking cell phones," CNET News, February 11, 2010, http://news.cnet.com/8301-13578_3-10451518-38.html (accessed March 21, 2011).

11.   Philip Zimmermann, *PGP Source Code and Internals* (Cambridge, MA: MIT Press, 1995).

12.   http://www.epic.org/crypto/export_controls/brenstein_decision_9_cir.html

13.   Kim Zetter, "U.S. Declassifies Part of Secret Cybersecurity Plan," *Wired,* March 2, 2010, http://www.wired.com/threatlevel/2010/03/us-declassifies-part-of-secret-cybersecurity-plan/ (accessed March 21, 2011).

14.   Declan McCullagh, "Feds weigh expansion of Internet monitoring," CNET News, March 4, 2010, http://news.cnet.com/8301-13578_3-10463665-38.html (accessed March 21, 2011).

15.   Matt Cover, "Senate Democrats Pass Bill Allowing Govt to Collect Addresses, ATM Records of Bank Customers," CNSNews.com, May 21, 2010, http://www.cnsnews.com/node/66439 (accessed March 21, 2011).

16.   Charlie Savage, "U.S. Tries to Make It Easier to Wiretap the Internet," *New York Times,* September 27, 2010, http://www.nytimes.com/2010/09/27/us/27wiretap.html (accessed March 21, 2011).

17.   John Adams' abstract of James Otis' argument, in L. Kevin Wroth and Hiller B. Zobel, eds., *The Legal Papers of John Adams* (Cambridge, MA: Harvard University Press, 1965).

18.   Omnibus Counterterrorism Act of 1995 (S. 390), http://thomas.loc.gov/cgi-bin/bdquery/z?d104:s.00390: (accessed March 21, 2011).

19.   David Cole and James X. Dempsey, *Terrorism and the Constitution: Sacrificing Civil Liberties in the Name of National Security* (Los Angeles, The New Press, 2002).

20.   Paul Rosenzweig, "Terrorism is not just a crime," American Bar Association, Patriot Debates, http://www.abanet.org/natsecurity/patriotdebates/206-2#rebuttal (accessed March 21, 2011).

21.   "Apology Note," *The Washington Post,* November 29, 2006, http://www.washingtonpost.com/wp-dyn/content/article/2006/11/29/AR2006112901155.html?nav=rss_nation/nationalsecurity (accessed March 21, 2011).

22.   Pete Yost, "FBI access to e-mail, Web data raises privacy fear," *Washington Post,* August 1, 2010.

23. *Doe* v. *Ashcroft*, U.S. District Court for the Southern District of New York, September 2004.

24. Dan Eggen, "Judge Invalidates Patriot Act Provision," *Washington Post*, September 7, 2007.

25. "Resolution on the USA Patriot Act and Related Measures That Infringe on the Rights of Library Users," American Library Association, January 29, 2003.

26. Jarrett Murphy, "Don't Call It 'Patriot Act II'," CBS News, September 19, 2003, http://www.cbsnews.com/stories/2003/08/19/national/main569135.shtml (accessed March 21, 2011).

27. "Surveillance Under the USA PATRIOT Act," American Civil Liberties Union, April 3, 2003, http://www.aclu.org/national-security/surveillance-under-usa-patriot-act (accessed March 21, 2011).

28. U.S. Supreme Court, *Michigan Department of State Police* v. *Sitz*, 1990, quoting *Alameida-Sanchez* v. *United States* (1973).

29. Thomas Jefferson, Letter to Colonel Charles Yancey, January 6, 1816.

30. Melvin L. Wulf, "On the origins of privacy; constitutional practice," *The Nation*, May 27, 1991.

31. Alexander Hamilton, *The Federalist*, No. 84, 582.

Amendment V

1.   Editorial, "The Limits of Property Rights," *New York Times*, June 24, 2005, http://www.nytimes.com/2005/06/24/opinion/24fri1.html (accessed March 22, 2011).

2.   Editorial, "Eminent Latitude," *Washington Post*, June 24, 2005, http://www.washingtonpost.com/wp-dyn/content/article/2005/06/23/AR2005062301698.html (accessed March 22, 2011).

3.   Legislative Center, Citizens Fighting Eminent Domain Abuse, http://www.castlecoalition.org/index.php?option=com_content&task=view&id=34&Itemid=119 (accessed March 22, 2011).

4.   Columbia University Statistical Abstract, Endowment Value, 1999-2000 to 2009-2010 (in billions of dollars), http://www.columbia.edu/cu/opir/abstract/endowment.html (accessed March 22, 2011).

5.   Doug Bandow, "Justice Done to Susette Kelo—A Few Years Too Late," *American Spectator*, March 13, 2009, http://spectator.org/blog/2009/03/13/justice-done-to-susette-kelo-a (accessed March 22, 2011).

6.   *Penn. Coal Co.* v. *Mahon*, U.S. Supreme Court, 1922.

7.   Jeanne Brokaw, "Does anybody give a hoot?" *Mother Jones*, Nov-Dec 1996, http://motherjones.com/politics/1996/11/does-anybody-give-hoot (accessed March 22, 2011).

8.   "Democrats More Hopeful," *New York Times,* January 30, 1894.

Amendment VI

1.   George Bancroft, *The History of the Formation of the Constitution of the United States,* 1882.

2.   Laura Kriho, "Passing on well-hidden information," guest editorial in the *Rocky Mountain News,* September 15, 1997.

3.   U.S. Supreme Court, *In re Oliver,* 333 U.S. 257, 1948, http://supreme.justia.com/us/333/257/case.html (accessed March 24, 2011).

4.   Laura Kriho, "Passing on well-hidden information," guest editorial in the *Rocky Mountain News,* September 15, 1997.

5.   "Holdout Juror Acquitted of Wrongdoing," Jury Rights Project, August 9, 2000 http://www.constitution.org/col/0809kriho.txt (accessed March 24, 2011).

6.   Hans Fantel, *William Penn: Apostle of Dissent* (New York: William Morrow & Co., 1974).

7.   William Blackstone, *Commentaries on the Laws of England,* 1765.

8.   *Debates on the Federal Constitution,* 1836 (remarks of Mr. Iredell, of North Carolina).

9.   Steven E. Barkan, "Jury Nullification in Political Trials," *Social Problems,* Vol. 31, October 1983.

10. Clay S. Conrad, "Jury Nullification as a Defense Strategy," Texas Forum on Civil Liberties and Civil Rights, 1995.

11. David E. Carney, *To Promote the General Welfare: A Communitarian Legal Reader* (Lanham, MD: Lexington Books, 1999).

12. Sam Howe Verhovek, "Larry Davis Cleared In the 1986 Slayings Of 4 Drug Suspects," *New York Times,* March 4, 1988.

13. Cicero, *De Officiis (On Duties),* 44 B.C.

14. Criminal Pattern Jury Instruction Committee of the United States Court of Appeals for the Tenth Circuit, "Duty to Follow Instructions," Criminal Pattern Jury Instructions.

15. Erick J. Haynie, "Populism, Free Speech, and the Rule of Law: The 'Fully Informed' Jury Movement and Its Implications," *The Journal of Criminal Law and Criminology,* Autumn 1997.

16.   *Patton* v. *United States*, U.S. Supreme Court, 1930.

17.   Justice William J. Brennan, *Jones* v. *Barnes*, 1983 (dissenting).

Amendment VII

1.   Ambrose Bierce, *The Devil's Dictionary*, 1911.

2.   William Shakespeare, *King Henry VI*, Act IV, Scene II.

3.   State Court Guide to Statistical Reporting, 2003, the National Center for State Courts.

4.   Associated Press, "Cabell schools to eliminate swing sets," *The Charleston Gazette*, September 1, 2010, http://wvgazette.com/News/201009010865?page=2&build=cache (accessed March 23, 2011).

5.   "Basketball Town Forced To Close," KCRA.com, September 30, 2007, http://www.kcra.com/r/14240061/detail.html (accessed March 23, 2011).

6.   Jill Whalen, "Man who sued Mt. Laurel pool out to clear name," Standard-speaker.com, February 9, 2010, http://standardspeaker.com/news/man-who-sued-mt-laurel-pool-out-to-clear-name-1.605820 (accessed March 23, 2011).

7.   Gary Klein, "In San Rafael, 'exploding' escargot ignite saucy lawsuit," *Marin Independent Journal*, November 12, 2010.

8.   L. Canter, "Man Sues Restaurant After Eating Entire Artichoke," www.foodanddrinkdigital.com, November 19, 2010, http://www.foodanddrink-digital.com/sectors/other-food-and-drinks/man-sues-restaurant-after-eating-entire-artichoke (accessed March 23, 2011).

9.   "The Drug Dealer Rick Ross Has Lost His Lawsuit Against the Rapper Rick Ross," NYMAG.com November 5, 2010, http://nymag.com/daily/enter-tainment/2010/11/the_drug_dealer_rick_ross_has.html (accessed March 23, 2011).

10.   *Liebeck* v. *McDonalds Et Al*, State of New Mexico at Albuquerque District, March 12, 1993.

11.   Thomas Jefferson, letter to L'Abbe Arnoux, July 19, 1789.

12.   *U.S.* v. *Callender*, U.S. Supreme Court, 1800.

13.   Jerry W. Knudson, "The Jeffersonian Assault on the Federalist Judiciary, 1802-1805: Political Forces and Press Reaction," *American Journal of Legal History*, 1970.

14.   Articles of Impeachment Against Samuel Chase, Art. IV, reprinted in Charles Evans, *Report Of the Trial Of the Hon. Samuel Chase*, 1805, Appendix at 4.

15.   Willard S. Randall, *Thomas Jefferson: A Life* (New York: Henry Holt & Co., 1993).

16.   Annette Gordon-Reed, *Thomas Jefferson and Sally Hemings: An American Controversy* (University of Virginia Press, 1997).

17.   Chief Justice John Jay, *Georgia* v. *Brailsford*, 1794.

18.   Section "1.01 General: Nature Of Case; Burden Of Proof; Duty Of Jury; Cautionary," Manual of Model Civil Jury Instructions for the District Courts of the Eighth Circuit, 2008.

19.   Rule 50(b), Federal Rules of Civil Procedure.

20.   Rule 50(a), Federal Rules of Civil Procedure.

21.   Robert H. Bork, "The End of Democracy? Our Judicial Oligarchy," *First Things,* November 1996, http://www.firstthings.com/article/2007/11/003-the-end-of-democracy-our-judicial-oligarchy-35 (accessed March 23, 2011).

22.   Note 22: "The Incorporation Debate," Exploring Constitutional Conflicts, http://law2.umkc.edu/faculty/projects/ftrials/conlaw/incorp.htm (accessed April 14, 2011).

23.   Bernie Marcus, guest editorial, "America's litigation crisis," *San Francisco Examiner*, September 7, 2004.

24.   Note 24: "Lawyers/Law Firms," OpenSecrets.org, http://www.opensecrets.org/industries/indus.php?ind=K01 (accessed April 14, 2011).

25.   James R. Copeland, "How the Plaintiffs Bar Bought the Senate," *The Wall Street Journal,* February 9, 2010.

26.   Eric Malnic, "GM Files Appeal of $1.2-Billion Verdict, Calling Trial Unfair," *Los Angeles Times,* December 12, 2007, http://articles.latimes.com/2000/dec/07/local/me-62370 (accessed March 23, 2011).

27.   Information available at www.100percent-compensation.co.uk/compensation_awards.htm (accessed March 23, 2011).

28.   *Kamilewicz* v. *Bank of Boston,* 7th Circuit, U.S. Court of Appeals, 2003.

Amendment VIII

1.   *Wabaunsee County* v. *Umbehr*, U.S. Supreme Court, 1996 (dissenting).

2.   *Furman* v. *Georgia*, U.S. Supreme Court, 1972 (Justice Thurgood Marshall, concurring).

3.   Robert H. Bork, *A Time to Speak* (Wilmington, DE: ISI Books, 2008).

4.   Erick Erickson, "William Henry Furman: A Postscript," RedState, 2004, http://archive.redstate.com/stories/archived/william_henry_furman_a_postscript (accessed March 24, 2011).

5.   William Blackstone, *Commentaries*, 1769.

6.   John Patterson, *The Bill of Rights: Politics, Religion, and the Quest for Justice*, (iUniverse, Inc, 2004).

7.   Debate in the Virginia Ratifying Convention, June 16, 1788; Philip Kurland, *The Founders' Constitution* (Liberty Fund Inc., 2000).

8.   Bernard Schwartz, *The Great Rights of Mankind: A History of the American Bill of Rights* (Lanham, MD: Rowman & Littlefield, 1992).

9.   Joseph Story, *Commentaries on the Constitution of the United States* (Boston, 1833).

10. As quoted in *Kennedy* v. *Louisiana*, http://www.supremecourt.gov/opinions/07pdf/07-343.pdf (accessed March 24, 2011).

11. John Stinneford, "The Original Meaning of the 'Unusual': The Eighth Amendment as a Bar to Cruel Innovation," *Northwestern University Law Review*, Vol. 102, No. 4, 2008.

12. *Fruman* v. *Geogia*, U.S. Supreme Court, 1972. (Justice Warren Burger, dissenting)

13. Scott Shane, "Waterboarding Used 266 Times on 2 Suspects," *New York Times*, April 19, 2009, http://www.nytimes.com/2009/04/20/world/20detain.html (accessed March 24, 2011).

14. "58% Favor Waterboarding of Plane Terrorist To Get Information," Rasmussen Reports, December 31, 2009.

Amendment IX

1.   Notes on the State of Virginia, Q.XVIII, 1782.

2.   Matthew 7:12.

3.   Babylonian Talmud, tractate Shabbat 31a.

4.   Seneca, *De Beneficiis*, III, 20.

5.   Charles H. McIlwain, *The Growth of Political Thought in the West: From the Greeks to the End of the Middle Ages* (New York: Cooper Square Press, 1932).

6.   Cicero, *De Legibus* (Keyes translation), book 1, section 28.

7.   St. Thomas Aquinas, *Summa Theologica*, Q. 95, A. 2.

8.   Richard Price, *Observations on the Nature of Civil Liberty*, 1776, reprinted in: Bernard Peach, *Richard Price and the Ethical Foundations of the American Revolution* (Durham, NC: Duke University Press, 1979).

9.   Pauline Maier, *American Scripture: Making the Declaration of Independence* (New York: Alfred A. Knopf, 1993).

10. Thomas Paine, *Rights of Man*, 1791.

11.   Ayn Rand, *Capitalism: The Unknown Ideal* (New York: New American Library, 1966).

12.   Kelly Shackelford, "Why the Texas Textbook Wars Matter to Every American," FOXNews.com, March 11, 2010, http://www.foxnews.com/opinion/2010/03/11/kelly-shackelford-texas-textbook-social-studies-standards-american-history/ (accessed March 30, 2011).

13.   Interview with David Barton, founder and president of Wallbuilders, November 17, 2010.

Amendment X

1.   James Madison, Speech in the Virginia Ratifying Convention on Control of the Military, June 16, 1788.

2.   Federalist No. 45 (James Madison).

3.   "The Articles of Confederation," http://www.Constitution.org/cons/usa-conf.htm (accessed May 2, 2011).

4.   Matt Cover, "When Asked Where the Constitution Authorizes Congress to Order Americans To Buy Health Insurance, Pelosi Says: 'Are You Serious?'" CNSNews.com, October 22, 2009, http://cnsnews.com/news/article/55971 (accessed March 25, 2011).

5.   Video available at http://www.youtube.com/watch?v=W1-eBz8hyoE (accessed March 25, 2011).

6.   "Help Fund the Lawsuit–Donate," Firearms Freedom Act, March 4, 2011, http://firearmsfreedomact.com/state-by-state/ (accessed March 25, 2011).

7.   Dr. James McHenry, one of Maryland's delegates to the Convention, first published in *The American Historical Review,* vol. 11, 1906. When McHenry's notes were included in *The Records of the Federal Convention of 1787,* ed. Max Farrand, vol. 3, appendix A, (1911), a footnote stated that the date this anecdote was written is uncertain.

8.   Stephen Ohlemacher, "Nearly half of U.S. households escape fed income tax," Associated Press, April 7, 2010.

9.   William J. Watkins Jr., *Reclaiming the American Revolution,* 2004.

10.   Opinion by Senior United States District Judge Roger Vinson, *State of Florida* v. *U.S. Department of Health and Human Services,* January 31, 2011, http://lawprofessors.typepad.com/files/florida-v.-u.s..pdf.

11.   Opinion by Judge Gladys Kessler of the United States District Court for the District of Columbia, *Margaret Peggy Lee Mead* v. *Eric H. Holder,* February 22, 2011, http://graphics8.nytimes.com/packages/pdf/national/20110223healthMemoMead.pdf (accessed May 2, 2011).

12. President Barack Obama interview on WBEZ-FM, a Chicago-based radio station on January 18, 2001.

13. "State of the Union Message to Congress," Franklin D. Roosevelt, January 11, 1944, http://www.fdrlibrary.marist.edu/archives/address_text.html (accessed March 25, 2011).

14. Barack Obama's "senior seminar" paper, written at Columbia University. The subject of this paper, which totaled 44 pages, was American government, and the title was "Aristocracy Reborn."

15. Federalist, No. 10

16. Andrew Napolitano, "Third-Ranking Democrat In House, James Clyburn, Admits Most Of What They Do Not Authorized By The Constitution," The American View, http://www.theamericanview.com/index.php?id=1465 (accessed March 25, 2011).